Business Valuation Case Law Yearbook 2017 Edition

BVR
What It's Worth
1000 SW Broadway, Suite 1200, Portland, OR 97205
(503) 291-7963 • www.bvresources.com

BVR

What It's Worth

Editor: Sylvia Golden

Publisher: Sarah Andersen

Managing Editor: Monique Nijhout-Rowe

Senior Copy Editor: David Solomon

Chair and CEO: David Foster

President: Lucretia Lyons

Chief Revenue Officer: Lisa McInturff

Customer Service Manager: Retta Dodge

Print/PDF ISBN: 978-1-62150-103-9

EPUB ISBN: 978-1-62150-104-6

Library of Congress Control Number: 2017932823

Table of Contents

Introduction

Dear Reader,

Valuation and damages represent two of the most hotly contested issues in civil litigation, as the cases derived from *BVLaw*[1] and featured in this annual compendium show. They cover all areas of law: bankruptcy, damages, divorce, ESOP, patent disputes, and tax disputes. And they make it clear that financial experts are critical to the success (or failure) of a case and judges are becoming more sophisticated (and assertive) in examining valuation- and damages-related claims.

All the cases impart lessons—about applicable legal principles, approved and discredited valuation methodology, and the act (art) of presenting expert opinions. Therefore, this collection benefits both the generalist as well as the specialist.

By way of sneak preview, some of the most talked-about cases arose in the statutory fair value context, with several pivoting on the applicability of the discount for marketability (DLOM).

At the cusp of 2015, New Jersey issued its third appellate decision in the *Wisniewski v. Walsh* case. This long and acrimonious dispute among the family members of a trucking business featured luminaries of the valuation world squaring off over the best method for determining the value of the dissenting (selling) shareholder's interest. What makes the case even spicier is the court's early decision to employ the DLOM as a way of punishing the oppressor, that is, the dissenting shareholder. The later rounds of litigation focused on the issue of whether the prevailing discounted cash flow analysis included the requisite DLOM. The court's appellate division agreed with the trial court that it did not and affirmed the lower court's DLOM rate. The decision has triggered a spirited discussion as to whether the court "got it right" in terms of the facts of the case and the use of a valuation tool such as DLOM to impose a legal sanction.

A decision in the spring of 2016 from the Delaware Court of Chancery has proven just as controversial. In *In re Appraisal of Dell,* the Chancery concluded the merger consideration did not represent fair value even though the company's board took great pains to stage a sound sales process. As if it were anticipating the reaction from financial experts and other commentators, the court went

1 This book features the court cases that were analyzed and presented in the *BVLaw* database in 2016. *BVLaw,* published by Business Valuation Resources, is an exclusive collection of 3,700-plus court cases and accompanying analysis concerning business valuation issues including economic damages, lost profits, estate and gift tax, divorce, shareholder repression, partnership dissolution, securities litigation, and more. Every day, *BVLaw* legal experts track published decisions from the courts in all 50 U.S. states and federal jurisdictions—including the Delaware Court of Chancery and U.S. Tax Courts—guaranteeing that you stay current on all the very latest valuation law.

through great length (115 pages) to explain its reasoning. Its opinion resembles a treatise on appraisal jurisprudence and is a must-read for any expert practicing in front of the Chancery. *Dell* is one the several key Chancery decisions appearing in this yearbook.

In the bankruptcy area, two decisions in particular were noteworthy for their differing take on the issue of equity committee. Given the tough legal standard, equity holders rarely succeed in persuading the court that a formal committee is necessary to represent their interests in reorganization discussion. However, they succeeded in *In re Horsehead Holding Corp.* After hearing testimony from equity holders, as well as lawyers for the debtors and creditors, the court decided something did not smell right about the valuations the debtor had presented and said it was willing to "go[], frankly, out on a limb" in terms of the legal requirements that shareholders show a substantial likelihood of recovery to equity. A transcript of the court hearing offers valuable insight into the arguments the equity holders (all sophisticated investors) and lawyers made to bolster their positions. The *Horsehead* decision also stands in marked contrast to the "no-equity-committee" approach the court in *In re Sunedison* took. The latter case is also included in this book.

In 2016, several divorce cases dealt with the issue of how to treat any appreciation in value for separate or gifted assets. One that stands out is *In re Marriage of Kerkhoff*, an Iowa case, in which the chief judge of the Court of Appeal wrote a dissenting opinion saying this was "a troublesome issue throughout the country." Different states, the judge noted, handle appreciation differently, and the results have been "chaotic and inconsistent." The dissenting opinion offers a recommendation for simplifying the appreciation analysis in order to achieve a fairer outcome.

Readers of this book also will see there was no shortage of economic damages disputes, some of them raising *Daubert* issues. A perfect example is *Washington v. Kellwood Co.*, a lost profits case involving an upstart sportswear apparel company that sought millions of dollars in damages based on the defendant marketing company's breaches of promises. The plaintiff expert based his calculation on a problematic yardstick analysis. Although his analysis survived a *Daubert* challenge, the court (a different judge) post-trial struck down the jury's multimillion-dollar award, which was rooted in the very expert opinion the court earlier had admitted. The court's thoughtful post-trial decisions explain in great detail why an expert's opinion might be admissible but represent insufficient evidence of lost profits.

This book has more in store, including an analysis of the years' most impactful ESOP and intellectual property cases, and enables readers to up their game by developing a deeper understanding of the current litigation landscape.

Sincerely,

Sylvia Golden, Esq.
Executive Legal Editor

Court Case Summary Table

Presented in order of case type, then by jurisdiction.

Case Name	Date	State/ Jurisdiction	Court	Summary	Page
Bankruptcy					
In re Mercury Cos. (In re Mercury II)	10/09/15	Federal/ Colorado	United States Bankruptcy Court	'Reasonably Equivalent Value' Analysis Meets FMV Standard, Court Says	158
Burtch v. Opus, LLC (In re Opus East, LLC) (I), (II)	03/23/15	Federal/ Delaware	United States Bankruptcy Court	Bankruptcy Court's Going-Concern Valuation Weathers Appeal	46
	03/31/16	Federal/ Delaware	United States District Court		46
In re Horsehead Holding Corp.	05/02/16	Federal/ Delaware	United States Bankruptcy Court	'Dramatic' Valuation Adjustment Justifies Equity Committee	123
Post-Confirmation Comm. for Small Loans, Inc. v. Martin	03/31/16	Federal/ Georgia	United States District Court	*Daubert* Flexible as to Solvency Determination for Multiple Debtor Entities	190
In re Case No. 800 Bourbon St.	11/20/15	Federal/ Louisiana	United States Bankruptcy Court	Court Rebuffs Attempt to Allocate Excess Value to Intangible Assets	51
In re Sunedison, Inc.	08/11/16	Federal/ New York	United States Bankruptcy Court	Debtors' Balance Sheet Not Reliable Indicator of Assets' Market Value	220
Hanckel v. Campbell (In re Hanckel)	12/11/15	Federal/ South Carolina	United States Bankruptcy Court	Bankruptcy Court Favors DCF to Value Dissociated Interest	116
In re Cole	03/24/16	Federal/ Virginia	United States Bankruptcy Court	Why Divorce Valuation Does Not Accord With Chapter 7 Liquidation Analysis	59
Breach of Fiduciary Duty					
In re Estate of Bittner (Bittner I), (Bittner II)	09/17/14	Pennsylvania	Probate Court	Shareholder Agreement Sparks Suit Over Discount Use in FMV Calculation	32
	01/21/16	Pennsylvania	Superior Court of Pennsylvania (Court of Appeals)		32
Contract					
St. Jude Med. S.C., Inc. v. Biosense Webster, Inc.	04/12/16	Federal/ 8th Circuit	United States Court of Appeals	8th Circuit Validates Employment Contract and Damages Related to Breach	215
Healthcare v. Orr	01/20/16	California	Court of Appeals	Buyer's Failure to Assign Value to Practice Goodwill Nullifies Noncompete	121
PECO Logistics, LLC v. Walnut Inv. Partners, L.P.	12/30/15	Delaware	Court of Chancery of Delaware	Value Determination Accords With Parties' Contract, Chancery Says	181
Pattridge v. Starks	02/24/16	Louisiana	Court of Appeals	Breach of Noncompete Means Damages for 'Loss Sustained' *and* Lost Profits	174
Spencer Franchise Servs. of Ga. v. WOW Café & Wingery Franchising Account, LLC	04/15/16	Federal/ Louisiana	United States District Court	Rebuttal Opinion Helpful to Jury Because Valuation 'Not a Common-Sense Subject'	212
Congel v. Malfitano	05/18/16	New York	Supreme Court of New York, Appellate Division	Unilateral Partnership Dissolution Exacts Steep Price From Wrongdoer	67
Bruno v. Bozzuto's, Inc.	11/19/15	Federal/ Pennsylvania	United States District Court	Court Excludes Pro Forma-Based Economic Damages Analysis	42
Covol Fuels No. 4 v. Pinnacle Mining Co.	02/04/16	Federal/ West Virginia	United States District Court	Defendant's Obfuscatory Tactics to Preclude Expert Testimony Fail	73
RMS of Wisconsin, Inc. v. S-K JV	05/16/16	Federal/ Wisconsin	United States District Court	Flawed Lost Profits Analysis Leaves Plaintiff Bereft of Damages Evidence	199

Case Name	Date	State/ Jurisdiction	Court	Summary	Page
Damages (incl. Lost Profits)					
Marten Transp., Ltd. v. Plattform Adver., Inc.	07/26/16	Federal/ Kansas	United States District Court	Court Distinguishes Between Proving Fact of Damage and Amount	151
Mattress Closeout Ctr. IV, LLC v. Panera, LLC	07/15/16	Federal/ Michigan	United States District Court	Court Deems Future Lost Profits Formula an Exercise in Speculation	155
Lane v. Lampkin (Lampkin II)	10/08/15	Mississippi	Supreme Court	High Court Finds Trial Court's Damages Assessment Unsound	145
Washington v. Kellwood Co. (Kellwood II), (Kellwood III)	07/15/16 09/30/16	Federal/ New York	United States District Court	Court Sets Aside Big Lost Profits Award Based on Bad Yardstick Analysis	237
Bocek v. JGA Assocs., LLC	03/23/16	Federal/ Virginia	United States District Court	Court Snubs Lost Earnings Analysis Based on 'Incomplete Use' of Data	35
Dissenting Shareholder					
Pearson v. Westervelt Co.	01/08/16	Alabama	Court of Civil Appeals	Demand for Executive Compensation Data Lacks 'Proper Purpose'	178
In re Appraisal of Dell Inc.	05/31/16	Delaware	Court of Chancery of Delaware	Chancery Rejects Deal Price Based on Unquantifiable 'Sales Process Mispricing'	17
In re DFC Global Corp.	07/08/16	Delaware	Court of Chancery of Delaware	Chancery Achieves Fair Value by Blending Three 'Imperfect Techniques'	81
In re ISN Software Corp. Appraisal Litig.	08/11/16	Delaware	Court of Chancery of Delaware	Chancery Relies on 'Simple and Powerful' DCF for Fair Value	126
Merion Capital LP & Merion Capital II LP v. BMC Software	10/21/15	Delaware	Court of Chancery of Delaware	Uncertainty Over Key Inputs Compromises DCF, Chancery Says	161
In re Trulia Stockholder Litig.	01/22/16	Delaware	Court of Chancery of Delaware	More Valuation Data Do Not Ensure Fair Class Action Settlement	223
Rubin v. Bedford	12/24/15	Illinois	Appellate Court of Illinois	Expert's Poor Grasp of Valuation Issues Undercuts Shareholder Suit	203
Wisniewski v. Walsh (Wisniewski II)	12/24/15	New Jersey	Superior Court, Appellate Division	Affirmation of DLOM Rulings Augurs End to Shareholder Fight	246
ESOP					
Perez v. Bruister (Bruister II)	05/03/16	Federal/ 5th Circuit	United States Court of Appeals	In Unusual ESOP Case, 5th Circuit Validates FMV Computation	185
Fish v. GreatBanc Trust Co.	09/01/16	Federal/ Illinois	United States District Court	'Persuasive' Defense Expert Testimony Defeats ESOP Overpayment Claims	98
Estate and Gift Taxation					
Estate of Dieringer v. Commissioner	03/30/16	Federal	United States Tax Court	Manipulation of Valuation of Bequeathed Stock Sinks Charitable Contribution Claim	87
Federal Taxation					
Estate of Giustina v. Commissioner (Giustina III)	06/13/16	Federal	United States Tax Court	Tax Court Corrects Prior Valuation of LP Interest to Startling Result	106
H.W. Johnson v. Commissioner	05/11/16	Federal	United States Tax Court	Return on Equity Analysis Undergirds Reasonable Compensation Claim	112
Redstone v. Commissioner	12/09/15	Federal	United States Tax Court	Subsequent Transaction Too Remote to Allow for Reliable Valuation	195
Fraud					
MSKP Oak Grove, LLC v. Venuto	06/29/16	Federal/ New Jersey	United States District Court	Expert Prevails by Documenting Adherence to Valuation Standards	168

Case Name	Date	State/ Jurisdiction	Court	Summary	Page
Intellectual Property					
Akamai Techs., Inc. v. Limelight Networks, Inc.	11/16/15	Federal/ Federal Circuit	United States Court of Appeals	No Legal Barrier to Expert's Adjusted Lost Profits Analysis	15
Commonwealth Sci. & Indus. Research Organisation v. Cisco Sys.,	12/03/15	Federal/ Federal Circuit	United States Court of Appeals	Court's Damages Model for SEP Infringement Fails Apportionment Rules	63
Ericsson, Inc. v. D-Link Sys. (D-Link II)	12/04/14	Federal/ Federal Circuit	United States Court of Appeals	Pivotal Ruling on Damage Calculation for SEP Infringement	95
3M Innovative Props. Co. v. GDC, Inc.	07/22/16	Federal/ Minnesota	United States District Court	No Automatic Bar to Royalties Accruing After Life of Patent	11
Arctic Cat v. Sabertooth Motor Group	08/09/16	Federal/ Minnesota	United States District Court	Court Nixes Royalty Calculation Relying on Unalike Prior Licenses	23
Luminara Worldwide, LLC v. Liown Elecs. Co.	05/18/16	Federal/ Minnesota	United States District Court	Court Clarifies Rule 26 Protection for 'Reporting' and 'Non-Reporting' Experts	148
Deflecto, LLC v. Dundas Jafine Inc.	11/04/15	Federal/ Missouri	United States District Court	Court Decides *Daubert* Attack 'Misses the Mark'	78
Judicial Dissolution (incl. Withdrawal, Buy Out)					
Curran v. Curran	01/12/16	Connecticut	Superior Court	Parties' Valuation Contract Precludes Review of Minority Discount	76
Wagner v. Wagner	04/27/16	Idaho	Supreme Court	High Court Pushes Back on Mandatory Discounts in Fair Value Determinations	233
In re Discontinuance & Disposition of P.K. Smith Motors, Inc.	03/09/16	Louisiana	Court of Appeals	Dodgy Real Estate Valuation Compromises Dependent Business Valuation	91
Verghetta v. Lawlor	03/09/16	New York	Supreme Court of New York (Trial Court)	No Place for DLOM and Tax Affecting in N.Y. Fair Value Determination	227
Jafar v. Mohammed	04/12/16	Texas	Court of Appeals	In Buyout, Income-Based Expert Appraisal Beats Other Value Indicators	129
Marital Dissolution					
Moore v. Moore	03/10/16	Arkansas	Supreme Court	In Controversial Move, High Court Strikes Active Appreciation Rule	166
Witt-Bahls v. Bahls	02/03/16	Florida	Court of Appeals	Court Rejects Bright-Line Rule for Valuing Appreciation of Nonmarital Assets	249
In re Marriage of Johnson	12/02/15	Illinois	Appellate Court of Illinois	Comparable Transaction Exposes Error in Court's Enterprise Goodwill Ruling	133
In re Marriage of Kerkhoff	08/31/16	Iowa	Court of Appeals	Divided Court Addresses Issue of Appreciation of Gifted Property	135
Baumboree v. Baumbouree	07/13/16	Louisiana	Court of Appeals	Spouse's Unilateral Stock Agreement Sets Value in Divorce Action	25
Lacoste v. Lacoste	07/19/16	Mississippi	Court of Appeals	Court Disapproves of Nonexpert Valuation of Key Marital Asset	143
Kminek-Nierenberg v. Kenneth Nierenberg	09/08/16	New Jersey	Superior Court, Appellate Division	Court Digs Through Appreciation Issues in Complex Divorce Case	139
Gifford v. Gifford	10/22/15	New York	Court of Appeals	Service Business Valuation Triggers Double Dip Rule	105
Berger v. Berger	12/31/15	Ohio	Court of Appeals	Lay Testimony About Offer to Buy Represents Admissible Valuation Evidence	28
Nieman v. Nieman	12/14/15	Ohio	Court of Appeals	Ohio Appeals Court Clarifies Provision on Tax Affecting at Divorce	171
Code & Code	08/17/16	Oregon	Court of Appeals	Court Upholds Inclusion of Premarital Value in Property Distribution	57

Case Name	Date	State/ Jurisdiction	Court	Summary	Page
Grant v. Grant	05/12/16	Tennessee	Court of Appeals	Appeals Court Signs Off on 'Slight' DLOM in Minority Interest Valuation	109
Sternat v. Sternat	10/28/15	Wisconsin	Court of Appeals	Business Debt Renders Expert's Lack of BV Credentials Inconsequential	218
Securities					
Showers v. Pfizer, Inc. (In re Pfizer Inc. Sec. Litig.)	04/12/16	Federal/ 2nd Circuit	United States Court of Appeals	2nd Circuit Chafes at Wholesale Exclusion of Loss Causation Testimony	207
Cdx Holdings, Inc. v. Fox (Fox II)	06/06/16	Delaware	Supreme Court of Delaware	High Court Dissent Rebukes Chancery's Analysis in Option Valuation Case	53
Broyles v. Cantor Fitzgerald & Co.	06/07/16	Federal/ Louisiana	United States District Court	Is Expert Opinion Based Solely on Experience Admissible?	40
State Taxation (incl. Ad Valorem)					
Wheelabrator Bridgeport, L.P. v. City of Bridgeport	02/02/16	Connecticut	Supreme Court	Highest Court Rebukes Trial Court Over Flat-Out Bar of DCF Approach	242
Corrigan v. Testa	05/04/16	Ohio	Supreme Court of Ohio	Key Tax Ruling From Ohio Supreme Court Concerning Pass-Through Entity	70

Court Case Digests

Presented in alphabetical order.

3M Innovative Props. Co. v. GDC, Inc.

Citation: 2016 U.S. Dist. LEXIS 96253
Date of decision: July 22, 2016
Country: US
State/Jurisdiction: Federal/Minnesota
Court: United States District Court
Type of action: Intellectual Property
Experts: Donald Gorowsky (plaintiffs); unknown (defendants)
Judge: Frank
SIC: 3714 Motor Vehicle Parts and Accessories (except truck and bus bodies, trailers, engine and engine parts, motor vehicle electrical and electronic equipment, motor vehicle steering and suspension components, motor vehicle brake systems, and motor vehicle transm
NAICS code: 336390 Other Motor Vehicle Parts Manufacturing

No Automatic Bar to Royalties Accruing After Life of Patent

A damages expert in the patent arena must reckon with the element of causation: "But for" the infringement, the patent holder would have made additional profit. In a recent *Daubert* case, the plaintiffs' expert successfully demonstrated that his lost profits calculation based on the *Panduit* test as well as on two-supplier and market share analyses was admissible. The court also discussed when and why it is acceptable to factor payments that occur after the expiration of the patented technology into a reasonable royalty calculation.

Backstory. The plaintiffs, the 3M companies, invented a thermally stable acoustical insulation that was used in cars for noise reduction. The product sells under the name Thinsulate Acoustic

Insulation (TAI). It dominated the market until the defendants, wanting a slice of the market, began selling a similar insulation that sells under the brand Sonozorb.

3M sued, claiming Sonozorb infringed its protected TAI version, and pursued lost profits and reasonable royalty damages based on expert testimony. The defendants challenged the expert opinion as to both damages theories under *Daubert*.

Comprehensive lost profits analysis. To qualify for lost profits, a patent holder must show that, "but for" the infringement, it would have made the infringer's sales. A standard way of proving lost profits is the four-part *Panduit* test. Other ways to examine causation are the two-supplier analysis or, if there are more than two suppliers, a market share analysis.

The plaintiffs' expert used all of these methods.

Panduit *test. Panduit* requires the patent holder to establish that: (1) there was demand for the patented product; (2) there were no noninfringing alternatives; (3) the patent holder had the manufacturing and marketing capability to exploit demand; and (4) the amount of profit the patent holder would have made but for the infringement.

As to Factor 1, the expert found sales of 3M's TAI and the defendants' Sonozorb were proof that there was not only demand, but also growing demand for the protected product. He also noted that the defendants' developing a product whose key features were based on the plaintiffs' patent was evidence of demand.

Regarding Factor 2, the expert analyzed the relevant market, the plaintiffs' share of the market, and potential noninfringing substitutes. He found the plaintiffs and the defendants were the only companies that made and sold insulation products that combined the features the consumer demanded and the plaintiffs' patent provided—high-level acoustic performance, low weight, and a resistance to degradation. This was a two-supplier market and there were no noninfringing alternatives, the expert decided.

Regardless, he performed a market share analysis in which he assigned a 10% share of the market to a third player for purposes of the "but for" analysis. Factoring out the defendants' infringing sales, the plaintiffs' relative market share would be about 81%, the expert found. But, in his opinion, the third party's product was inferior to the plaintiffs' and the defendants' products because it was susceptible to degradation. The expert ultimately concluded this was not a true, noninfringing substitute; consequently, the market was a two-supplier market.

As to Factor 3, the plaintiffs' expert said testimony from the plaintiffs' marketing and manufacturing executives showed the companies were capable of fulfilling the defendants' sales. 3M had underutilized manufacturing capability in the U.S. and was able to speed up the start dates for already-planned U.S.-based capability increases to meet the added demands related to the defendants' sales. Also, 3M had relationships that enabled it to make, at a minimum, its market share portion of the defendants' sales. Therefore, the plaintiffs were entitled to 100% of the defendants' infringing sales, the expert decided.

Concerning Factor 4, the plaintiffs' expert first determined the defendants' infringing sales through the expiration of the patent. He found the defendants' sales were subject to accelerated re-entry damages (ARD), that is, some recovery to compensate the patent holder for loss of profits after the expiration of the patent based on the infringer's accelerated future competition with the patent holder. Under the ARD theory, the infringement during the life of the patent allows the infringer to make a faster and more meaningful entry into the market in the post-expiration period.

The expert then calculated the portion of sales the plaintiffs would have made but for the infringement and adjusted for 3M's higher sales price. He next determined 3M's incremental profit margin and calculated the plaintiffs' lost profits.

The defendants said all aspects of the plaintiff experts' analysis were flawed, resulting in an unreliable calculation. A sales analysis of TAI and Sonozorb did not demonstrate there in fact was demand among the defendants' customers for TAI, the defendants contended. The plaintiffs and the defendants sold different acoustical insulation at different prices to different customers, and there was no evidence that the defendants' customers would switch to 3M's product in a "but for" world.

The defendants further alleged the plaintiffs' expert falsely assumed that an acoustical insulation product that did not have the patented level of thermal stability would not last the life of a car.

Moreover, the defendants claimed they had a noninfringing Sonozorb version available during the damages period. Relatedly, they argued the plaintiffs' expert did not investigate whether customers actually demanded all the "advantages" the patented product provided. The defendants contended the presence of a noninfringing alternative would put into question the market share and the two-supplier analysis the plaintiffs' expert undertook.

Further, they said, the plaintiffs' expert did not sufficiently quantify the plaintiffs' additional manufacturing capacity.

Finally, they objected that the lost profits calculation included sales the plaintiffs would not have made but for the alleged infringement. Applying the ARD theory, the expert impermissibly extended the life of the patent in that he included sales that would occur after the patent had expired based on four-year supply commitments the defendants had made with third parties.

The court found none of the arguments were a basis for excluding any of the lost profits analysis under existing case law. The Federal Circuit has held that, if the patent owner and the infringer are the only suppliers of the product, causation may be inferred. Also, it is reasonable to assume that the patent holder would have made the infringer's sales, assuming the patent holder had the manufacturing and marketing capacities. And lost profits may be based on profit share where there are multiple competitors.

In the instant case, the court found that, in applying the two-supplier and market share methods and in following the *Panduit* test, the plaintiffs' expert had used accepted damages methods and principles. The court advised the defendants to challenge the analysis by presenting opposing damages expert testimony and cross-examining the plaintiffs' expert.

Royalty dispute is factual. The plaintiffs' expert noted that at a minimum the plaintiffs were entitled to a reasonable royalty. He used the *Georgia-Pacific* framework and concluded, in a hypothetical negotiation before the infringement, the plaintiffs and the defendants would have agreed on a "running royalty" of at least 8% of the defendants' sales and a lump sum for other infringing acts.

The defendants argued the analysis was based on the plaintiffs' research and development expenditures that were unrelated to the patented product. The expert did not tie the 8% rate to the claimed invention and did not attempt to value the invention. The evidence showed that customers did not place any value on the protected features such as the claimed level of thermal stability. Also, the royalty analysis improperly included royalties on sales occurring after the expiration of the patent.

The plaintiffs countered that the defendants' objections represented disputes over facts and conclusions, not over methodology. Those needed to be explored at trial. Moreover, it was appropriate to include the patent holders' research and development costs and consider the infringer's savings in these areas. Finally, the royalty rate did not include post-expiration sales but royalties for supplier commitments the defendants made during the lifetime of the patent.

The court again sided with the plaintiffs. Most of the challenges were factual and went to the weight of the testimony, it said.

It noted that, under U.S. Supreme Court law, collecting royalties that accrued after the expiration of a patent was unlawful. However, this was not what the plaintiffs' damages expert in the instant case proposed, the court clarified. Rather, the expert's hypothetical negotiation took into account royalties owed to the plaintiffs for multiyear supply contracts the defendants had entered into during the term of the patent in dispute. The contracts happened to go beyond the life of the patent. Courts have found this type of patent licensing agreement "acceptable," the court in the instant case said.

Consequently, it also admitted the reasonable royalty testimony.

Akamai Techs., Inc. v. Limelight Networks, Inc.

Citation: 2015 U.S. App. LEXIS 19848
Date of decision: Nov. 16, 2015
Country: US
State/Jurisdiction: Federal/Federal Circuit
Court: United States Court of Appeals
Type of action: Intellectual Property
Experts: Dr. Keith Ugone
Judge: Linn
SIC: 7374 Computer Processing and Data Preparation and Processing Services
NAICS code: 518210 Data Processing, Hosting, and Related Services

No Legal Barrier to Expert's Adjusted Lost Profits Analysis

In a protracted patent case, the defendant challenged the jury's lost profits award to the plaintiff, claiming it relied on unsound expert testimony. The price disparity between the defendant's infringing product and the plaintiff's protected product was too great to support the expert's adjusted market share analysis underlying the lost profits calculation. The Federal Circuit rejected the argument.

Direct competitors. Both parties were content delivery network providers that competed with each other. However, Akamai, the plaintiff, is the dominant force in the market. It has one of the world's largest distributed computing platforms that is responsible for serving between 15% and 30% of all Web traffic. Limelight Networks, the defendant, initially sold technology that did not infringe, but in spring 2005 it introduced its contested software. In 2007, Akamai, jointly with the Massachusetts Institute of Technology, sued Limelight for violating its protected technology.

Early in the proceedings, a jury found Limelight liable and awarded Akamai approximately $40 million in lost profits, $1.4 million in reasonable royalty damages, and $4 million in price erosion damages. But the district court (D. Mass.) overturned the jury's verdict based on noninfringement. Numerous rounds of appeal followed that culminated in the reversal of the district court's ruling on infringement.

When the case returned to the Federal Circuit for a resolution of all remaining issues, the defendant argued there were other grounds for striking down the jury's verdict. One was that the district court erred when it allowed Akamai's damages expert to present a flawed lost profits analysis. The crux of the problem was that the expert failed to establish the necessary "but for" connection between Limelight's infringement and Akamai's lost profits. Limelight's products cost half as much as Akamai's. Akamai's expert either failed to account for the effect of this disparity in his lost profits calculation or he did so in an arbitrary way. According to Limelight, Akamai did not lose customers to Limelight. Rather, considering the huge price difference, both companies served different markets. Consequently, lost profits were legally unavailable to Akamai, Limelight claimed.

'Relatively inelastic' market. At trial, Akamai's expert showed that, in 2005, when Limelight first released the infringing software, it had a 5% market share, compared to Akamai's 79.8% market share. In 2006, Limelight's market share had more than doubled, to 10.7%. In contrast, Akamai's share had dropped to 74.7%. The expert next calculated the market share Akamai would have had "but for" the infringement. For 2005, he found it would have been 81%, and for 2006 it would have been 79.9%. He explained he did not have sufficient data to calculate the market share for 2007 but assumed it would have been the same as in 2006. He said that, to be on the conservative side, he decided to reduce Akamai's market share by 3%, and he also excluded 25% of the lowest earning customers of Limelight. The reason was that those customers were the most price-sensitive and least likely to buy Akamai's considerably more expensive service if Limelight's products were not in the market. By the expert's calculation, Limelight's infringing sales totaled about $87.5 million.

The expert explained how the price disparity affected his lost profits calculation in greater detail. Assuming a world without the infringing product, he said he first assumed that Akamai would sell its technology to some of Limelight's customers for double the price Limelight was charging. He also assumed that, even though not all of Limelight's customers would buy Akamai's service, about 75% of Limelight's sales would have gone to Akamai because demand for Akamai's technology was "relatively inelastic," that is, unaffected by price changes. Akamai's costs were "revenue-generating costs," he pointed out. This meant customers would be more willing to spend money on Akamai's products. Further, notwithstanding some price sensitivity, demand for the product did not change as much as the price. There was no question that both companies were in direct competition. Limelight in statements had acknowledged that Akamai was its biggest competitor and had said that the two companies were "head and shoulders above the rest of … Limelight's competition." Also, demand for the products was driven by end-users not customers. And, even though Limelight introduced an infringing service at a lower price, Akamai remained the dominant player in the market. The expert allowed that using 75% as the number of sales Akamai could have made but for the infringement was a "judgment call." He ultimately concluded Akamai lost approximately $74 million in profits because of the infringement.

The Federal Circuit found the district court's admitting the expert's adjusted lost profits analysis was proper. The reviewing court rejected Limelight's market segmentation argument based solely on price disparity. Rather, the Federal Circuit said, the evidence showed that Akamai and Limelight were direct competitors. Moreover, Akamai's expert gave reasons why the market for the infringing technology was relatively inelastic. The expert's 25% adjustment was "sufficiently grounded in economic principles," the Federal Circuit found. "Whether this discount was sufficient is not a legal challenge to the availability of lost profits, but as to the amount of lost profits," the court added. It pointed out that Limelight, in its briefs, did not question the amount of lost profits, only the availability. The Federal Circuit sent the case back to the district court for reinstatement of the damages.

In re Appraisal of Dell Inc.

Citation: 2016 Del. Ch. LEXIS 81
Date of decision: May 31, 2016
Country: US
State/Jurisdiction: Delaware
Court: Court of Chancery of Delaware
Type of action: Dissenting Shareholder
Experts: Prof. Bradford Cornell (petitioners); Prof. Glenn Hubbard (respondents)
Judge: Laster
SIC: 5045 Computers and Computer Peripheral Equipment and Software (merchant wholesalers except those selling computers, equipment, and software via retail method)
NAICS code: 423430 Computer and Computer Peripheral Equipment and Software Merchant Wholesalers

Chancery Rejects Deal Price Based on Unquantifiable 'Sales Process Mispricing'

The Delaware Court of Chancery's favoring the value derived from a post-merger discounted cash flow analysis over the deal price in the Dell statutory appraisal action stunned the world of high finance. How was it possible that the merger price did not reflect fair value when the company's board and Michael Dell, who led the management buyout that gave rise to the lawsuit, seemingly performed according to script? What about the Chancery's recent decisions that expressly considered the merger price a better indicator of fair value than any results from the DCF and other valuation methods? In a 115-page decision that is heavy on appraisal jurisprudence but relatively light on valuation methodology, the Chancery explained its findings.

Market pessimism. Michael Dell founded the company in 1983. In 1988, it went public. He left in 2004 but returned in 2007. Once back in charge, he decided to transform the company by reducing its reliance on PC sales and pursuing an expansion into enterprise solutions and services. Between 2010 and 2014, the company spent about $14 billion on acquiring new businesses. Michael Dell and the company's management believed that over the long term the enterprise division would prove successful and the company would be able to grow its PC business by about 1% to 2% per year. In January 2011, management prepared a "sum-of-the-parts" analysis that valued the company at $22.49 per share (based on line of business) and $27.05 per share (based on business unit).

However, the company stock traded at $14 per share. Michael Dell recognized that the market still considered the company a PC business, and the outlook for that sector was increasingly grim. In a June 2012 meeting with analysts, Michael Dell and management tried to communicate their optimism, suggesting 12% annual growth in software sales and 22% growth in services revenue. Management also announced a $2 billion cost savings initiative. Market observers remained skeptical, and the company's stock price declined to about $12 per share.

Meanwhile, Michael Dell began talking to two financial sponsors about a management buyout (MBO). He straightaway informed the company's board of directors, saying he did not want to proceed without the directors' approval. The board formed a special committee, which hired

JPMorgan Chase & Co. as its financial advisor. At that time, the company's earnings call for the second quarter of FY 2013 showed an 8% revenue decline and a 13% drop in earnings per share. Dell seemed undaunted: "We're transforming our business, not for a quarter or a fiscal year, but to deliver differentiated customer value for the long term." In contrast, analysts described the company as a "sinking ship" and its turnaround strategy as "fundamentally flawed."

Focus LBO analysis. In fall 2012, JPMorgan made a presentation to the committee about the feasibility of an MBO considering "the basic math by which financial sponsors determine what they are willing to pay in an acquisition transaction." It noted that a sponsor typically expected to obtain a return on its equity investment within three to five years in an outright sale, public offering, or recapitalization. "Financial buyers evaluate investments with an internal rate of return (IRR) analysis, which measures return on equity," JPMorgan explained. And "IRR will be used as the primary means to determine the appropriate purchase price by a sponsor."

JPMorgan also said that it was not very likely that financial sponsors other than the two with whom Michael Dell had talked or any strategic bidders would be interested in buying the company. The upshot was that throughout the process JPMorgan and other financial advisors, including Goldman Sachs, prepared valuations based on a leverage buyout (LBO) analysis. By that calculation, JPMorgan suggested a financial sponsor wanting to achieve a range of IRRs of 20% to 25% would be willing to pay in the range of $11.75 per share to $13.00 per share or $13.25 per share to $14.25 per share, if it engaged in further recapitalizations of the company. Goldman Sachs, using the same company forecasts as JPMorgan did, said a sponsor could pay about $16.00 per share and still achieve a five-year IRR of 20%.

In late 2012, the market's outlook for the PC industry and Dell, the company, became even more pessimistic and the committee, concerned that management projections were too optimistic for purposes of "valuation and sell-side estimates," hired Boston Consulting Group (BCG) to prepare an independent set of forecasts. As a result of the negative outlook, one of the financial sponsors dropped out and the other—the eventual buyer—proposed to buy the company for $12.70 per share. The committee found the offer "inadequate."

BCG said the low valuation did "not match apparent company strengths." Instead, it reflected "investor concerns." JPMorgan agreed that investors were focused on short-term results at the expense of the company's long-term value. Michael Dell, himself, made a presentation to the board explaining the strategic initiatives he planned to pursue once the company was a private company and noting an MBO would be in the best interest of the company's shareholders "because they would receive a portion of the potential upside from these initiatives without bearing the risk."

Third-party projections. In early 2013, BCG prepared a series of projections. The most consequential ones in terms of the later trial expert valuations were two that turned on the company's likelihood of achieving $3.3 billion in cost savings. Publicly, management had only announced $2 billion in savings to give itself a "cushion." Under one scenario, the "BCG 25% Case," BCG assumed the company would be able to realize 25% of the savings. BCG believed that goal was achievable and resulted in the most reasonable set of projections. The "BCG 75% Case" assumed the company would realize 75% of the savings. The committee was doubtful about this scenario, which implied margins for FY 2015 that were higher than the company or its competition had ever achieved.

Another set of projections, the "Bank Case," related to a presentation the buyout group and Michael Dell made in fall 2013 to banks that would finance the merger. The forecasts assumed lower gross profit and EBITDA relative to an earlier set of projections submitted to banks but higher revenues. The presentation modeled $3.6 billion in cost savings, with $2.6 billion appearing in the forecasts and $1 billion as a separate line item.

Go-shop period. Also, in early 2013, the committee hired a second financial advisor, Evercore, to conduct a potential go-shop period. In pitching itself for the job, Evercore prepared a DCF analysis that valued the company at between $14.27 per share and $18.40 per share. Its LBO analysis suggested a range of between $12.36 per share and $16.08 per share assuming an IRR of 15% to 25%.

Negotiations between the buyout group and the committee kept going. The committee wanted $13.75 per share, and the buyout group offered $13.50 per share. Under threat of a stalemate, Michael Dell himself offered to roll over his shares at a lower price than what public stockholders would receive. Ultimately, the parties agreed to a $13.65-per-share price, which both financial advisors considered fair to unaffiliated stockholders from a financial point of view.

The merger agreement provided for a 45-day go-shop period. During that period, there were two offers of promise, one by Blackstone Management Partners LLC and the other by Carl Icahn. Blackstone suggested the company's existing shareholders could elect to receive a cash payment of at least $14.25 per share or a package of stock in a new entity worth $14.25 per share and subject to a cap on the total amount of equity that the new entity would issue. Icahn proposed a similar transaction offering stockholders a combination of cash and stock subject to a cap on the amount of cash. Evercore found the proposal amounted to a value of between $13.37 per share and $14.42 per share.

Ultimately, neither bid went anywhere, but both had the effect of bumping up the original merger price. In a final bid, the buyout group agreed to pay an additional $0.10 per share, increasing the total merger consideration to $13.75 per share. It also agreed to a special cash dividend of $0.13 per share. A majority of the holders of outstanding shares approved the deal.

Fair value determination a different animal. However, a number of shareholders filed a petition under Delaware's appraisal status asking the Chancery for a fair value determination. The court, performing a discounted cash flow analysis that drew on analysis from both sides' experts, achieved a value of $17.62 per share. In other words, Michael Dell sold the company for about $7 billion too little.

The crux of the Chancery's decision is that a statutory appraisal determination is not an inquiry into a breach of fiduciary duty claim. "In a fiduciary duty class action, the court is faced with the question of holding individual directors personally liable for having breached their duties to the stockholders," the court explained. "An appraisal action asks a substantially more modest question: did the stockholders get fair value for their shares in the merger?" According to the court, "a sale process might pass muster for purposes of a breach of fiduciary claim and yet still generate a sub-optimal process for purposes of an appraisal." This was the case here. No one breached a duty to the shareholders. In fact, the board, the committee, and its advisors "did many praiseworthy things," the court noted. Regardless, factors related to the process "undercut the relationship between the Final Merger Consideration and fair value," the court found.

Presigning phase problems. The problems started with the presigning phase, which produced an original merger price ($13.65 per share) that was below fair value, the Chancery said.

The paramount problem was that the players all were financial sponsors—there was no outreach to strategic bidders—and all the valuations driving the merger were premised on LBO models, which calculate what a financial investor would be willing to pay to achieve a certain internal rate of return.

In contrast, "fair value" under the applicable statute is "the value to a stockholder of the firm as a going concern as opposed to the firm's value in the context of an acquisition or other transaction." The court noted that the company conceded that an LBO model was not "oriented toward solving for enterprise value." Here, JPMorgan performed a going-concern analysis using the DCF method and showed a value of between $20 per share and $27 per share. But, said the court with emphasis, "using the *same projected cash flows* in an LBO model," JPMorgan found a financial buyer would pay a maximum of $14.13 per share—if the price were any higher, the sponsor could not achieve a minimum 20% IRR over five years. Assuming the buyer wanted to achieve IRRs in the range of 20% to 25%, the likely range of prices was even lower, JPMorgan determined.

The financial sponsors behaved as the committee's financial advisors predicted they would, and they used similar LBO models. Competition between or among financial sponsors depends on their willingness to sacrifice IRR, but it "does not lead to intrinsic value," the court observed. Michael Dell and the committee also did not focus on fair value, the court added. In fact, in its proxy to the shareholders, the committee stated it did not pursue a premerger going-concern valuation but used other metrics, such as what the LBO models indicated a financial sponsor would pay. "As a practical matter, the Committee negotiated without determining the value of its best alternative to a negotiated acquisition," the court said.

The court also noted a "valuation disconnect" between the market's perception and the company's operative reality. The market focused on short-term results and on the company's $14 billion investment to transform itself, but this narrow view might cause it to "excessively discount the value of long-term investments," the court said. It also noted that proposing an MBO when the stock market is low meant using the low stock price to anchor price negotiations. Empirical evidence shows that the ensuing sales process is more likely to generate an undervalued bid, the court said. Here, all the participants to the transaction recognized the value disconnect, the court observed. In fact, Michael Dell and management tried to convince analysts that the company was worth more. Even though, during the sales process, the committee and its advisors used the market price as a key input, the court observed. "In fact, the trading price was the only quantitative metric the Committee cited in the Company's proxy statements when explaining its recommendation that stockholders approve the merger," the Chancery pointed out.

Post-signing issues. The post-signing go-shop period did not cure the initial undervaluation, the court found. True, the Blackstone and Icahn bids that came in during the go-shop period led to a 2% increase in the final merger consideration, but they ultimately went nowhere. If anything, the court said, the two bids showed that the original merger price was too low. Worse, in terms of the respondents' case, the fact that the two bids exceeded the final merger price "undercut the notion that the Final Merger Consideration provided fair value," the court observed.

DCF analysis tops merger price. To determine fair value, the court turned to the DCF analysis—the method both parties' experts used, albeit to startlingly different effect. The petitioners' expert said the company had a fair value of $28.61 per share on the merger closing date; the respondents' expert said the value was $12.68 per share. "Two highly distinguished scholars of valuation science, applying similar valuation principles, thus generated opinions that differed by 126%, or approximately $28 billion. This is a recurring problem," the Chancery observed.

Neither expert analysis was entirely credible, the court found. The petitioner expert's result suggested that the merger undervalued the company by $23 billion. "Had a value disparity of that magnitude existed, HP or another technology firm would have emerged to acquire the Company on the cheap," the court noted. On the other hand, the respondent expert's result was below the merger price. If, as the court found, the deal price undervalued the company, the respondent expert's valuation did even more so.

The court declined to "exhaustively describe the DCF methodology" but instead discussed areas of major disagreement between the experts and its preferences.

Forecasts. The projected cash flows underlying the experts' analysis accounted for much of the difference in value, the court said. The petitioners' expert used the BCG 25% Case and BCG 75% Case and weighted them equally. He also considered the Bank Case. The respondents' expert used the BCG 25% Case but adjusted for weaknesses, including the risk that these forecasts were stale by the time of the merger. They were prepared in January 2013 and never updated. The adjustments included updating revenue projections based on PC industry data and updating revenues flowing from the sale of secondary products. Moreover, the expert adjusted for stock-based compensation and created a five-year transition period in the projections to better capture the company's operative reality and the likely schedule for the transformation plan to show results.

He also found the Bank Case reasonable but adjusted to account for nonrecurring restructuring expenses and stock-based compensation.

The Chancery normally is skeptical about litigation-driven adjustments, the court noted. It prefers valuations "based on contemporaneously prepared management projections." In this instance, however, the respondents' expert "persuasively justified his changes." The court agreed that, even though the BCG projections were "impressively thorough, with over 1,100 assumptions," they risked being out of date by the time the merger closed (the valuation date). It found the Bank Case was perhaps too optimistic, but ultimately it approved of both sets of forecasts, as adjusted by the respondents' expert.

Tax considerations. Taxes also figured prominently in the valuations. The petitioners' expert used a 21% tax rate throughout his forecast period based on rates in the valuation's models the company's financial advisors prepared. The respondents' expert used a 17.8% rate during the projection and transition periods but a 35.8% marginal tax rate for the terminal period. He justified the latter by citing to academic literature.

The court adopted the petitioner expert's 21% rate. It pointed out the company had not paid taxes at the marginal rate since at least 2000. In the five years leading up to the merger, it paid effective rates of between 16.5% and 29.2%. Its cash tax rates ranged from 9.6% to 24.1%. The low effective rate stemmed from the company's "indefinite reinvestment election," meaning the company represented to auditors that it planned to defer indefinitely paying U.S. taxes on overseas profits. To suggest, as the respondent expert's model did, that the company would in the near future pay a marginal tax rate of 35.8%, not to mention perpetually, contradicted historical practice, the court found.

The respondents' expert also deducted $2.24 billion for deferred taxes attributable to the company's foreign earnings and profits. However, the evidence showed the company's effective tax rate accounted for the deferred taxes and the company did not plan to repatriate funds. Consequently, "a proper valuation would have to back out any deferred taxes on foreign earnings from its effective tax rate," the Chancery found.

Finally, the respondents' expert deducted a contingent liability of $3.01 billion from the enterprise value for unrecognized tax benefits. This liability equaled 100% of the reserve the company was required to have on its balance sheet to cover unpaid taxes in the event a tax position it had taken earlier proved incorrect (FASB Interpretation No. 48 (FIN 48)).

To subtract the full FIN 48 liability was excessive, the court found. However, there was evidence that the company would pay out $650 million from the FIN 48 reserve in connection with a dispute resolution. The court said it was reasonable to subtract this amount as a nonoperating liability.

Equity risk premium. The experts disagreed over every input, except the risk-free rate, in computing the company's weighted average cost of capital. Notably, the petitioners' expert used a forward-looking equity risk premium of 5.50%, whereas the respondents' expert used a blended historical and supply-side ERP of 6.41%. The court adopted neither approach but opted for a supply-side ERP of 6.11%.

Beta. The petitioners' expert arrived at a beta of 1.35 by analyzing peer companies. The respondents' expert generated a beta of 1.31 by analyzing weekly observations over a two-year period. The court favored the respondent expert's approach, noting a "beta specific to the Company is more targeted than a blended beta calculated from peer companies, particularly when both experts opined that the Company had few peers."

In the final analysis, the court arrived at a WACC of 9.46%.

The court concluded that in this case the sales process "functioned imperfectly as a price discovery tool." At the same time, it was impossible to quantify the "sales process mispricing." Accordingly, the Chancery decided not to give any weight to the final merger price but rely exclusively on the result of its DCF analysis as the indicator of fair value.

Arctic Cat v. Sabertooth Motor Group

Citation: 2016 U.S. Dist. LEXIS 105583
Date of decision: Aug. 9, 2016
Country: US
State/Jurisdiction: Federal/Minnesota
Court: United States District Court
Type of action: Intellectual Property
Experts: Unknown (plaintiff); Melissa Snelson (defendants)
Judge: Tunheim
SIC: 5571 Motorcycle Dealers
NAICS code: 441228 Motorcycle, ATV, and All Other Motor Vehicle Dealers

Court Nixes Royalty Calculation Relying on Unalike Prior Licenses

A recent *Daubert* case in a trademark dispute explores the criteria courts use to decide whether a royalty calculation based on prior licensing agreements is reliable enough to qualify as admissible. The case featured a noted damages expert who, it seems, tried to make the most of scant or problematic evidence, but whose damages opinion the court excluded in its entirety. The takeaway: Not any licensing agreement will do to develop a creditable rate.

Dueling infringement claims. The parties in this case traded allegations of trademark infringement over the name "Wildcat." The plaintiff designed, built, and sold snowmobiles, all-terrain vehicles, and side-by-sides. The defendants, two related companies and their owner, sold custom-made V8 motorcycles. Both parties at one point filed trademark applications for the use of the Wildcat mark. It appears neither party succeeded in securing an approval from the patent and trademark office.

In January 2013, the plaintiff sued the defendant, claiming infringement, deceptive trade practices, and unfair competition. The defendant countersued, alleging similar wrongdoing by the plaintiff.

At issue in this pretrial opinion was the admissibility under Federal Rule of Evidence 702 and *Daubert* of the reports the defendants' damages expert submitted.

In her initial report, the expert merely discussed how she would calculate the damages to the defendant based on a hypothetical royalty rate. She noted she did not have sufficient information—examples of the plaintiff's licensing agreements for similar marks—to perform an actual calculation. She said a complete analysis would focus on the licensing agreement the defendant and the plaintiff would have developed had the plaintiff not infringed on the mark. The initial expert report did mention an agreement the defendants had made with a third party that required the licensee to pay 25% of his net profits resulting from the retail sales of products using the defendants' mark. In reality, however, the licensee paid only "a few thousand dollars." The agreement had since expired.

As part of discovery, the plaintiff provided information about four trademark licensing agreements it had or had had in place. The defense expert "updated" her report by calculating a royalty rate based on her analysis of three of the four agreements.

None of the agreements were between the plaintiff and the defendants. Under two of the agreements, the plaintiff licensed its trademarks to third parties for use with cold-weather footwear and "ride-in" toy vehicles. Under a third agreement, the plaintiff paid to use a well-known company's trademarks (the Remington marks) on the plaintiff's ATV accessories. The defense expert said she was not able to determine a royalty rate related to the fourth agreement.

Extrapolating from the rates in the three agreements, the defendants' expert claimed the plaintiff would have paid the defendants a royalty of between 2% and 5% for use of the Wildcat mark. This rate translated into the plaintiff owing the defendants between $3.4 million and $8.4 million, the defendants' expert concluded.

Missing link. The plaintiff claimed the opinion was too speculative to assist the trier of fact and should be excluded.

The defendants maintained at a minimum one of the agreements was on point. The defendants' licensing their trademark to the plaintiff was comparable to the plaintiff's obtaining a license for the Remington mark for ATV accessories. The licensing in the instant case would have been for something akin to ATV accessories, the defendants contended. Therefore, there was a valid basis for the defense expert's royalty calculation.

The defendants also argued that case law suggested that the reliability of the calculation was best addressed through the adversarial process and not at the admissibility stage.

The court found all of those arguments unconvincing.

At the outset, the court noted that expert testimony generally is admissible if it is reliable and helps the jury understand the evidence or a contested fact. "Although the factual basis of an expert's opinion is generally an issue of credibility rather than admissibility, an expert's opinion should be excluded if it is so fundamentally unsupported that it can offer no assistance to the jury," the court noted. (internal citation omitted)

The court explained that courts typically permit recourse to a "purportedly reasonable hypothetical royalty rate" for damage calculations "where the hypothetical rate is based on prior licensing agreements between the parties in the litigation or involving the licensing of the at-issue marks to other parties." But when the rate estimate is based on some other consideration, courts are less willing to allow the use of a hypothetical royalty rate.

This was the situation here, the court observed. It was impossible to predict from the three licensing agreements forming the basis of the expert's calculation what the plaintiff would have paid to license the defendants' mark.

For one, none of the agreements dealt with the mark at issue in the case. Second, the defendants were not a party to any of the agreements. Moreover, the circumstances in two of the agreements were different from the posture in the instant case. In the two agreements, the plaintiff licensed its marks to a third party. In the instant case, the assumption was that the defendants would have licensed their mark to the plaintiff.

The court found it "highly unlikely" that an agreement between the parties would have resembled the agreement the plaintiff and Remington had made, observing both of those companies were "established, storied companies with well-known marks," whereas the defendants were new to the market.

The court also noted there was reason to doubt the reliability of the expert testimony. An actual agreement between the defendants and a third party focused on the mark in dispute and specified a 25% royalty rate and yet the licensee paid only a few hundred thousand dollars. Here, the expert determined a far lower royalty rate, between 2% and 5%, and arrived at damages amounting to millions of dollars. A calculation that relied on royalty agreements not involving the defendants and not involving the mark at issue was "so speculative that it would offer no assistance to the jury," the court concluded.

It declined to admit the expert testimony.

Baumboree v. Baumbouree

Citation: 2016 La. App. LEXIS 1388
Date of decision: July 13, 2016
Country: US
State/Jurisdiction: Louisiana
Court: Court of Appeals
Type of action: Marital Dissolution
Experts: Mark Shirley (wife/appellant); unknown (husband/appellee)
Judge: Keaty
SIC: 8011 Offices and Clinics of Doctors of Medicine (except mental health specialists, HMO medical centers, and ambulatory surgical and emergency centers)
NAICS code: 621111 Offices of Physicians (except Mental Health Specialists)

Spouse's Unilateral Stock Agreement Sets Value in Divorce Action

An issue that often arises in divorce cases involving a professional is what to do with the shareholder agreement the owner-spouse signed. Does it set the value of the owner's interest? Citing precedent, a majority of a Louisiana appeals court recently said yes, no matter that the nonowner spouse had refused to sign the agreement and the contract addressed the disposition of the owner spouse's stock in circumstances other than divorce. The decision triggered a noteworthy dissent.

'Subjective and static value.' Louisiana is a community property state. The husband was a pediatrician. During the marriage, he bought one share in a medical group for $1,000. More than 10 years later, the shareholders signed a stock subscription agreement in tandem with a shareholder agreement that specified that in the event of death, incapacity, disqualification, or termination of employment the corporation would buy back each share for $1,000. "At no time and under no circumstances shall the Corporation be called upon to pay more," the agreement stated.

The husband signed the contract, but the wife refused. At the time, the couple was separated and contemplating divorce. Some nine months later, there was a final divorce decree that the wife subsequently contested. By trying to subpoena financial documents from the medical corporation, it appears the wife tried to dispute the value of the husband's share in the practice.

The corporation resisted discovery, and the husband filed a motion asking the trial court to rule as a matter of law that the value of his share for purposes of marital distribution was $1,000.

The wife opposed the motion. She claimed the stock was community property, and the agreement was not applicable to her because she had not signed it. Moreover, the agreement fixed the value of the husband's share only in four situations in which there was a buyback. Those situations did not include divorce and/or partition of community property.

The wife also retained a CPA who stated in an affidavit that he was asked to value the husband's medical practice. The expert explained that to do a valuation he needed to identify and quantify two "distinct intangible assets": goodwill and going-concern value. He said it was necessary to determine the fair value of the stock in the context of the partition. He noted the "subjective and static stated value contained in the shareholder agreement excludes all of the necessary elements which must be considered in quantifying either the 'fair market value' or 'fair value' of the community property."

The trial court ruled in favor of the husband and also granted the corporation's request to nullify the wife's subpoena.

'Fundamentally flawed' argument. The wife appealed the ruling to the state Court of Appeal. In finding error with the trial court's ruling, she made essentially the same arguments against the validity of the shareholder agreement she had made to the trial court in the earlier proceeding. Relying on the shareholder agreement meant assigning "an arbitrary price ... not based on any indicia of financial value" to value the husband's use and enjoyment of the ownership interest, the wife contended.

The appeals court began its analysis by saying the wife's argument was "fundamentally flawed." Under applicable case law, "transfer restrictions affecting community property consisting of corporate stock that were contractually agreed to by one spouse are binding on the noncontracting spouse," the court explained.

It went on to say that stock transfer restrictions did not affect the ownership of the stock "but merely qualify the privilege of the disposition of the stock." Here, the court said, even though the stock issued to the husband was in his name only, it was community property. However, the right to manage the stock exclusively belonged to the husband, the owner-spouse. The wife's refusal to sign the agreement did not affect the applicability of the contract's stock valuation, the appeals court said.

Case law was clear that it was inappropriate to consider the goodwill of the husband or the goodwill of the other stockholders in valuing the husband's share, the court noted. Here, the appeals court also dismissed as "irrelevant" the statements the wife's expert had made regarding the need to ascertain goodwill and going-concern values related to the company. If the husband were forced to sell his one share back to the corporation, all he would receive was $1,000, the court added. Consequently, the appeals court upheld the trial court's value determination.

More to stock ownership. Two judges dissented. At the outset, they disagreed with the majority's claim that the wife's argument was "fundamentally flawed."

The dissent said the law was clear that a spouse in whose name stock in a corporation was registered had the authority to enter into an agreement that contained transfer restrictions. However, no authority supported the husband's claim that the value determination in the stock agreement had to be used in a partition action.

Under the applicable statute, ownership, the dissent explained, is "the right that confers on a person direct, immediate, and exclusive authority over a thing. The owner of a thing may use, enjoy, and dispose of it within the limits and under the conditions established by law."

The dissent noted that, although in this case the stock agreement set the value in case of disposition of the stock in four specific situations, the agreement did not fix the value for the husband's use and enjoyment of the stock. Owning a share in the corporation had value to the husband "outside of a disposition in the few enumerated circumstances," the dissent said.

As specific examples, the dissent pointed to shareholder voting rights, a right to receive dividends or distributions, and a right to receive part of the proceeds in case of liquidation. "Each of these rights inures some benefits to [the husband], and such must be valued for the purposes of the partition," the dissent stated.

Because none of the circumstances the stock agreement addressed were present in the instant case, the valuation in the agreement was inapplicable, the dissent maintained. The trial court was obligated to determine the value of the stock to the owner-spouse outside the context of these limited circumstances, the dissent said. It concluded a remand to the trial court was appropriate.

Berger v. Berger

Citation: 2015 Ohio App. LEXIS 5336
Date of decision: Dec. 31, 2015
Country: US
State/Jurisdiction: Ohio
Court: Court of Appeals
Type of action: Marital Dissolution
Experts: John D. Davis (husband); Robert A. Ranallo (wife)
Judge: Wright
SIC: 1711 Plumbing, Heating, and Air-Conditioning (except environmental controls installation; and septic tank, cesspool, and dry well construction)
NAICS code: 238220 Plumbing, Heating, and Air Conditioning Contractors

Lay Testimony About Offer to Buy Represents Admissible Valuation Evidence

In an Ohio divorce case, the wife appealed the trial court's exclusion of a friend's testimony as to his offer to buy the husband's company. She also attacked the prevailing expert's valuation, both in terms of the expert's qualifications and methodology. The appeals court declined to second-guess the lower court's rulings on the parties' expert opinions. But it found the trial court missed the issue in the case, the valuation of the contested company, when it brushed aside a real-world offer to buy as irrelevant. This case includes a useful discussion on valuation methodology and gives insight into how an expert's arguments play to the court.

A 'real' offer? The husband owned a 99.85% equity interest in a privately held company that owned and operated manufacturing companies in the United States, Mexico, and China. Part of the husband's interest was separate property that the husband either had received as a gift from his parents or had acquired prior to the marriage.

A major point during the divorce proceedings concerned the valuation of the company and the valuation of the marital portion of the husband's interest, that is, the appreciation in value during the marriage. However, the court's opinion does not provide great detail (legal and factual) on the issue of separate property.

Both parties retained business valuation experts whose testimony the trial court admitted. At the same time, the wife tried to introduce testimony from a former employer and friend who, she said, had made a written offer to pay $12 million for 80% of the company's stock; under the offer, the husband would retain a 20% interest in the company and would stay on for another five years.

The trial court, after asking the husband whether the company was for sale and hearing the husband say that it had never been for sale, refused to admit the testimony of the wife's employer/friend, finding it was not relevant. The court said: "An offer for sale for a company that's not even for sale? People can offer any kind of monetary amount for a company that they're never going to have to pony up the money for because it's not for sale." The wife testified on direct examination that she thought the company was worth $15 million based on the friend's offer to buy.

Experts' different views of the company. Neither of the business valuators came close to valuing the company at $15 million. But the experts also disagreed sharply with each other's valuation of the company and, even more, the valuation of the marital portion of the company.

The wife's expert portrayed the company as "very diversified" because its entities made different products and catered to a varied clientele. He explained that, generally speaking, diversification was a good thing: It meant less risk to a business because, if one part did not perform well, its other segments would not suffer negative consequences. The wife's expert allowed that there was some risk to the husband's business because the husband and certain "key" employees were "so integral" to the company's operations.

The wife's expert valued the company under a market approach, an asset approach, and an income approach. Under the market approach, he said he looked to the Standard Industrial Classification Codes (SIC codes) to find comparable companies and concluded the company was worth $14 million.

Under an asset-based analysis, he found the company was worth $7.8 million. However, neither he nor the opposing expert relied on the result from this valuation methodology in determining the final value.

Under the income approach, the wife's expert performed a discounted cash flow (DCF) analysis based solely on the company's management projections. Ultimately, he relied on the DCF result to conclude the fair market value of the husband's interest in the company, on a controlling basis, was $10.5 million.

The husband's expert saw the company in a completely different light. It was not "diversified" but "fragmented," he said. According to him, a diversified company had a common core, which a fragmented company lacked. The subject company and its subsidiaries shared a management team, but the subsidiaries had nothing in common. They served different segments of the population. The expert pointed out that the company grew by acquiring businesses, not organically. This meant going into debt. He described the company as highly leveraged and at risk of not having enough cash to cover its debt. He said part of the reason for his lower valuation of the company was its increase in debt ($5.6 million), which lowered the fair market value.

In terms of methodology, he rejected the market approach, finding there were no companies comparable to the husband's company considering its "eclectic" nature. He criticized the wife's expert for looking to publically traded companies as comparables. Those companies, he said, had sales in the billions whereas the subject company had sales of only $40 million during the relevant years. He also objected to the use of the SIC codes whose categories, he thought, did not capture the nature of the husband's company.

The husband's expert's asset-based valuation showed the company was worth about $6.5 million, but the expert did not rely on it.

Instead, he relied on the income approach. He explained that he used a capitalization of earnings approach to determine the company's historical cash flow. He explained it was "key" to look at a company's past performance to obtain a complete picture of any company.

He also used a DCF analysis to determine the company's future performance. He considered management projections but cautioned that the company did not ordinarily prepare projections—only at the request of its bank. Therefore, the projections were "optimistic." In reviewing projections for 2008, 2012, 2013, and 2014, he found the company had not met its goals for 2008 and 2012. Part of the reason was the economic slowdown, he allowed, but part of it was that the optimistic nature of the projections, he concluded.

The parties' experts disagreed over the need to look at a company's past performance. The wife's expert said doing so in this case would not provide reliable information as to the company's ability to generate cash flow considering the recession. In contrast, the husband's expert maintained a buyer would want to see how the company had done in the past rather than simply rely on projections.

According to the husband's expert, the company's fair market value was about $7 million.

Disagreements over determining appreciation in value. Under Ohio law, even though part of the husband's interest in the business was separate property, the wife had a right to part (generally 50%) of any appreciation in value that occurred during the marriage.

The wife's expert relied on gift tax returns to value the marital portion of the business. He concluded it was worth nearly $9.4 million.

The husband's expert arrived at a value of a bit over $4 million. He explained that, even though considering gift tax returns was "useful," there were other factors to consider that in this case suggested there was no appreciation during the marriage. He said that, early in its history, from 1993 to 1997, the company showed income of about $2.5 million. In contrast, later, from 2007 to 2011, the income had dropped to about $1.2 million. As the husband's expert saw it, the husband now owned more of a company that was worth less.

The wife's expert relied on gift tax returns from the early years, when there was more income and less debt, the husband's expert claimed. He said that, under the income approach as he performed it, the final value of the appreciation was about $4 million. (The court's opinion states two slightly different figures as to the fair market value of the appreciation. It does not provide details on valuation methodology.)

The trial court credited the valuations the husband's expert proposed. It approved of the expert's two-part income approach, and it credited the expert's observations that the company's growth was by acquisition and at the cost of increasing its debt and that the company was not performing "as well as it did before." The fair market value of the marital portion of the business was about $4 million, the trial court found.

Wife says Pratt would not approve. In appealing the judgment at the state Court of Appeals, the wife launched a series of attacks against the trial court's judgment, including its value determinations. Most of the arrows missed their targets, but the wife's claim that it was error to exclude the testimony of her employer/friend to buy most of the company for $12 million had traction with the appeals court.

"To conclude that what [the friend] was willing to pay for the company was not relevant because the owner was not willing to sell disregards the ultimate issue—the value of [the company]," the Court of Appeals said. There was evidence that the offeror had done a review of the company's financial performance and had received "other information" from the wife's attorney. It appeared he had significant knowledge if he was willing to pay $12 million for 80% of the company, the appeals court said. The offer was evidence of a valuation based on the market approach, the Court of Appeals decided.

It added that any issues as to how believable the offeror was as a witness or how sound his method for arriving at this offer was went to credibility, not to the relevance and admissibility. Credibility issues were best addressed during cross-examination.

The appeals court found the erroneous exclusion of relevant valuation testimony was sufficient to remand, and it ordered the trial court "to revisit" the valuation of the company. It instructed that, in so doing, the trial court had to consider not only the expert testimony, but also allow the offeror to testify about his offer and the bases for it.

The wife's attacks on the prevailing expert testimony were less successful. Some of them lacked support in case law or revealed a misreading of the record or misstatement of the testimony, the appeals court found. For example, the appeals court dismissed the wife's claim that the trial court erred when it accepted the conclusions of the husband's expert over those of the wife's expert because her expert was more qualified. Unlike the husband's expert, the wife's expert previously had been appointed as a special master to perform complex business valuations. The appeals court said it was not clear why such an appointment made one expert's testimony more credible than the other's and that the wife failed to state a reason or provide case law to support her claim.

The wife contended the husband's expert conceded that he did not complete a market-based valuation. Not doing so made his opinion "worthless," she argued. The appeals court disagreed. First, the expert was only required to consider all three of the valuation approaches. He did not have to complete them. Here, the husband's expert explained that no companies were similar to the subject company. Consequently, his abandoning the market approach was not a surprise, the appeals court said.

The wife maintained that the husband's expert applied a discount for lack of marketability that was too high—21.3%—considering the husband was the majority owner of the company. Also, the expert improperly relied on studies involving minority owners.

The husband countered that his expert explained that the "fragmented nature" of the company would make it more difficult to sell the company: Because it would take longer to sell the company, the rate of the marketability discount was higher. Also, the husband said, his expert was able to justify the use of the contested studies because the stocks at issue were restricted in nature. This is what affected the expert's analysis of the marketability discount, not the minority position of the stocks, the husband claimed.

The appeals court dismissed the issue by noting the trial court had discretion to believe the explanation the husband's expert gave for using "minority owner studies."

Finally, the wife argued Shannon Pratt, "the undisputed and acknowledged expert with respect to business evaluation procedure," would not approve of the methodology the husband's expert used to value the company. Accordingly, the trial court should have rejected the valuation.

The trial court was under no obligation to accept Pratt's methodology just because of his reputation, the Court of Appeals said.

Based on the trial court's improper exclusion of relevant valuation testimony, the Court of Appeals ordered the lower court to redetermine the value of the company as well as the value of the marital portion of the company.

In re Estate of Bittner (Bittner I), (Bittner II)

Citation: 2014 Pa. Dist. & Cnty. Dec. LEXIS 857
Date of decision: Sept. 17, 2014
Country: US
State/Jurisdiction: Pennsylvania
Court: Probate Court
Type of action: Breach of Fiduciary Duty
Judge: Livengood
SIC: 5812 Eating Places (full-service restaurants)
NAICS code: 722511 Full-Service Restaurants

Citation: 2016 Pa. Super. Unpub. LEXIS 179
Date of decision: Jan. 21, 2016
Country: US
State/Jurisdiction: Pennsylvania
Court: Superior Court of Pennsylvania (Court of Appeals)
Type of action: Breach of Fiduciary Duty
Experts: Joshua Lefcowitz (executors); none (appellants)
Judge: Olson
SIC: 5812 Eating Places (full-service restaurants)
NAICS code: 722511 Full-Service Restaurants

Shareholder Agreement Sparks Suit Over Discount Use in FMV Calculation

Are discounts a given in a fair market value determination? This question was at the heart of a buyback dispute involving two closely held family businesses and an ambiguous shareholder agreement that governed the transaction. The executors and the beneficiaries of the decedent minority shareholder's estate argued over whether the plain language of the agreement prohibited the application of discounts for lack of marketability and lack of control. The court resorted to business valuation expert and lay opinion testimony to resolve the issue.

Interests in closely held family companies. The decedent owned minority interests in two closely held family entities. The decedent's will specified that his wife and son were each beneficiaries of 25% of the decedent's residual estate. The shareholder agreement applicable to both companies provided that each company had an option to buy back all of the decedent's common stock at a price equal to the fair market value (FMV) of the stock, which the companies were prepared to do.

A key provision in the shareholder agreement stated in relevant part that the fair market value of the stock being transferred meant "that amount determined by the Shareholders to be the per share fair market value of the Company issuing such Common Stock … for the calendar year of the transfer, multiplied by the number of shares of Common Stock being transferred." The provision went on to say that, if the shareholders failed to determine the "per share fair market value" of the company for the year of transfer, the company should hire a CPA to determine that value.

After the decedent died, the co-executors of his will (the decedent's brother and a bank) valued the stock by applying discounts for lack of marketability (DLOM) and lack of control. The combined value of the stock was slightly less than $720,000.

Discounts 'inherent' in FMV concept. The beneficiaries contested the stock's valuation. At a hearing in front of the probate court, they claimed the plain language of the shareholder agreement militated against the use of discounts. In calculating the FMV of the stock, "no discounts should have been applied, that the value should have been calculated on a pro rata basis." They claimed that, in discounting the value of the decedent's stock, the executors violated the agreement and breached their fiduciary duty. According to the beneficiaries, the pro rata valuation of the shares was about $1.1 million.

The executors countered the language of the agreement was ambiguous. Consequently, there was a need for the introduction of extrinsic evidence (parole evidence) to clarify the terms of the contract. The probate court agreed to hear testimony on the matter.

The beneficiaries, standing by their position that the shareholder agreement was unambiguous, offered no testimony or evidence.

The executors presented expert witnesses and lay testimony to support their interpretation of the agreement. A representative of the bank that served as co-executor testified that "discounts for lack of marketability and lack of control when there's a calculation of fair market value" of minority shares in a closely held corporation are "always" a "component of developing the fair market value" of the shares.

The CPA who was retained by the issuing companies to value the stock in this matter testified that the term "fair market value," as it appeared in the shareholder agreement, was well defined in the business valuation community. "When you're valuing a minority interest in a closely-held business as [here, the term includes] adjustments for the lack of control and lack of marketability that exists with that non-controlling ownership interest." The expert went on to say, "the term 'per share fair market value' equates to the fair market value of the equity interest being valued."

According to the expert, "discounts for lack of control and lack of marketability are inherent in the fair market value concept" for minority interests in closely held corporations. He added that a prior valuation of the stock of the issuing companies also adjusted for lack of control and lack of marketability and none of the stockholders objected to the valuation. The expert noted that not accounting for lack of control and marketability in a fair market value determination was "nonsensical" because without the discounts "the corporations would be forced to buy the shares back at a price that was higher than fair market value."

Finally, the decedent's brother who was one of the signatories of the shareholder agreements said that, when using the term "fair market value," it was not his intent to "just take the total company value and then just distribute the *pro rata* portion of it."

Ambiguity as to meaning of FMV. Following the hearing, the probate court found the agreement was "inherently ambiguous." It said the agreement's requirement that the share price be the "per share fair market value of such Company" allowed for two reasonable interpretations.

Under the beneficiaries' interpretation, there was a need "to calculate the total fair market value of the entire company first and then simply divide by the number of shares." According to the court, "this interpretation assumes that 'fair market value' specifically refers to the 'Company.'"

Under the co-executors' equally reasonable interpretation, the shareholder agreement required an assessment of the fair market value of the shares themselves, "including an analysis of the specific shares to be transferred," followed by a calculation of the value of the transferred shares, the court said. This interpretation assumed that "fair market value" refers to the shares themselves as opposed to the company as a whole, the court added.

The court said it was necessary to consider parole evidence to uncover the meaning of the agreement's provisions. The court also noted with disapproval the beneficiaries' failure to produce any testimony or evidence, and it adopted the executors' interpretations and discounted value. However, the court did note that the executors' interpretation "renders the method of calculation [the requirement that the per share value be calculated, then multiplied by the number of shares being transferred] as surplusage." But, said the court, this interpretation "does not gut the clear and essential mandate that the stock be assessed at 'fair market value.'"

Valuation affirmed. The beneficiaries unsuccessfully challenged the ruling at the state's intermediary appellate court, which adopted the lower court's ruling with approval. The appeals court declined to comment on the appellants' various claims. Accordingly, the decedents' shares in the issuing companies were subject to a DLOM and discount for lack of control.

Bocek v. JGA Assocs., LLC

Citation: 2016 U.S. Dist. LEXIS 38259
Date of decision: March 23, 2016
Country: US
State/Jurisdiction: Federal/Virginia
Court: United States District Court
Type of action: Damages (incl. Lost Profits)
Experts: Joseph Estabrook (plaintiff); Hempstead & Company (defendant)
Judge: Cacheris
SIC: 8011 Offices and Clinics of Doctors of Medicine (except mental health specialists, HMO medical centers, and ambulatory surgical and emergency centers)
NAICS code: 621111 Offices of Physicians (except Mental Health Specialists)

Court Snubs Lost Earnings Analysis Based on 'Incomplete Use' of Data

A doctor sued a business partner for losing the opportunity to acquire a medical practice at a certain price and with it the ability to earn a living. The appeals court validated his breach of fiduciary claim against the defendant and remanded for a trial on remedies. The plaintiff's expert testimony did not go well. The trial court found the expert used inappropriate methods (income and market approaches) or applied them incorrectly. The expert's lost earnings calculation was the product of speculation, it said. A critique running through the court's opinion—and one that comes up in many cases—is that the plaintiff's expert chose to consider only the data that were favorable to the plaintiff while ignoring real-world numbers and facts.

Backstory. The plaintiff was a board-certified allergist. From 2007 until his firing in 2010, he worked as a full-time physician and medical director at a multioffice medical practice. In 2007, his salary was $225,000, plus an additional $45,000 in benefits. He agreed with the practice's owner that he would receive yearly salary increases of $60,000 up to a total of $200,000. Because the practice had done well in prior years, there was an expectation that it would continue to grow and result in the opening of a new office. After the practice's owner died in 2008, the plaintiff's salary continued to rise, such that in 2009 and 2010, the plaintiff earned over $500,000 a year, including benefits.

But the business suffered after the owner's death. In 2009, the company's gross revenue dropped by 7.8%. In 2010, it declined by another 3.8%. Net earnings fell even more sharply. The data showed that in 2007 the company's gross revenues were over $4.7 million; in 2010, they were about $4.3 million. Notwithstanding the decline in the company's performance, the plaintiff's baseline salary almost doubled during the same period.

In October 2010, the plaintiff was fired amid allegations of improprieties, including sexual harassment, and a dispute over his high salary. A few days later, he signed a consulting agreement with the defendant and the defendant's company to explore the possibility of opening a new medical practice. Shortly thereafter, the plaintiff suggested to the defendant that the deceased owner's estate might be willing to sell the assets of the medical practice (the plaintiff's former place of employment).

The plaintiff did not disclose the various reasons for his firing to the defendant, but he insisted the defendant leave the plaintiff's name out of any negotiations with the estate. Ultimately, the defendant secured an option to buy the practice's assets for $1 million.

Shortly before the acquisition went through, the defendant discovered the allegations against the plaintiff and terminated his contract with the latter. In response, the plaintiff demanded the defendant either abandon the deal or transfer the opportunity to acquire the practice for $1 million to the plaintiff. The defendant went ahead as planned, and, in June 2011, a court approved the $1 million acquisition.

Meanwhile, the plaintiff filed a complaint against the defendant claiming, among other things, breach of fiduciary duty. Initially, the trial court found the defendant was under no obligation to the plaintiff and, therefore, did not breach any duty. The 4th Circuit Court of Appeals disagreed and remanded the case for a new trial on the issue of remedies.

During the new trial, the plaintiff claimed he was entitled to over $1.2 million in damages related to the lost opportunity to acquire the subject company's assets as well as $2.1 million in lost income. Both parties presented expert opinions.

Loss or no loss of business opportunity? The plaintiff argued that, but for the defendant's breach, he would have been able to buy the practice for $1 million. The damage he suffered from losing the opportunity was the amount of the medical practice's fair market value minus $1 million.

The plaintiff's expert used an income and a market approach to calculate the company's FMV.

For the income approach, the expert relied on the capitalization of earnings method, which showed the company was worth about $2.6 million in June 2011, not accounting for discounts. Based on revenue from the first five months of 2011, the expert projected the company's revenue for the year would be $4.6 million. He increased projected revenue by 5% and determined the company's "profitability rate" (i.e., ratio of earnings before taxes to revenue) would be 13.96%. Applying the profitability rate to the $4.6 million in projected revenue resulted in a normalized net annual earnings figure of $639,400 before taxes and about $478,300 after taxes. The expert then applied a "mid-year convention adjustment factor," which produced an annual net income of $532,800. Finally, he applied a 20.2% capitalization rate to arrive at the $2.6 million valuation.

Under the market approach, he relied on the merger and acquisition method. He derived pricing variables by looking at 21 companies whose annual revenue ranged from $144,000 to $125 million. He subsequently applied the variables to the subject company's projected revenue of $4.6 million and EBT of $639,400 and weighted both outcomes at 50% each. Using a 10% discount for lack of marketability (DLOM), he concluded the company was worth a little less than $2.3 million.

Based on the weighted average of the results from the income and market analyses, he concluded the company was worth about $2.2 million in June 2011—the date on which the defendant took ownership of the practice. Subtracting the $1 million actual sales price from the expert's valuation resulted in a loss to the plaintiff of $1.2 million.

In contrast, the defendant relied on the 2010 valuation a financial consulting firm had prepared for the practice—a few months before the plaintiff was fired. The appraiser favored an asset-based approach because the practice was marginally profitable in 2009 and "neither the Company's recent history nor the near-term outlook for the Company suggest growing revenues or positive earnings." The appraiser also performed a market-based analysis as a cross-check and concluded the subject company was worth about $620,000 in August 2010.

There was evidence that the defendant early in the due diligence process leading up to the $1 million acquisition believed the business was worth around $3 million. He testified that his opinion changed when he found out, sometime after the acquisition in 2011, that the practice had engaged in inappropriate billing practices. After changing accounting procedures, gross revenue dropped "tremendously," the defendant said—about $3 million in 2012. It was then, he said, that he believed the business's value was "somewhere south" of $600,000. He said he stopped working for the business in August 2012. The only payment he ever received related to its operation was about $75,000 in salary. His business partner—an investor in the acquiring entity—earned the same amount for managing the subject company in 2011. The defendant maintained that in the final analysis the 2010 appraisal report accurately valued the company.

The court agreed with the defendant. It found the most credible valuation method was the asset approach, resulting in the 2010 valuation. The appraiser's pessimistic near-term outlook for the company was accurate considering the business showed a net profit of less than $6,000 in 2010, and it recorded substantially decreased revenue in 2011, the court said.

Expert's inconsistent view. The court rejected the plaintiff expert's calculation for a number of reasons. It noted that the capitalization of earnings approach required "[s]tabilized earnings or cash flows expected to continue into perpetuity." Considering this premise, the approach was "ill-suited" to valuing the subject company, which showed steady declines in gross revenue and net earnings after the prior owner's death in 2008. The court also faulted the expert for assuming the plaintiff could have returned the company to its past profitability had he been an owner of the business. Considering the plaintiff had no experience with the business side of a medical practice and intended to fire the practice's then manager and reduce offices and staff after the acquisition, the assumption of an improved performance was "speculative," the court observed.

What's more, the expert did not apply the income approach in a reliable manner, the court said. To project business earnings for 2011, he decided to use revenue from the first five months of the year only. Using that revenue and growing it by 5%, he arrived at revenue for the entire year of $4.6 million when the company actually earned only $3.8 million. Moreover, revenue during those few months did not align with revenue from the prior two years, when it had steadily declined. Also, considering the plaintiff did not work at the company in 2011, the revenue figure from the first five months was not a reliable indicator of the company's success under the plaintiff's ownership, the court added.

It pointed out a contradiction in the expert's position by citing to a case from 2000 in which the expert had attacked another expert's capitalization of earnings calculation as unreliable because it was based on revenue figures that "were atypical of both the historic performance of the company and any legitimate projection of its future earnings."

Finally, the court found there was no justification for growing revenue by 5% considering in reality revenues in 2009 and 2010 had decreased. During those years, the practice was under the plaintiff's management. The court noted that the expert developed the profitability rate based on estimates from the company's most profitable years when it was under the leadership of the deceased owner. Had he considered the company's performance during the plaintiff's subsequent, two-year tenure as medical director, the valuation would have been much lower, the court said.

The expert's market-based analysis was equally unreliable for the simple reason that the companies he selected to derive pricing variables bore no reliable resemblance to the subject practice, the court decided. The set of "comparables" included 13 businesses with revenue below $1 million and four businesses with revenue over $20 million. Two of the four businesses had revenue over $100 million.

By crediting the $620,000 business valuation, the court concluded the plaintiff would have had to pay more for the company than it was worth and, therefore, suffered no damages from losing the opportunity to buy it.

Lack of reliable earnings indicators. The plaintiff also demanded $2.1 million as compensation for lost income. This amount, he said, represented the salary he would have been able to pay himself as the owner of the practice. He relied on an estimate from his expert that suggested the plaintiff lost between $1.23 million and $1.37 million by not employing himself from February 2011 through 2015.

The expert first calculated a baseline salary of over $447,000 by averaging the plaintiff's income from 2009 and 2010. He then made a 4% upward cost of living adjustment and also added $60,500 in annual benefits before discounting to present value and adjusting for various mitigation scenarios. For example, he relied on an industry salary database to determine the median annual salary for an allergist working in a practice with 10 physicians was about $235,000, not including $30,000 in benefits. At the time the plaintiff was fired, the practice had five physicians: four were part-time, and the plaintiff was full-time. The plaintiff also was the only board-certified allergist. The expert said he did not consider the business's post-sale performance because he worked off the assumption that the plaintiff would run the business. In reality, the defendant and his business partner were in charge.

According to the defendant, if he had known why the plaintiff was fired, he never would have entered into a business relationship with him. As it was, the defendant immediately terminated the contract he had with the plaintiff once he had confirmed the information he eventually received.

The court discredited the lost earnings calculation from the plaintiff's expert. It noted the "incomplete use of information," that is, the expert's decision to base the baseline salary on the plaintiff's highest earnings years, while ignoring the much lower earnings from 2007 and 2008. It pointed out that the plaintiff's 2009 salary was nearly twice as much as his salary from 2007 when he was essentially managing the same caseload. The plaintiff's salary grew automatically even though the practice's revenues and profits declined, the court observed again. Consequently, the salary increased as a percentage of gross revenue from 4.77% in 2007 to 10.46% in 2010. Considering the plaintiff's salary was a burden on the business and contributed to the plaintiff's termination, relying on the 2009 and 2010 salaries as a basis for estimating future earnings put the entire calculation in question, the court said.

Further, the expert did not account for other factors that would have interfered with the practice's future success such as the plaintiff's plan to fire the practice's manager, the loss of some patients during the interval between the plaintiff's termination and the approval of the sale, and likely cuts in offices and staff. The court also mentioned potential workplace tensions stemming from the plaintiff's return to the practice given the circumstances of his firing, which, it suggested, could negatively affect profitability.

Also, the court found the expert attributed salary and benefits too early—starting in February 2011 instead of June 2011 (the official approval of the sale). While this inaccuracy may not seem a grievous mistake, the court found it actually caused the expert to overestimate earnings by between $100,000 and $115,000. According to the court, this overestimation lowered the court's confidence in the quality of the expert's work product even further.

Similarly, it criticized the expert's use of industry data that based salaries for allergists on a practice of 10 physicians when the subject practice only had five doctors.

All told, the court found there was a dearth of evidence as to what salary the plaintiff reasonably could have earned had he become an owner of the practice starting in mid-2011. It decided the most reliable indicator was the defendant's testimony that the defendant and his business partner paid themselves $75,000 each in 2011 for managing the newly acquired practice. Accordingly, the court awarded the plaintiff $150,000 in lost income.

Broyles v. Cantor Fitzgerald & Co.

Citation: 2016 U.S. Dist. LEXIS 74597
Date of decision: June 7, 2016
Country: US
State/Jurisdiction: Federal/Louisiana
Court: United States District Court
Type of action: Securities
Experts: Theodore Urban (plaintiffs); unknown (defendants)
Judge: Brady
SIC: 6211 Security Brokers, Dealers, and Flotation Companies (oil lease and gas lease brokers offices)
NAICS code: 523999 Miscellaneous Financial Investment Activities

Is Expert Opinion Based Solely on Experience Admissible?

Experts and attorneys know that under *Daubert* and Rule 702 testimony based on nothing more than the expert's "because I say so" (ipse dixit) is destined to be excluded. But what about testimony that is based on the expert's experience alone? A recent *Daubert* ruling in a tangled securities fraud case provides an answer that may surprise testifying experts.

Extensive relevant experience. The plaintiff-investors were a group of 12 individuals and three retirement systems. They alleged that they suffered financial losses after the defendant CEO of an investment firm tricked them into investing millions of dollars in "pooled asset" hedge funds. Instead of pursuing individual investment strategies, the funds essentially all invested in doomed collateral debt obligations (CDOs). Other financial firms assisted in the fraudulent transactions, the plaintiffs alleged.

The plaintiffs hired a lawyer with extensive experience in the field of securities industry regulation. He explained that for over 20 years he had served as general counsel for a major regional broker and investment advisor. In this capacity, he was a member of the company's board of directors and the board's executive committee. He also was a trustee of the firm's employee pension and benefit plans. He managed the firm's legal and compliance departments, which meant ensuring the firm cooperated with and responded to all regulatory investigations and litigation matters. Moreover, before joining the private sector, he had worked for nine years as a staff attorney and manager at the Securities and Exchange Commission and Commodity Futures Trading Commission.

During his deposition, he was asked to comment on a statement from a defense expert that, even though the defendants "were aware of regulatory exposure arising out of the SEC investigation, they did not know that it could also lead to private civil litigation, such as this case."

The plaintiff's expert rejected this argument as "not reasonable or consistent with my experience in the industry." Regulatory investigations into transactions that involve significant customer losses were a "reasonable predictor of potential regulatory and/or civil liability," the plaintiffs' expert said. He further stated that he did not know the statistics, but, based on his experience in the industry, he believed "a relatively high percentage ends up in civil litigation."

In their *Daubert* motion, the defendants argued this opinion was inadmissible because the expert had not performed an analysis but merely cited to his experience.

The plaintiffs contended experts were able to qualify and render opinions based solely on their experience in the field.

Explain how and why. The court sided with the plaintiffs. "Despite the requirements set forth in *Daubert*, a proffered expert's experience may be used to determine whether they are qualified as an expert under FRE 702 [Federal Rule of Evidence 702]," the court noted.

The court cited to statements from the advisory committee in 2000, when Rule 702 was amended to incorporate the *Daubert* requirements. "Nothing in this amendment is intended to suggest that experience alone—or experience in conjunction with other knowledge, skill, training or education—may not provide a sufficient foundation for expert testimony," the committee notes state.

They go on to say that "the text of Rule 702 expressly contemplates that an expert may be qualified on the basis of experience. In certain fields, experience is the predominant, if not sole, basis for a great deal of reliable expert testimony."

The cardinal rule for an expert relying on experience alone is to "explain how that experience leads to the conclusion reached, why that experience is a sufficient basis for the opinion, and how that experience is reliably applied to the facts," the advisory committee notes say.

The court found the plaintiffs' expert met those requirements. He showed he had had years of experience in the relevant field, securities regulation, and in the financial industry, and he discussed "the basis of his opinion in regards to his experience in the industry."

The court admitted the testimony. It noted the defendants were free to explore concerns regarding the reliability of the opinion in "vigorous cross-examination."

Bruno v. Bozzuto's, Inc.

Citation: 2015 U.S. Dist. LEXIS 156339
Date of decision: Nov. 19, 2015
Country: US
State/Jurisdiction: Federal/Pennsylvania
Court: United States District Court
Type of action: Contract
Experts: James N. Dragotto, Dr. Murli Rajan (plaintiffs); John A. Slavek, David M. Duffus (defendant)
Judge: Brann
SIC: 5411 Grocery Stores (except convenience stores, freezer plans, and grocery stores with substantial general merchandise)
NAICS code: 445110 Supermarkets and Other Grocery (except Convenience) Stores

Court Excludes Pro Forma-Based Economic Damages Analysis

A damages strategy misfires. In a breach of contract case, two highly educated experts working together on a case relied on the opposing side's data for their damages calculation. They did not test the information and in a subsequent report refused to revise their discounted cash flow analysis despite their access to newly uncovered sales data. The defects in the experts' calculations went to the core of the damages analysis and rendered the latter inadmissible under *Daubert*, the court found.

'Infamous plot twist.' Trouble started before the litigation. The plaintiffs, a married couple, owned and operated a small supermarket chain, Bruno's Market Inc. The wife, a CPA with nearly 20 years of experience, was in charge of the books. The defendant was a wholesale distributor.

Around the time the plaintiffs contemplated suing the defendant for the alleged breach of a supply agreement related to their flagship store, the wife destroyed all financial and accounting records. This impropriety came to light during discovery, when the defendant asked the plaintiffs to produce all records reflecting on the financial operations of the business during the relevant period. In response, the plaintiffs' attorney informed the defendant "none of the documents requested in your letter exist." During her deposition, the wife admitted that she "threw [the] records out." She said "the paper copies went in the trash" and the business computer was "thrown out" as well. The court later called this "the most infamous plot twist in the life of this six-year-old litigation."

The wife's admission caused the defendant to claim the missing information prevented it from developing its defense and asked the court to sanction the plaintiffs. The court reserved judgment because the plaintiffs argued some key financial information was available via its third-party payroll and accounting service.

Defendant disavows early projections. However, the intentional destruction of evidence came to haunt the plaintiffs when it came to show damages. They retained two experts—one, a J.D., MBA, and the other, a Ph.D., MBA—who used a discounted cash flow (DCF) analysis to calculate damages. The experts prepared two joint reports, one in 2011 and one in 2014.

Since initially no financial data were available from the plaintiffs, the experts decided to use one of the defendant's sales projections from 2007 (prior to the litigation) for their cash flow calculation. The projections appeared in an internal document termed "pro forma." According to the defendant's vice president of sales, the defendant typically used a pro forma to decide whether or not to make a loan to another party and "to determine the break-even point of a store's operations." The contested 2007 pro forma served the same purpose in the instant case. It helped the defendant decide not to enter into an agreement with the plaintiffs, whereby the defendant would have supplied the plaintiffs' store with groceries and paid off one of the plaintiffs' outstanding loans.

The contested 2007 pro forma pegged the plaintiffs' sales at $150,000 per week. But even before the plaintiffs' experts prepared their first expert report, the defendant revised its projections when it learned, before the litigation, that the plaintiffs' weekly sales figures for the relevant period actually were fluctuating around $110,000, a number that suggested a decline in sales. A new pro forma showed that the plaintiffs' sales were no more than $120,000 per week.

Further, after the plaintiffs' experts had submitted their first report in 2011, the plaintiffs' attorney was able to retrieve data that showed that total sales for the relevant period were about 6.21 million, which translated into approximately $120,000 in sales per week. The data also showed that the plaintiffs' business lost over $188,000 overall during the relevant period and over $199,000 in the months preceding the closing of the plaintiffs' flagship store.

However, in their 2014 report, the plaintiffs' experts basically reused the sales projections from the defendant's 2007 pro forma document rather than the actual sales figures. They made one minuscule adjustment, which assumed that net sales for 2007 were approximately $7.57 million instead of $7.6 million. In both reports, the experts also noted that they relied on the gross margin and total expense figures stated in the contested 2007 pro forma.

In their depositions, the plaintiffs' experts were adamant that they did not independently verify the numbers. "I did not project anything. I used [the defendant's] report," one expert testified. And "I think we've tried to make that totally clear to everyone through this whole matter that the basis for our calculations are numbers provided by [the defendant].... I relied on their expertise in that field."

The experts did not remember exactly how they obtained the contested pro forma or how the defendant arrived at the $150,000 projected weekly sales. Nor did they seem to know what the purpose of the pro forma was. "I'm not concerned with what the numbers are if they [the defendant] feel this is what the numbers would be," the first expert said. In terms of verifying the defendant's numbers by reviewing the source books and records, he noted, "all of the scrutiny was done by [the defendant]. I did not feel that there was a need to." And, he added, "I relied on [the defendant]'s being the experts." When asked just how much he relied on the defendant's expertise, the expert replied, "One hundred percent." The second expert adopted the same stance. When asked whether he did any separate analysis of the competition in this line of business, he said, "No, I did not."

The defendant also hired two experts, who were CPAs and had business valuation credentials. Upon review of the plaintiff experts' first report, the defense experts sharply criticized the opposing experts' "unbridled" use of the pro forma. The sales projections were unreliable, the defense experts said, because the plaintiffs' missing financial data at that time made it difficult to assess the store's profitability during the year immediately preceding the litigation or determine the financial condition of the market in the three years prior to the litigation. One of the experts suggested that the plaintiffs were doing poorly for reasons unrelated to the defendant's conduct and might have had to close their flagship store because of financial problems rather than the defendant's conduct.

After the plaintiffs' experts submitted their second report in 2014, the defendant filed a *Daubert* motion to exclude all expert damages testimony and asked the court again to sanction the plaintiffs for destroying evidence.

'Garbage-in-garbage-out' problem. The defendant argued the plaintiffs' experts adopted the sales projections in the 2007 pro forma without independent analysis or verification of the numbers. The experts essentially took a "no questions asked" approach when selecting the inputs for their DCF analysis. Moreover, the defendant's subsequent analysis proved the weekly sales projections were "grossly" overstated when compared with the sales the plaintiffs actually made. Consequently, the defendant at that time rejected the contested pro forma figures. Further, the defendant used the pro forma for one specific purpose: to determine the break-even point in its loan analysis. The pro forma was not intended to project sales or potential contract damages, the defendant noted. By relying on the $150,000 weekly sales figures rather than the actual $120,000 figure, the plaintiffs' experts created over $1.3 million in annual sales "out of thin air," the defendant argued. The effect of this improper extrapolation was further compounded with each year projected into the future.

According to the plaintiffs, the contested projections were "inherently" reliable because they were the product of the defendant's analysis, and they were not self-serving. The plaintiffs further contended that any disagreement over the expert testimony went to the weight and not the admissibility of the financial evidence.

The court sided with the defendant. It expressed "surprise" over the decision by the plaintiffs' experts to disregard the restored financial data even though they had received the revised data and reviewed the downward-adjusted sales numbers. The court observed that, under controlling case law, experts who do not independently test the accuracy of data fail the jurisdiction's *Daubert* reliability requirement. Verification of the figures was particularly important in the instant case because the plaintiffs' experts lacked industry knowledge, the court said. It also considered the experts' decision to rely on the contested pro forma figures self-serving: Doing so "unquestionable yielded a significantly higher damages estimation than what would have resulted had the experts conservatively employed the actual data."

The court observed both experts were "wholly unfamiliar with the methodology or purposes underlying the pro forma." They neither participated in the data collection nor in the creation of the pro forma; instead, "they merely took what Defendant gave them." During testimony, the experts were unable to answer questions such as whether the contested pro forma was based on a market study, how many pro formas the defendant generated, and which pro forma was the one on which the defendant ultimately relied.

In an aside, the court wondered whether the experts "were not given the full story or if proceeding with the $150,000 pro forma was entirely their own decision based upon its evident propensity to yield the highest damages output."

The court rebuffed the plaintiffs' weight-versus-admissibility argument, which it said was a common objection by proponents of contested expert testimony. Although federal courts may overlook certain "surface-level flaws" related to methodology or data collection, they decline to do so when the evidence is so defective as to be "completely unhelpful to the trier of fact." Here, the flaws in the expert analysis went "directly to the core of the contested opinions" and made it impossible to produce a meaningful ex post recalculation or restatement of the data, the court found.

It acknowledged that the DCF analysis was a generally accepted and widely used technique. But "inputting inflated projections into a discounted cash flow model in an attempt to arrive at a contract damages figure warps the true purpose of such models, especially when contradictory data exists." The court agreed with the defendant that the plaintiff's damages analysis suffered from the "garbage in, garbage out" problem.

In striking down the plaintiffs' expert opinions in their entirety—reports and testimony—the court added:

> The role of an expert witness in federal court is thus necessarily an active one—it requires, at a minimum, an appropriate mix of careful fact-gathering and constructive analysis, two hallmarks in any expert methodology assuring that the proffered opinions stand on good footing and proceed with a tested analysis.

Finally, to highlight the compounding effect of the experts' use of an inflated base quantity, the court attached the following exhibit:

	Pro Forma	Actual 2007
2007	7.5728	6.2116
2008	7.8000	6.3979
2009	8.0340	6.5898
2010	8.2750	6.7875
2011	8.5233	6.9912
2012	8.7790	7.2009
2013	9.0423	7.4169

Burtch v. Opus, LLC (In re Opus East, LLC) (I), (II)

Citation: 2015 Bankr. LEXIS 923
Date of decision: March 23, 2015
Country: US
State/Jurisdiction: Federal
Court: United States Bankruptcy Court
Type of action: Bankruptcy
Experts: Quentin Mimms (trustee); Daniel Lentz (defendants)
Judge: Walrath
SIC: 6552 Land Subdividers and Developers, Except Cemeteries
NAICS code: 237210 Land Subdivision

Citation: 2016 U.S. Dist. LEXIS 42955
Date of decision: March 31, 2016
Country: US
State/Jurisdiction: Federal/Delaware
Court: United States District Court
Type of action: Bankruptcy
Experts: Quentin Mimms (trustee/appellant); Daniel Lentz (defendants/appellees)
Judge: Andrews
SIC: 6552 Land Subdividers and Developers, Except Cemeteries

Bankruptcy Court's Going-Concern Valuation Weathers Appeal

A Chapter 7 bankruptcy case, which was appealed, includes a valuable analysis for solvency experts of the prevailing tests for deciding when a company is insolvent. Establishing the insolvency date is critical as it determines what type of valuation the expert must perform. In reviewing the Bankruptcy Court's insolvency findings, the appellate court also discussed the use of a liquidation discount under a going-concern analysis.

Insolvency date dispute. The debtor company was part of a network of regional entities that developed, built, and sold commercial real estate projects as soon as possible rather than holding them. For each project, it created a special purpose entity (SPE). The debtor's operation focused on the Northeastern and Mid-Atlantic regions. Its parent company owned other entities that provided financial, payroll, architectural, and other services to the debtor and other entities within the network.

In addition to loans from within the network, the debtor had a $20 million unsecured line of credit with Bank of America (BoA) and obtained construction financing from outside banks. The debtor operated successfully from 1994 until 2008. But, after the collapse of the financial markets beginning in fall 2008, the company became unable to sell its real estate projects and secure financing to complete projects in the works. As a consequence, in July 2009, it filed for Chapter 7 bankruptcy.

In 2011, the trustee sued the debtor and a gaggle of related entities as well as individuals, alleging 67 counts of wrongdoing. The trustee pursued recovery under various legal theories, including avoidance of fraudulent and preferential transfers. The outcome in terms of a number of claims turned on the issue of insolvency.

At trial, the trustee and the defendants presented expert testimony, and both experts disagreed sharply on when the debtor became insolvent. The trustee's expert proposed it was as early as December 2006 under two of the controlling insolvency tests. In contrast, the defendants' expert said the debtor was not insolvent until July 2009, when it filed for bankruptcy.

The Bankruptcy Court sided with the defendants' expert and ruled for the defendants on the insolvency.

Balance sheet test. The experts first squared off on the balance sheet test, which defines insolvency as the financial condition in which an entity's debts exceed its property at fair value.

Both experts agreed that, as of June 30, 2008, the company's liabilities were between $237 million and $242 million. But they disagreed over the valuation of the debtor's assets.

The trustee's expert contended that, under this test, the debtor became insolvent as early as June 2008. Even though it reported $317 million in assets on its June 2008 financial statements, the fair value of the assets was only $153 million to $196 million. He explained he used the liquidation value of the assets because certain creditors held demand notes from the debtor and could ask to be paid back at any moment. Also, the debtor needed additional capital to cover its current operating expenses. And it was required to reduce its line of credit from BoA to zero by August 2008.

The defendants' expert used a going-concern analysis. He said that, while it's true that GAAP require that demand notes be recorded as current liabilities, the notes generally are not considered matured and payable until there is an actual demand for repayment. Here, the notes specified that there would be no payment until five days after the creditors made a written demand. There never was a demand for payment, and, therefore, the notes never became mature, the defendants' expert reasoned.

Concerning the August 2008 deadline to pay down the third-party line of credit, the expert explained that the debtor knew about the requirement and repaid the loan to BoA without liquidating any assets. Consequently, there was no justification for using a liquidation value based on that argument.

The Bankruptcy Court credited the defense expert's testimony in favor of using a going-concern valuation. Citing applicable case law, the court said: "A business does not have to be thriving in order to receive a going concern valuation. Before the going concern valuation is to be abandoned, the business must be 'wholly inoperative, defunct or dead on its feet.'"

Besides the points the defendants' expert made, the court pointed to other signs of commercial viability after June 2008. The debtor was able to sell several projects above liquidation value as late as the third quarter of 2008, the court said. Moreover, the debtor had an agreement to sell a project in Washington, D.C., that had a fair market value of $93 million and was to close in October 2008 or November 2008. The intended buyer had made a $5 million nonrefundable earnest-money deposit in May 2008 to the debtor's SPE that owned the project. The debtor and the buyer worked together into early 2009, leaving the debtor optimistic that the buyer would not give up on its deposit and the sale would go through. However, in January 2009, it became clear that the debtor would be unable to close the sale.

The court concluded the debtor was insolvent under the balance sheet test no earlier than Feb. 1, 2009.

Alternative tests, same conclusion. The court found an analysis of the debtor's financial situation under the alternative insolvency tests supported its insolvency date determination.

Inadequate capital and cash flow tests. As the trustee's expert saw it, without loans from related entities, the debtor lacked the capital necessary to continue its operations past December 2006. Therefore, it was insolvent as of that date under the "inadequate capital" and the "cash flow" tests. The inadequate capital test determines whether, at the time of transfer of assets, the debtor had insufficient or "unreasonably small" capital. The cash flow test asks whether, at the time of transfer, the debtor intended to incur or believed it would incur more debt than it could repay.

The defendants' expert noted that into early 2009 the debtor regularly paid its bills as they came due. It continued to operate the real estate business during that time and was able to complete and sell seven of its projects in the ordinary course of business. He dismissed the objection from the trustee's expert that for purposes of determining cash flow insolvency it was irrelevant whether the debtor continued to operate and pay its bills if it only did so because of its ability to borrow in a manner unrelated to its own creditworthiness.

According to the defense expert, the opposing expert failed to acknowledge that the debtor was able to obtain third-party loans between December 2006 and December 2008 because it had its own $20 million credit line from BoA. The ability to obtain credit from BoA showed the bank had confidence in the debtor's financial strength, the expert maintained.

In terms of cash flow, the trustee's expert performed an analysis of the debtor's projections, as adjusted by the expert, that he said showed "the debtor's capitalization metrics were among the worst in the industry." He alleged its net working capital averaged -$80 million and the availability of highly liquid assets to pay liabilities was below the industry's lowest quartile. He added that, between 2000 and 2008, the debtor only recorded positive cash flow twice from operations. He considered this "chronic" negative cash flow further indication that the debtor had unreasonably low capital for its operations.

The defendants' expert claimed the trustee expert's use of liquidity ratios to compare the debtor's financial condition to that of its peers and show inadequate capitalization was a flawed approach. The trustee's expert used real estate investment trusts (REITs) that were not similar to the debtor because they typically bought and held commercial real estate, whereas the debtor built and promptly sold its projects.

Moreover, because of the debtor's business model (with its uneven and unpredictable cycle of sales), the compared ratios were ineffective indicators of the debtor's ability to sustain its operations. In fact, the trustee's expert admitted as much when he said he only used this approach as a "sanity check."

The defense expert also objected to the "adjusting" the opposing expert did to the debtor's projections and cash flow to show inadequate cash. Because the debtor's financial statements did not differentiate between current and noncurrent assets and liabilities, the trustee's expert created data necessary to perform his current ratio analysis. The defense expert noted that the adjusted cash flow projections indicated a $7 million cash shortfall in the first five months of 2007 that did not actually occur. The debtor's forecasts were reasonable and showed the debtor had adequate capital between December 2006 and March 2008.

The court found the defendants' expert persuasive. Apropos the adjustments the trustee's expert made, the court noted, "[C]ash flow projections created by expert witnesses for litigation purposes are inherently suspect." Here, the debtor's projections were reasonable in terms of what the debtor expected to sell and borrow. In terms of adequate capital, the court noted that, even though the debtor periodically experienced "cash flow timing issues," it was able to deal with them by borrowing from BoA or a related-party lender. The debtor also obtained capital infusions from the parent company or triaged projects or sold an asset. The debtor's primary source of capital was its retained earnings, the court found. Through its operations and additional equity contributions from the parent company, the debtor's equity increased from $12 million to $75 million by the end of 2008, the court noted. Financials that KPMG audited confirmed solvency through at least March 2008, the court observed.

According to the Bankruptcy Court, the debtor slipped into insolvency because of the "unexpected depth and breadth of the market collapse after the bankruptcy filing of Lehman Brothers in September 2008." The debtor's management did not initially understand how severe the market downturn was or the detrimental effect it would have on the debtor. Management's projections indicated the debtor would be profitable through the end of 2008. Although the capital markets had begun to freeze by then, the debtor still believed it would be able to profit from the anticipated closing on the Washington, D.C., project.

The debtor only revised its forecasts at the end of January 2009, when it assumed for the first time that the project had turned into a flop. It knew that, without the sale, the debtor would run out of cash. And it did so.

In sum, the "unreasonably small capital" test and the "cash flow" test confirmed the court's finding under the balance sheet test: that the debtor was not insolvent until Feb. 1, 2009. Therefore, transfers that occurred before that date were not avoidable, the court concluded.

Ultimately, the Bankruptcy Court found for the trustee on seven of the alleged 67 counts and for the defendants on the remaining 60 counts.

Liquidation discount inappropriate. The trustee appealed the judgments with the federal district court (D. Del.), which handles bankruptcy appeals in this jurisdiction. Among other things, the trustee assigned error to the Bankruptcy Court's insolvency date determination. It was wrong for the court to value the debtor's assets under a going-concern analysis rather than a liquidation analysis prior to Feb. 1, 2009, the trustee contended. Further, even under the mistakenly applied going-concern valuation, the Bankruptcy Court erred in crediting the defense expert's opinion and rejecting the testimony of the trustee's expert.

The appellate court went over the insolvency tests and the evidence in front of the Bankruptcy Court and found there was adequate support for the Bankruptcy Court's use of a going-concern valuation based on the February 2009 insolvency date.

In terms of expert testimony, the reviewing court noted that the trustee "makes much of the fact" that the Bankruptcy Court rejected the trustee expert's analysis because he used the liquidation value of the assets, as opposed to the going-concern value. This proposition oversimplified the reasoning informing the Bankruptcy Court's decision to reject the trustee expert's valuation, the district court found.

The trustee's expert essentially applied a 40% to 50% "liquidation discount" to the debtor's assets because he assumed the debtor had to sell its real estate within a month. The Bankruptcy Court rejected this assumption and found the discount was incompatible with a going-concern valuation.

The district court agreed. It pointed out that "a liquidation discount may be appropriate, even under a going concern analysis, to account for the 'conversion of assets into cash during a reasonable time.'" Prior cases have upheld a 12-month-to-18-month period for the sale of operating assets, whereas, in the instant case, the trustee's expert allowed for 30 days. A sale within a period this short amounted to a forced sale rather than a sale within a reasonable time, the district court noted. Therefore, the Bankruptcy Court did not clearly err when it found the trustee expert's valuation did not align with the applicable going-concern valuation.

Moreover, the defendants' expert did not blindly rely on the debtor's financial statements but examined company records and independently tested the reliability of those statements. The Bankruptcy Court did not err in favoring the defense expert's insolvency analysis, the district court concluded. It affirmed the Bankruptcy Court's judgment.

In re Case No. 800 Bourbon St.

Citation: 2015 Bankr. LEXIS 3963
Date of decision: Nov. 20, 2015
Country: US
State/Jurisdiction: Federal/Louisiana
Court: United States Bankruptcy Court
Type of action: Bankruptcy
Experts: Patrick Gros (debtors); Ellis J. Roussel (creditor)
Judge: Magner
SIC: 5813 Drinking Places (Alcoholic Beverages)
NAICS code: 722410 Drinking Places (Alcoholic Beverages)

Court Rebuffs Attempt to Allocate Excess Value to Intangible Assets

After years of fighting among the owners of two related companies, the companies filed for bankruptcy and sold their assets as a package. In the latest round of the proceedings, the debtors petitioned the court for the right to deviate from the previously sanctioned formula for allocating the sales proceeds between the companies. The court's decision includes an informative discussion of the methods—multiple of earnings approach versus capitalization rate approach—experts proposed for valuing one of the assets, a well-known bar and nightclub.

Old allocation plan. The Chapter 11 debtors were two New Orleans businesses: "800 Bourbon," whose only asset was real estate, and "Oz," a popular dance club that rented the real estate and also owned a warehouse. The companies shared common ownership, but the owners' infighting led to two bankruptcies, a state court receivership, and finally the sale of the combined assets to pay off the companies' debts. The debtors had explored the possibility of selling each company's assets separately, but they decided a package sale would produce a greater return to creditors. The bankruptcies were jointly administered to minimize administrative costs.

Initially, the debtors filed a joint disclosure statement and plan for reorganization that proposed to sell the combined assets for $4.75 million, unless a higher or better offer presented itself. The debtors committed themselves to allocating $3.6 million (75.79%) of the sales price to 800 Bourbon's real estate and the remainder $1.15 million to Oz (24.21%)—the club and the warehouse. The debtors claimed, and the court agreed, that this allocation formula would ensure the payment of all secured and unsecured claims as well as take care of administrative and priority debt.

Just prior to confirmation of the reorganization plan, a better offer came along. An auction produced a bid to buy the assets of both debtors for $8.175 million. Subsequently, the debtors asked the court to change the allocation formula. Two main creditors objected to the debtors' new allocation approach. One of the creditors also objected to the debtors' valuation of Oz's dance club.

Recalibrating club's value. Under the new plan, the debtors proposed to allocate only $3.475 million to 800 Bourbon based on a real estate appraisal at the time of auction. The debtors argued that, since the real estate was 800 Bourbon's only asset and the price of real estate was easy to determine and would essentially have remained constant, the only explanation for the difference in sales price was that the debtors earlier had miscalculated the value of Oz. The increase in price had to be attributable to Oz's intangible assets, that is, the club's goodwill and trade name, the debtors maintained.

To support their position, they offered the testimony of their accountant, who lacked expertise in business valuation but qualified as an expert in restaurant accounting. He explained how the debtors would report the sale on their tax returns. Under generally accepted accounting principles (GAAP), the debtors had to specify the price attributable to each of the various assets. This meant using the appraised values for each tangible asset and allocating any difference to goodwill. In other words, goodwill represented a plug category when the sales price exceeded the aggregate appraised value of the assets.

He also noted that one common way for determining the value of an ongoing business, such as Oz's dance club, was to use a multiple of earnings approach. After adjusting for the savings Oz made during the administration of its case, the expert found that Oz had annual earnings of about $383,000.

The court explained that GAAP was not controlling in this situation. The tax implications of the sale were of little consequence to the allocation of the sales price. As for the multiple of earnings approach, the court observed that a "rough valuation" of a going concern typically was three to five times annual earnings, which suggested that Oz's value resulting from this approach was approximately $1.91 million.

One of the creditors claimed that a valuation from its appraiser indicated Oz was worth only about $1.5 million. In fact, even though that appraiser qualified as a business valuation expert, he declined to provide a valuation of Oz because of his limited access to information. Instead, he explained an alternative method for valuing the business, using a capitalization rate formula. This approach, he said, required first determining the company's annualized net income. Because of his lack of access to the company's financials, he adopted the annual earnings figure the debtors' expert calculated. He next developed the capitalization rate applicable to the earnings to calculate the company's value. He explained the various components making up the cap rate, including company-specific risk, industry risk, and size premium, and ultimately decided on a capitalization rate of 14.62%.

He said he originally added a large—40%—control premium to account for the history of the company. As he saw it, the prior infighting of the owners had a negative effect on the earnings of the business. However, the sale of the business to a single owner would lead to an increase in income by as much as 10%, he assumed.

He explained that he initially did not factor industry or company-specific risks into his cap rate determination but found they would account for an additional 4%. An increase in the cap rate meant a reduction in the control premium to 10%, he said. Using this valuation method, the company was worth about $2 million. It was appropriate to add approximately $534,000 to account for its furniture, fixtures, inventory, and the warehouse, he said. This approach yielded a total value of $2.534 million for Oz.

Synergistic value. The court rejected the debtors' claim that only Oz's asset—the dance club—had the potential to increase in value. It noted that 800 Bourbon's asset—real estate—was valued based on the income it could generate and on comparable sales data. According to the court, "no one would seriously argue that either factor will remain constant." The court observed that appraisals "capture the value of an asset for a snapshot in time." Only time would tell whether or not an asset's present value would change, the court said.

The court further explained that all of the debtors' assets were sold as a package, not piece by piece. Allocating the value from the real estate appraisal to 800 Bourbon and the rest of the sale price to Oz "would not account for the synergy of the package," the court said. Because all the assets were combined in the sale, "the total effect was greater than the sum of the individual pieces." Accordingly, the increased value was to be apportioned between the companies in accordance with the method the disclosure statement set forth.

The court said that the expert valuations of Oz—based on a multiple of earnings or capitalization rate approach—suggested a range of values between $2 million and $2.534 million. If the court were to deviate from the allocation formula the debtors' disclosure statement detailed and were to adopt the debtors' new proposal, creditors of 800 Bourbon that had endorsed the original allocation formula would suffer adverse consequences. On the other hand, applying the agreed-upon formula to the new sales price did not lead to absurd results, the court found. Consequently, it decided to allocate almost $6.2 million (75.79% of the sales price) to 800 Bourbon and $1.98 million (24.21%) to Oz.

Cdx Holdings, Inc. v. Fox (Fox II)

Citation: 2016 Del. LEXIS 334
Date of decision: June 6, 2016
Country: US
State/Jurisdiction: Delaware
Court: Supreme Court of Delaware
Type of action: Securities
Experts: Unknown (Plaintiffs); Grant Thornton, PwC (Defendants)
Judge: Holland
SIC: 3829 Measuring and Controlling Devices, NEC (medical thermometers)
NAICS code: 339112 Surgical and Medical Instrument Manufacturing

High Court Dissent Rebukes Chancery's Analysis in Option Valuation Case

Almost a year ago, the Delaware Court of Chancery issued a noteworthy decision in a case featuring a medical science company that went through a controversial merger. The court sided with option holders who claimed the company's board of directors allowed for the undervaluation of the plaintiffs' shares. In a stinging rebuke to the financial firms working on the transaction, the Chancery said the work reached a "new low" in terms of "motivated" valuations. When the company appealed the decision with the Delaware Supreme Court, a majority of judges affirmed, but one dissenting judge had harsh words for the Chancery's analysis. The most recent ruling shows how much the evaluation of financial evidence depends on the judge.

Backstory. The flashpoint was Caris, a medical science company that developed advanced diagnostic and prognostic tools for special illnesses, including cancer. It had three subsidies. Two, TargetNow and Carisome (SpinCo.), were developing potentially lucrative treatments but were not making any profit. A third, Caris Diagnostic, was consistently profitable. To secure financing for TargetNow and Carisome and generate money for its stockholders, Caris sold its profitable enterprise in a spin/merge transaction to a third party, Miraca Holdings.

David Halbert, the founder and chairman of Caris, owned 70.4% of the company's fully diluted equity. A private equity fund owned another 26.7% interest, and Caris employees owned most of the remaining 2.9% in the form of stock options. The options were cancelled in connection with the merger.

A 2007 stock incentive plan said that each option holder was entitled to receive the amount by which the fair market value of a share covered by an option exceeded the exercise price. It required the plan's administrator to determine the FMV in good faith. The company's board of directors was the plan administrator. For purposes of the transaction, Caris assigned SpinCo. the value of $65 million and notified the option holders they would receive $0.61 per share.

The option holders sued in the Delaware Court of Chancery, contending the company breached the plan because members of the company's management, rather than board members, determined how much the option holders would receive. Also, the $0.61-per-share price was not a good-faith determination but the result of an arbitrary and capricious process.

The principal players (and individual defendants) in the transaction were Halbert and Gerald Martino, the company's executive vice president, chief financial officer, and chief operating officer.

The court found that Halbert and Martino wanted to achieve a tax-free spinoff. This meant Caris needed to show that the value of SpinCo. was lower than the basis. Martino, the Chancery decided, was most directly involved in manipulating the valuations underlying the transaction, and he set the value of the options. Halbert signed off on the value determination.

Martino used two major accounting firms in connection with the transaction. He instructed Firm 1 to provide a valuation of SpinCo. that ensured zero tax liability. The Chancery found Firm 1 did so by performing a transfer tax valuation instead of a fair market valuation. The defendants knew the nature of the valuation but used it to determine the consideration owed to the option holders, the Chancery found.

Firm 2 was to provide a second valuation opinion. In the past, it had performed sound stock-option-related valuations for the company, the court found. However, within the context of the merger, it abandoned its prior methodologies and produced a valuation "so much lower as to be itself suggestive of bad faith," the court found. Firm 2's work was basically a (sloppy) copy job of the analysis Firm 1 had done, the Chancery found.

The Chancery heard testimony from some board members about their opinions of the value of SpinCo. at the time of the merger. It noted the witnesses spoke "with conviction," but it discounted the testimony, considering it the product of "hindsight bias." Psychology defines hindsight bias as "the tendency for people with outcome knowledge to believe falsely that they would have predicted the reported outcome of an event," the Chancery explained.

The court concluded the board members never made the required FMV determination. They left the valuation to Martino, with Halbert approving it. Therefore, the Chancery said "the good faith standard arguably does not even apply."

It decided to apply the good-faith test to Martino's and Halbert's actions. It found the evidence showed they believed the spun-off companies had a much higher value, "around \$300 million," than the \$65 million determination used in the context of the merger. It also concluded that, even if they actually believed in the \$65 million valuation, they used a process that was arbitrary and capricious. By the Chancery's calculation, damages owed to the option holders were over \$16.26 million. (Find an extended discussion of *Fox v. Cdx Holdings*, 2015 Del. Ch. LEXIS 194 (July 28, 2015), as well as the court's opinion, at *BVLaw*.)

Short approval from court's majority. In appealing the decision with the state Supreme Court, the company assigned a number of errors to the Chancery's findings. A main argument was the Chancery mistakenly focused on the conduct of the company's officers, particularly Martino, instead of the board members' conduct.

The Supreme Court's majority declined to revisit the evidence. It noted that findings of historical fact were subject to a "clearly erroneous" standard of review. The reviewing court must defer to the trial court's credibility determinations as well as findings related to physical and documentary evidence or inferences from other facts, the majority observed.

It pointed out that it was the Chancery's prerogative to discredit the trial testimony of defense witnesses and instead rely on contemporaneous evidence that suggested at the time of the transaction they believed TargetNow was about to become profitable and Carisome would succeed in producing a marketable product. Based on interest from several strategic buyers and advice from the company's financial advisor, they believed TargetNow could be sold for anywhere from \$150 million to \$300 million, the Chancery had found.

In sum, the record supported the Chancery's findings and the Chancery arrived at its findings through an "orderly and logical deductive reasoning process," the Supreme Court's majority said. Therefore, it upheld the Chancery's judgment in favor of the option holders.

All-out dissenting opinion. One judge issued a lengthy dissent in which she maintained there was no reason in this case to defer to the Chancery's factual findings. For one, by finding the board did not act to determine Spinco.'s FMV, the Chancery failed to make the requisite finding that the board acted in bad faith. To make matters worse, the Chancery then applied the good-faith test only to the conduct and beliefs of Halbert and Martino. If the Chancery believed the board members had not acted, it should have examined whether a majority of the board *intentionally* failed to act in the face of a duty to act, the dissent said with emphasis. To show an intentional failure to act "typically requires an extraordinary set of facts," which were not present in this case, the dissent said.

The dissent was particularly critical of the Chancery's embrace of the "hindsight bias" theory when assessing the credibility at trial of board members. Members of the high court "should be skeptical of court rulings predicated upon social science studies, particularly, where, as here, such theories impact a trial court's own post-trial impressions of the testimony offered," the dissent said.

According to the dissent, comments the Chancery made immediately after trial, such as "the credibility of the people on the [B]oard who made these decisions" was "very, very strong," seemed to be accurate and sincere accounts of the Chancery's impressions of trial testimony. In contrast, the Chancery's ultimate findings seemed based solely on the Chancery's own hindsight bias and were "logically disconnected from the record of evidence before it, from the trial court's own immediate, on-the-record impressions of the trial, and from the requirements of the legal test established by the Plan."

The dissent discounted the "contemporaneous" evidence the Chancery relied on in favor of the "collective statements of the directors who testified at trial." These statements, the dissent said, showed the internal valuations by the company's financial advisors predated critical events that caused the value of the spun-off companies to drop around the transaction date. Digging deeper into the record, the dissent also noted that the Chancery made no findings that any of the company's directors, excepting Halbert, knew of the flaws in the value analyses the accounting firms performed. To the extent management acted in bad faith, the dissent noted, "knowledge of bad faith cannot be imputed from an executive or even from a director to the entire Board on the basis of this record."

The dissent said the facts suggested the board determined the stock's FMV. Based on legal advice, the board hired an independent advisor to assist with the determination. Minutes of a telephonic meeting showed that Accounting Firm 1 reviewed its $65 million valuation with board members, who then authorized the final transaction based on the valuation, the dissent stated. Finally, the dissent, citing again to trial testimony from board members, pointed out some witnesses said the valuation Firm 1 had provided was in line with or even higher than the values the witnesses had assigned to the spun-off companies at the time of the transaction.

In sum, the dissent found the state Supreme Court owed no deference to the Chancery's findings of fact. The Chancery was wrong to rely on the problematic hindsight bias theory in evaluating the credibility of board members, the dissent found. The Chancery should have credited the trial testimony of the board members, which was evidence that the board satisfied its obligations under the plan, the dissent concluded.

Code & Code

Citation: 2016 Ore. App. LEXIS 1003
Date of decision: Aug. 17, 2016
Country: US
State/Jurisdiction: Oregon
Court: Court of Appeals
Type of action: Marital Dissolution
Experts: Kramer (wife/appellee); Gary Schaub (husband/appellant)
Judge: Egan
SIC: 8043 Offices and Clinics of Podiatrists
NAICS code: 621391 Offices of Podiatrists

Court Upholds Inclusion of Premarital Value in Property Distribution

An Oregon divorce case includes a noteworthy discussion on the goodwill valuation of the owner-spouse's professional practice. The wife's expert asserted the majority of goodwill was enterprise goodwill, whereas the husband's expert contended most of the goodwill was personal to the husband. What complicated the valuation was that the business started out as separate property. Although the husband's expert determined the premarital value of the practice, the trial court decided to treat the entire business as a marital asset.

Husband argues zero value. The husband was a podiatrist who owned his own, successful practice before marrying the wife. Based on a five-year average, the husband's personal income was nearly $310,000. This amount was considerably higher than the average income for a podiatrist in the state. Medicare and insurance reimbursements made up the majority of the income.

The valuation of the practice was the sticking point in the divorce proceedings. Both sides offered expert testimony.

The wife's witness used an excess earnings approach and determined goodwill overall was worth $600,000. He said he "looked at numerous conditions surrounding [the husband's] practice, including competition and the use of his name and his business name or not and other factors." The expert considered 60% of goodwill—$360,000—to be enterprise goodwill and the remainder personal goodwill. He concluded the value of the enterprise goodwill plus the value of tangible assets was the value of marital property subject to equitable distribution.

The husband's expert decided the fair market value of the practice was $365,000. It included total goodwill, assets, and accounts receivables. He determined there were liabilities in the amount of $122,000. Consequently, the net FMV was $243,000.

He maintained that enterprise goodwill typically was anywhere from 0% to 33%. Here, considering the location of the practice, staff, website, telephone number, type of patient, insurance plans, and new patient referral sources, the enterprise goodwill amounted to 24% of the entire goodwill, he found. Accordingly, the enterprise goodwill was worth $72,000 and the personal goodwill was worth $227,000. In subtracting the personal goodwill from the net FMV, the appraiser concluded $16,000 was the value that was subject to equitable division.

The husband's expert also prepared a valuation of the business as of the year immediately preceding the marriage. He concluded collections at that time were 51% of the collections at the time of divorce.

Building on the expert testimony, the husband argued the business had zero value for purposes of marital distribution.

The trial court disagreed with the husband's assessment. It found the wife's expert more credible and adopted his valuation "with a slight modification." Specifically, the court subtracted the liabilities the husband's expert determined from the $360,000 enterprise goodwill valuation the wife's expert proposed. The court then added in the value of equipment and supplies and accounts receivables and arrived at an FMV for the practice of $304,000.

The court awarded the husband the business and used the FMV of the business to divide all the assets equally. Before the court entered final judgment, the husband objected, arguing case law required the court to award the premarital value of the business to the husband. The court noted its "finding was based upon assets becoming commingled and living together," and it declined to change its ruling.

Oregon goodwill jurisprudence. The husband challenged the trial court ruling at the state's Court of Appeals. He asserted the trial court's goodwill calculation was wrong. Moreover, the trial court made a legal error in not assigning the premarital value of the business to the husband.

The appeals court noted that under Oregon law enterprise goodwill is subject to marital distribution, but personal goodwill, "which is largely indistinguishable from the individual's future earning capacity," is not.

Goodwill calculation. The husband claimed there was no evidence to support the goodwill calculation. The wife's expert "merely pulled a number out of thin air for enterprise goodwill." Further, this expert used an improper methodology and lacked the "proper credentials to make the valuation."

The appeals court noted it was obligated to uphold the trial court's findings if supported by "any" evidence. Here, the wife's expert submitted testimony and a report, which qualified as "any evidence." At trial, the husband failed to object to the expert's credentials and did not challenge admission of the expert report and testimony, "which included the method [the wife's expert] used and the factors he considered in determining goodwill." Consequently, there was evidence to support the trial court's goodwill findings, the appeals court said.

Premarital value. The husband noted that he had owned the practice more than a decade before marriage. At trial, only his expert had submitted an opinion on the business's premarital value, which the wife did not dispute. Moreover, she had not contributed to building the business. Therefore, the premarital value of the business was not a marital asset.

The wife countered that under the law the trial court had the authority to divide the premarital value as long as the court's determination was "just and proper" under the circumstances. She noted the husband did not argue that the trial court misapplied the statutory or equitable "just and proper" considerations.

The appeals court sided with the wife. It noted that the applicable statute directs trial courts to divide property in a way that is "just and proper in all the circumstances." Property includes real and personal property "that either or both of the parties hold at the time of dissolution, including property that the parties had brought into the marriage." Ultimately, the appeals court said, the trial court's decision turns on whether the property division is equitable in view of all of the circumstances of the parties.

The appeals court noted that, although the husband offered evidence of the premarital value of the business, neither he nor the wife "made a specific argument to the trial court on how to treat that premarital value." When the husband subsequently objected, the trial court explained its decision was based on the commingling of assets and other factors, including how the distribution of assets and debts squared with the parties' circumstances, the length of the marriage, and the contribution to the process.

The Court of Appeals concluded the trial court used the correct analytical framework to arrive at its final value determination and affirmed.

In re Cole

Citation: 2016 Bankr. LEXIS 932
Date of decision: March 24, 2016
Country: US
State/Jurisdiction: Federal/Virginia
Court: United States Bankruptcy Court
Type of action: Bankruptcy
Experts: Robert Raymond (wife/creditor); Dean Heinberg, Bruce Matson (husband/debtor)
Judge: Phillips
SIC: 8021 Offices and Clinics of Dentists
NAICS code: 621210 Offices of Dentists

Why Divorce Valuation Does Not Accord With Chapter 7 Liquidation Analysis

How meaningful is a valuation that was prepared for one type of case in another context? This was the key issue in a combined divorce and bankruptcy case centering on the husband's minority interest in a dental practice. Following the divorce, the husband filed for Chapter 13 bankruptcy and asked for confirmation of his plan. The issue was whether the plan could meet the applicable liquidation test. The Bankruptcy Court said its decision depended on the value of the husband's interest, which, in turn, depended on whether the court was required to adopt, or could simply adopt, the valuation prevailing in the divorce case or had to find a reliable indicator of value elsewhere.

Divorce valuation based on intrinsic value. At divorce, and subsequently during bankruptcy, the husband owned a 25% interest in a dental practice that he had acquired in 2008 for $325,000.

Under a controlling shareholders' agreement, if a shareholder wanted to dispose of his shares, the corporation had a first right of refusal. If it decided not to buy the shares, the other shareholders "shall be obligated to purchase and the Offering Shareholder shall be obligated to sell all of the remaining shares." The agreement included a formula for determining the purchase price for the shares.

At divorce, for purposes of equitable distribution, the trial court determined the value of the husband's interest. Both parties presented valuation expert testimony.

The wife's expert calculated the going concern of the dental practice as a whole, taking 25% of the total. He concluded the husband's share was worth $212,000. The wife's expert also valued the shares using the formula in the shareholders' agreement. The formula value, he said, represented "an absolute floor" in terms of the amount the husband would be able to command from the other shareholders. Based on this calculation, the husband's interest was worth at least $114,200, the wife's expert concluded.

The husband's expert contended the husband's interest was worth about $15,800. He declined to assign any value to the patient records or the goodwill of the practice.

The trial court explained that, based on Virginia law, the applicable standard of value for a valuation done in the context of divorce was the intrinsic value of the business. The intrinsic value is "inherently—and deliberately—a very subjective concept that attempts to determine the worth of the business interest to these parties." The court adopted the value the wife's expert proposed—$212,000—and rejected the valuation of the husband's expert, in part, because it gave no value to "patient charts."

Valuation for Chapter 7 liquidation. Three months after the divorce, the husband filed for Chapter 13 bankruptcy and petitioned the Bankruptcy Court for plan confirmation. In his bankruptcy schedules, he listed the value of the practice at $15,800—the value his expert stated in the divorce proceedings.

The proposed funding of the Chapter 13 plan was $66,000. The plan contemplated monthly payments to the trustee and a $13,000 payment to cover the wife's priority claim of domestic support obligations. This left about $41,800 to cover the claims of unsecured creditors—primarily the wife. The total amount of unsecured claims was about $189,500. Not accounting for present value of future payments, the plan would allow for a distribution of 22% of unsecured claims.

The wife and the trustee objected to the confirmation, arguing the plan failed to meet the liquidation test applicable under the Bankruptcy Code's section 1325(a)(4). In essence, the test requires that creditors in a Chapter 13 bankruptcy receive present value payments that are at least equal to the amount the creditors would receive in a Chapter 7 case. The calculation involves two value determinations: (1) the value of property to be distributed to each unsecured creditor under the plan including administrative costs; and (2) the amount each unsecured creditor would receive if the estate were liquidated in a hypothetical Chapter 7 case, considering administrative costs.

The husband claimed his plan met the test. According to a provision in the plan, "[i]f this case were liquidated under Chapter 7, the debtor(s) estimate that unsecured creditors would receive a dividend of approximately 6%."

The crux of the wife's argument was that the divorce court's valuation of the husband's interest was controlling. If that valuation was applied in a Chapter 7 liquidation analysis, the plan did not qualify for confirmation, she said.

In a valuation hearing in front of the Bankruptcy Court, both parties offered testimony from the same experts that had valued the interest for the divorce proceedings. Moreover, the husband presented the opinion of an experienced Chapter 7 trustee.

The husband's expert maintained that, in the context of a Chapter 7 liquidation, the husband's practice as a "personal-services company" had "zero" value because the liabilities of the business exceeded the value of its assets. Again, the expert placed no value on patient records or goodwill.

The husband's Chapter 7 expert said he had reviewed relevant documents, including an operating agreement, the shareholders' agreement, a balance sheet, and other financial data. He said that, if he were appointed as a Chapter 7 trustee to administer the husband's bankruptcy estate, he would abandon the interest because he did not believe there was "anyone who would pay anything in the open market for that twenty-five percent interest." He added that he assumed that, following the bankruptcy, the husband would be able to practice dentistry somewhere else and would compete with the person acquiring his interest—a fact that would deter potential buyers.

The wife's expert said he had valued some 300 medical practices, including 75 to 100 dental practices, but very few in the context of a Chapter 7 liquidation. He rejected the opposing valuation expert's claim that the patient records had no value. On the contrary, the wife's expert said, "[F]ar and away the most significant asset of any dental practice is its patient base." He adhered to his earlier methodology—basing the value on a division of proceeds after the sale of the whole practice rather than the liquidation of the husband's 25% interest. But, based on updated financial information, he made a downward adjustment, finding the interest was worth $203,000, rather than $212,000.

At the same time, the wife's expert—who was the only expert witness valuing the interest in the event of a buyout—made an upward adjustment to the value he had determined under the shareholders' agreement. Based on the agreement's formula, the interest was worth about $161,300, rather than $114,200.

Revaluation not precluded. The Bankruptcy Court first dealt with the wife's argument that, since the divorce court had decided the valuation issue, the matter could not be relitigated under the collateral estoppel doctrine.

The husband contended that he was not precluded from revisiting the issue since the valuation that prevailed in the divorce proceedings was based on the intrinsic value of the business. This was not the standard of value applicable under Section 1325(a)(4), he said. Relying on expert testimony, the husband emphasized the impediments a Chapter 7 trustee would encounter when trying to market this minority interest in a personal services corporation. The expert testimony showed that the interest had no value in the open market, the husband contended.

The court agreed and disagreed with both sides on different arguments.

It agreed with the husband that collateral estoppel did not apply. Equitable distribution proceedings in Virginia require a valuation "which represents the property's intrinsic worth" to the parties. The valuation the wife's expert offered, and which the divorce court adopted, was based on the value of the interest to the husband and wife, the Bankruptcy Court observed.

In contrast, in the context of a hypothetical Chapter 7 liquidation, Section 1325(a)(4) required a Chapter 7 trustee "to reduce to money the property of the bankruptcy estate" by selling or disposing of the property in other ways, the court explained. "This is different from determining the intrinsic value, or its worth to the parties, in a divorce proceeding," the Bankruptcy Court added.

In an alternative argument, the wife claimed that the going concern value her expert used for his most recent valuation was the appropriate measure of value for purposes of the Chapter 7 liquidation test.

This argument also had no traction with the Bankruptcy Court. It noted that the valuation of the wife's expert was based on the going concern of the entire dental practice, from which the expert then calculated the value of 25%. But there was no evidence that the husband, or a Chapter 7 trustee stepping into his shoes, had the power to force a sale of the practice as a going concern to maximize the husband's minority interest in the proceeds. A Chapter 7 trustee would have only the rights the husband as a minority shareholder in the practice had, the Bankruptcy Court pointed out.

At the same time, the court rejected the husband's claim the interest had zero value. The failure by the husband's expert to assign any value at all to the patient records or to the goodwill of the practice meant the value determination was "fatally flawed," the court said. The husband's interest "has value in the form of the Practice's invested capital, accounts receivable, goodwill, employment contracts with staff, and patient relationships, all of which are part of the bankruptcy estate," the Bankruptcy Court explained.

Moreover, since the husband as the debtor had the burden of showing that his interest had no value, he had to do more than simply enumerate the impediments a Chapter 7 trustee would face in trying to liquidate the asset, "particularly where there is evidence to suggest that the asset has more than a nominal value." Here, the evidence suggested the debtor's interest would have "significant" value in a Chapter 7 liquidation, the court said.

As the wife's expert showed, under the shareholders' agreement, the debtor had the right to compel the other shareholders to buy out his interest for a price derived from the formula in the agreement. The wife's expert testified that the value resulting from the formula was $161,300. The Bankruptcy Court noted that neither of the husband's experts actually challenged this value determination. It discounted the claim by the husband's Chapter 7 expert that as trustee he would simply abandon the husband's interest. According to the court, the Bankruptcy Rules require the trustee to give notice of his intention; if there were any objections to it, the court would be required to hold a hearing. Here, it was reasonable to assume the wife would object.

The Bankruptcy Court concluded that it was fair to assume a Chapter 7 trustee in this case could recover the amount payable under the buyout provisions of the shareholder agreement. Therefore, the court valued the husband's interest in the practice at $161,300.

Given this value determination, which exceeded the husband's scheduled valuation of $15,800 by $145,500, the court found the husband's Chapter 13 plan failed to meet the liquidation test. Specifically, in a hypothetical Chapter 7 liquidation, there would be almost $178,500 available to pay the remaining creditors, or a distribution of 94% of their claims. In contrast, in this Chapter 13 case, under the proposed plan, there would only be a distribution of 22% of the unsecured creditor's claims. The Bankruptcy Court denied confirmation but allowed the husband, as debtor, to submit an amended plan.

Commonwealth Sci. & Indus. Research Organisation v. Cisco Sys.

Citation: 2015 U.S. App. LEXIS 20942
Date of decision: Dec. 3, 2015
Country: US
State/Jurisdiction: Federal/Federal Circuit
Court: United States Court of Appeals
Type of action: Intellectual Property
Experts: James Malackowski (plaintiff/appellee); Christopher Bakewell (defendant/appellant)
Judge: Prost
SIC: 4899 Communications Services, NEC (except ship to shore broadcasting, satellite communications, pay telephone concession operators)
NAICS code: 517919

Court's Damages Model for SEP Infringement Fails Apportionment Rules

Apportionment is key to determining damages in all patent infringement cases. But apportionment in the context of patents that are essential to standardizing technology, products, and services comes with its own rules. A guiding principle is that the royalty must only reflect the value of the patented technology's superiority, not any value resulting from its being adopted due to standardization. The Federal Circuit recently elaborated on this concept when it struck down a $16.2 million royalty award against Cisco, finding the trial court's damages model failed to account for standardization.

A prior licensing agreement. The plaintiff, Commonwealth Scientific and Industrial Research Organisation (CSIRO), was a research arm of the Australian government. CSIRO's work on wireless technology resulted in a patent that subsequently became included in the 802.11 wireless standard that provides protocols for products using the Wi-Fi brand. CSIRO pledged to license its technology on reasonable terms for the 802.11 and 802.11a standards, but it refused to provide assurance as to subsequent revisions of the standard.

In early 2001, the defendant, Cisco Systems, acquired a company, Radiata, which had a technology licensing agreement (TLA) with CSIRO for the patent in suit. The royalty rates in the TLA were based on the volume of chips sold. Cisco and CSIRO amended the TLA in 2001 and 2003. Under the agreement, Cisco paid CSIRO royalties in the amount of over $900,000 until 2007.

In 2004, CSIRO developed a rate card by which it proposed to license the patent to other Wi-Fi participants based on sales volume and the date of accepting CSIRO's offer.

In 2005, in informal rate discussions, Cisco's vice president of intellectual property suggested to negotiate a license with CSIRO based on a $0.90-per-unit rate. The parties talked but never reached an agreement.

In July 2011, CSIRO sued Cisco for infringement of its patent. Two years later the parties stipulated to Cisco's infringement, and the case headed to trial on damages. Both sides presented expert testimony.

CSIRO claimed the benefits to the 802.11 products that used the patented technology over products that did not use it were mostly attributable to the patented technology. Therefore, the value of the patent was the difference in profit between the infringing and the noninfringing 802.11 products. Accordingly, CSIRO's expert compared the market prices of the products at the time of the hypothetical negotiation and attributed Cisco's profit premiums to the patent. After adjusting based on his analysis of the *Georgia-Pacific* factors, he determined a hypothetical negotiation between the parties prior to infringement would have resulted in a volume-based royalty table with rates from $1.35 to $2.25 per unit sold. He concluded that total damages amounted to nearly $30.2 million.

Cisco's expert looked to the TLA rates for his damages calculation. He determined for one brand of the infringing products a rate based on chip sales was in the range of $0.04 to $0.37; for the other brand, the range was $0.03 to $0.33. In total, Cisco owned CSIRO just over $1.05 million, the expert decided.

Experts' models flawed. The trial court declared both models defective. It decided the final apportionment underlying CSIRO's damages model was "arbitrary." At the same time, it objected to the use of the TLA by Cisco's expert. It said that the original TLA between CSIRO and Radiata, Cisco's predecessor, was not the result of a "purely disinterested business negotiation" because some of Radiata's personnel had had ties to CSIRO. Also, the TLA had imposed considerable obligations on Radiata. According to the court, another obstacle to using the TLA rates was related to timing. CSIRO and Radiata signed the TLA in 1998, but a hypothetical negotiation involving CSIRO and Cisco would have taken place between 2002 and 2003. During the four-to-five-year interval, the "[c]ommercial viability of the technology escalated sharply," the trial court observed.

Moreover, the court declined to use the TLA because it based royalty rates on chip prices. That is "like valuing a copyrighted book based only on the costs of the binding, paper, and ink needed to actually produce the physical product. While such a calculation captures the cost of the physical product, it provided no indication of its actual value," the court said.

Instead, the trial court looked to CSIRO's 2004 rate card to potential licensees and Cisco's 2005 informal rate suggestion to CSIRO for data points. It decided "a range of $0.90 to $1.90 is a reasonable starting point for negotiations between the parties in 2002 and 2003." It then performed a *Georgia-Pacific* analysis to determine any potential downward or upward adjustment. Factors 8, 9, and 10 having to do with the advantages of the patented technology weighed in favor of an upward adjustment, the court found. Several other factors required a downward adjustment. In the end, the court found that the parties would have been in a substantially equal bargaining position in a hypothetical negotiation. It found the $0.90-to-$1.90 range was appropriate for one line of products, but it made a downward adjustment to the other line of products, from $0.65 to $1.38, because Cisco's 2005 offer did not apply to that brand.

All things considered, the court awarded CSIRO over $16.2 million.

'Untenable' proposition. Cisco attacked the judgment at the U.S. Court of Appeals for the Federal Circuit. It made three arguments in favor of overturning the award, which the court analyzed in turn.

Smallest salable unit. Cisco contended the trial court's methodology was wrong because damages were not based on the "smallest salable patent-practicing unit," in this case the wireless chip.

By way of background, the Federal Circuit explained that, whenever infringement claims concern multicomponent products, the "governing rule" is apportionment—damage calculations must separate the value of the infringing feature from the value of the other noninfringing features.

A related principle is that when a damages model apportions to a royalty base, it must use the smallest salable patent-practicing unit as the base. See *LaserDynamics, Inc. v. Quanta Comput., Inc.*, 694 F.3d 51 (Fed. Cir. 2012) (available at *BVLaw*). The aim underlying that principle is to avoid compensating the patent holder for nonprotected features and to avoid misleading the jury by emphasizing the value of the entire product regardless of the contribution of the patented component.

The Federal Circuit went on to say that since the trial court here used a model that did not involve apportioning from a royalty base, the smallest salable unit principle did not come into play. Instead the trial court looked to evidence of actual rate discussions, including Cisco's 2005 proposal to CSIRO to take a license for the patented technology at $0.90 per unit. This rate served as the trial court's lower end. For the upper end, the trial court looked to CSIRO's rate card license offer to the public, which specified a $1.90-per-unit rate. Because these rates reflected the value of the patented component "and no more," the trial court's damages model had "already built in apportionment," the Federal Circuit found.

Cisco's proposition that a damages model had to start with the smallest salable unit was "untenable," the Federal Circuit said. It contradicted law that sanctioned using rates from sufficiently comparable licenses as a starting point and then accounting for differences in the technology and the parties' economic circumstances. Comparable licenses reflect the market's actual valuation of the patent, the court observed.

In sum, the Federal Circuit found the trial court's use of a damages model that looked to the parties' informal license rate negotiations did not violate the apportionment principles.

Standardization. Cisco argued the trial court failed to account for any extra value the patent in suit derived from being essential to the 802.11 standard.

The Federal Circuit agreed, outlining the "unique considerations that apply to apportionment in the context of a standard-essential patent ('SEP')." The underlying idea is that patented technology that is incorporated into a standard and as such becomes widely adopted is not necessarily widely used because it is superior to other technology, but because it is necessary to comply with the standard.

To prevent compensation to the patent holder related to standardization, "a SEP must be apportioned to the value of the patented invention (or at least the approximate value thereof), not the value of the standard as a whole," the Federal Circuit held. The value of the technology is distinct from the value that "artificially accrues to the patent due to the standard's adoption," the court emphasized.

In explaining the guiding principles, the Federal Circuit extensively cited to its prior decision in *Ericsson v. D-Link Sys.*, 773F.3d 1201 (Dec. 4, 2014), which analyzed apportionment for SEPs. The Federal Circuit noted that the trial court in the instant case did not have the benefit of that ruling and, therefore, failed to account for standardization. For example, in analyzing the *Georgia-Pacific* factors, the trial court erroneously increased the royalty award because the patent in suit was essential to the 802.11 standard.

Specifically, the trial court expressly found that certain factors, including Factor 8, which considers "[t]he established profitability of the product made under the patent; its commercial success; and its current profitability," militated in favor of an upward adjustment. Instead, the trial court should have adjusted its *Georgia-Pacific* analysis to eliminate any value standardization contributed to the patented technology's commercial success, the Federal Circuit noted.

Further, the Federal Circuit said, the trial court did not account for the possibility that the parties' informally offered royalty rates, which it used as a starting point, and especially CSIRO's rate card rates, might have included some value accruing to the patent from the standard's adoption. Because the trial court's damages model failed to filter out any value stemming from standardization, the Federal Circuit vacated the award and remanded for a new reasonable royalty determination.

TLA. Cisco claimed the trial court's rejection of the TLA in favor of other licensing rate evidence, such as CSIRO's rate card and Cisco's informal 2005 rate proposal, was error.

The Federal Circuit agreed that the trial court's reasons for rejecting the TLA were not altogether sound. It noted the trial court's objection that the TLA was signed in 1998, several years before a hypothetical negotiation in 2002 and 2003, during which time the trial court said "[c]ommercial viability of the technology escalated sharply." The Federal Circuit pointed out this view ignored evidence that, during the intervening time, when the hypothetical negotiations would have taken place, CSIRO and Cisco twice amended the TLA and that, during the amendment process, CSIRO had leverage to renegotiate royalty rates.

The Federal Circuit added that the TLA was the only "actual" royalty agreement between the parties. It focused on chips, and it was reached before one of the later, relevant versions of the standard (802.11g) was adopted. In remanding for a new damages analysis, the Federal Circuit ordered the trial court to re-evaluate the relevance of the TLA given all of these considerations.

Congel v. Malfitano

Citation: 2016 N.Y. App. Div. LEXIS 3706
Date of decision: May 18, 2016
Country: US
State/Jurisdiction: New York
Court: Supreme Court of New York, Appellate Division
Type of action: Contract
Judge: Dickerson
SIC: 6512 Operators of Nonresidential Buildings (except stadium and arena owners)
NAICS code: 531120 Lessors of Nonresidential Buildings (except Mini ware houses)

Unilateral Partnership Dissolution Exacts Steep Price From Wrongdoer

What a difference a word makes. That's the lesson from a recent New York appellate ruling in a dispute in which a minority shareholder was found liable of wrongfully breaching the partnership agreement to secure a high price in the buyout of his shares. The plan went awry when the appellate court decided the shareholder's conduct justified the imposition of a significant minority discount. Policy concerns underlying New York's prohibition against the use of a minority discount in fair value proceedings did not come into play in this case, the court found, because the dispute turned on a statutory provision that required only that the wrongdoer be paid the "value" of his interest in the business.

One expert applies minority discount. In 1985, the plaintiffs and the defendant entered into an agreement to form a partnership that would own and operate a shopping center in upstate New York. The defendant was a general partner and held a minority—3.08%—interest. Twenty-one years later, he informed the other partners that he had decided to dissolve the partnership because of a "fundamental breakdown in the relationship between and among us as partners."

The plaintiffs claimed he decided to unilaterally dissolve the partnership in violation of the partnership agreement so they would have "to buy out ... his interest at a steep premium." The plaintiffs sued for damages for breach of contract and a declaration from the court that the defendant wrongfully dissolved the business.

The defendant asked the court to dismiss the complaint, contending the partnership was at will and of infinite duration. Therefore, he was free to dissolve it under a provision of New York's partnership law. In a series of trial and appellate decisions from 2008 and 2009, the courts found the partnership was not at will and the defendant was liable for wrongful dissolution.

The New York Supreme Court (trial court) then held a nonjury trial on the issues of damages to the plaintiffs owing to the defendant's conduct and the value of the defendant's interest pursuant to Partnership Law § 69(2)(c)(II). That provision says the partner who has caused the wrongful dissolution shall have "the *value* of his interest in the partnership, less any damages caused to his copartners by the dissolution ... but in ascertaining the value of the partner's interest the value of the good-will of the business shall not be considered." (emphasis added)

At the start of trial, the parties stipulated that the unadjusted value of the defendant's total interest in the business was $4.85 million as of the valuation date.

Both sides offered valuation expert testimony. Points of contention were whether the stipulated value included an element of goodwill that needed to be deducted and whether discounts for lack of marketability and lack of control were appropriate.

The plaintiffs' expert said, in order to determine the fair market value of the defendant's minority interest, it was appropriate to discount for lack of control. Based on a number of factors, including sales of comparable interests and provisions in the partnership agreement that restricted the rights of minority owners, the expert decided to apply a 66% minority discount.

The defendant's appraiser agreed that under normal circumstances a minority discount figured into calculating fair market value. But he did not apply the discount here because he "was advised, under the relevant statutes, that a minority discount was not applicable."

Trial court rejects minority discount. The trial court decided to apply a 15% discount for goodwill as well as 35% DLOM. But it found that case law involving the valuation of a minority shareholder's interest in a closely held corporation militated against the use of a minority discount.

The trial court referenced two seminal cases in support of its opposition to the minority discount. In the *Beway* case, New York's highest court found a minority discount was not appropriate in determining the "fair value" of a shareholder's interest within the meaning of Sections 623 and 1118 of New York's Business Corporation Law. It said imposing a minority discount would mean minority shares received a value below that of majority shares, in violation of the principle that all shares of the same class must receive equal treatment in shareholder buyouts. *Matter of Friedman v. Beway Realty Corp.*, 661 N.E.2d 972 (1995) (available at *BVLaw*).

In *Matter of Murphy*, an oppressive shareholder suit brought under Business Corporation Law §1104-a, the appellate court clarified that "New York law does not permit a 'minority discount'" but does permit a marketability discount. *Matter of Murphy v. United States Dredging Corp.*, 74 A.D.3d 815 (2010) (available at *BVLaw*).

In the instant case, all things considered, including damages to the plaintiffs because of the defendant's wrongful conduct, the trial court decided the value of the defendant's interest was about $857,000.

Value vs. fair value. The parties appealed and cross-appealed the ruling with the New York Supreme Court's appellate division. The defendant asked the reviewing court to revisit its earlier decision that he wrongfully had dissolved the partnership. The court declined to do so, letting the lower court's liability ruling stand.

The principal valuation issue was whether the trial court should have applied a minority discount in this case. Yes, said the appellate court.

The concerns giving rise to the prohibition against the imposition of a minority discount in cases such as *Beway* and *Murphy* did not figure into the current case, the appellate court found. It pointed out that *Beway* and *Murphy* required the determination of the "fair value" of a dissenting shareholder's interest under Business Corporation Law §§ 623 and 1118, whereas the instant case "involves the determination of the 'value' of the shares of a partner who has wrongfully caused the dissolution of a partnership pursuant to Partnership Law §69(2)(c)(II)."

It further noted that applying a minority discount in the context of valuing a partnership interest would not run afoul of the corporate statutory prohibition against treating holders of the same class of stock differently nor undermine the goal of appraisal statutes to protect shareholders from being coerced into selling at unfairly low values or encourage oppressive conduct (citing *Vick v. Albert*, 47 A.D.3d 482 (2008)) (available at *BVLaw*).

Where the "wrongful" conduct of a minority partner caused the dissolution, the concern that imposing a minority discount would encourage oppressive majority conduct was not relevant, the appellate court explained.

The court also found support in a decision from the Massachusetts Supreme Court. That court interpreted a Massachusetts partnership statute that was almost identical to the New York law, and it affirmed a trial court's ruling to apply a minority discount in determining the value of the one-third, minority interest of the partner who wrongfully caused the dissolution. The Massachusetts trial court properly applied a minority discount to ascertain the market value of the partner's minority interest in a going concern instead of determining the partner's proportionate share of the liquidation value of the partnership's assets, the Massachusetts high court found. Since the remaining partners exercised their right to continue the business, the latter had to be treated as a going concern, i.e., using a "nonliquidation-based" method to calculate the value of the minority partner's interest. The statute's express exclusion of goodwill from the valuation of the wrongdoer's interest supported this approach, the Massachusetts Supreme Court found, "as good will is an asset only if the partnership business is a going concern."

The New York appellate court found that reasoning applicable to the case in front of it. Here, as there, the partnership would continue. The defendant had no right to force a liquidation sale of the shopping mall and receive a proportionate share of the liquidation value of the asset.

In sum, the appellate court said the trial court should have applied a minority discount. As to the rate of the discount, the appellate court, without analysis or much comment, found the statement from the plaintiffs' expert that a 66% discount was appropriate to be "credible and supported by the record." It remanded for a new calculation of damages incorporating the 66% minority discount.

Corrigan v. Testa

Citation: 2016 Ohio LEXIS 1163
Date of decision: May 4, 2016
Country: US
State/Jurisdiction: Ohio
Court: Supreme Court of Ohio
Type of action: State Taxation (incl. Ad Valorem)
Judge: O'Connor
SIC: 5074 Plumbing and Heating Equipment and Supplies (Hydronics) (merchant wholesalers except those selling plumbing and hydronic heating equipment via retail method)
NAICS code: 423720 Plumbing and Heating Equipment and Supplies (Hydronics) Merchant Wholesalers

Key Tax Ruling From Ohio Supreme Court Concerning Pass-Through Entity

A taxpayer successfully challenged an Ohio statute that imposed income tax on capital gain that the out-of-state investor realized when he sold his majority ownership interest in a pass-through entity. Taxing that was based on nothing more than the fact that the entity conducted some of its business in Ohio was a violation of the United States Constitution, the state's Supreme Court ruled. While this case does not focus on valuation specifically, it does raise a novel tax issue regarding a pass-through company.

Realizing capital gain. In 2000, the taxpayer and business associates acquired a 79.29% stake in a limited liability company that produced sanitaryware. It had plants in Texas and California and did business across the country, including in Ohio. It was organized as a pass-through entity for tax purposes.

The taxpayer did not reside in Ohio.

The taxpayer was the principal co-owner and a member of the board of managers. He testified that he was not involved in the company's day-to-day operations but visited the company headquarters in Ohio for meetings that focused on growing the company. He said his role was "stewardship" rather than active management of the business.

In 2004, he and his follow investors sold their interests to a third party. As a result, the taxpayer realized over $27.5 million in capital gain. Because he did not live there, he did not allocate any amount of the gain to Ohio.

Five years later, in 2009, the state claimed he owed nearly over $847,000 (including interest) in taxes related to the sale. After paying $100,000, the taxpayer filed for a refund for that amount. The tax commissioner denied the claim, citing the applicable statute, R.C. 5747.212.

The statutory provision deals with "apportioning gain recognized by nonresident investor selling an investment in a closely-held business." In essence, it says that anyone who directly or indirectly owns at least a 20% interest in a pass-through entity during a three-year period including the taxable year owes income tax in proportion to the percentage of the entity's business during the three-year period.

The taxpayer subsequently appealed the decision with the Board of Tax Appeals. The board affirmed the commissioner's ruling but acknowledged it lacked jurisdiction to rule on the taxpayer's constitutional claims.

State tax authority has limits. The taxpayer petitioned the state Supreme Court for review. He argued the statute was unconstitutional both as applied to him and on the face of it.

At the beginning of its analysis, the high court noted that, under the U.S. Constitution's due process, a state can only impose tax if it has jurisdiction.

This means there must be a link between the state and the person and/or the activity the state seeks to tax.

Here, Ohio taxed "every individual *** residing in or earning or receiving income in this state." Because the taxpayer was not a resident of the state, the issue was whether he could be taxed based on income earned or received in the state.

As a general matter, Ohio's tax scheme differentiates between business income and nonbusiness income. The statute defines business income as income generated in "the regular course of a trade or business" and requires apportionment based on the percentage of a company's property, payroll, and receipts located in the state.

Nonbusiness income includes rents, royalties, and capital gains. The allocation is to a specific site. In case of capital gains from the sale of intangible personal property, the site for tax purposes is the taxpayer's domicile.

The Ohio Supreme Court found that, as the majority owner of a pass-through entity, the taxpayer was subject to tax on a portion of the distributive share of the income the business generated. That income was business income as to the taxpayer.

Here, the company did not generate profit, but the taxpayer was able to benefit from its losses by using them to offset other income and reduce taxes he owed in other jurisdictions.

The court noted that "in the ordinary course," the gain the taxpayer realized from selling his membership interest in the company would not be allocable to Ohio because the activity was the transfer of intangible property by a nonresident. However, here the state tried to take advantage of R.C. 5747.212, which specifically addressed the tax liability of pass-through entity investors.

Unitary-business theory. The taxpayer's principal argument was that Ohio had no authority to tax his capital gain unless it could show that his activities and his business were intertwined—that there was a "unitary business relationship."

The state argued that the unitary business relationship was irrelevant and did not address the role the taxpayer played in the company. Instead, it emphasized that the taxpayer's liability "is determined by the business done by *the entity in which the taxpayer has invested*" and claimed any income the investor realized, whether in the form of a dividend, capital gain from the sale of the investment, or the payment of a debt, was taxable to the nonresident investor.

The court dismissed this argument. It was "self-evident," the court noted, that a dividend has a more direct relationship to corporate earnings, which pay for the dividend, than does the capital gain from the sale of an ownership in the corporation.

Another argument the state offered, and which also failed, was that, because, under state law, the state was able to tax the gain from an asset sale of the business, it also should be able to tax the gain from the ownership interest.

Here, had there been an asset sale, the gain would have been realized at the corporate level; since the company was a pass-through entity, the nonresident taxpayer would have been liable for the Ohio-apportioned share. Taxation to the taxpayer in an asset sale was the "economically equivalent situation" of taxation in the form of the taxpayer's individual capital gain, the state claimed. Taxing one but not the other form of gain was elevating form over substance, the state suggested.

The state Supreme Court saw it differently. While it may appear to the parties that an asset sale and a sale of an ownership stake are different forms of the same economic substance, the court said, that does not mean the limitation on the state's taxing authority is insignificant. "Nor is it unusual that two different methods of achieving the same economic result could have drastically different tax implications," the court added.

In sum, because the state failed to show that the taxpayer's activities were "unitary with" those of the business, Ohio had no authority to tax the nonresident taxpayer on capital gain resulting from the sale of his ownership interest in the pass-through entity.

However, the court declined to rule that the statute itself was unconstitutional, noting the taxpayer failed to show that "there exists no set of circumstances under which the statute would be valid." Conceivably, a taxpayer might engage in the business in a way that created a unitary-business situation, the court concluded.

Covol Fuels No. 4 v. Pinnacle Mining Co.

Citation: 2016 U.S. Dist. LEXIS 14151
Date of decision: Feb. 4, 2016
Country: US
State/Jurisdiction: Federal/West Virginia
Court: United States District Court
Type of action: Contract
Experts: Vincent Thomas (plaintiff); unknown (defendant)
Judge: Berger
SIC: 1241 Coal Mining Services (except site preparation and related construction activities on a contract basis)
NAICS code: 213113 Support Activities for Coal Mining

Defendant's Obfuscatory Tactics to Preclude Expert Testimony Fail

In a breach of contract action, the defendant challenged the testimony of the plaintiff's damages expert by arguing it had become irrelevant because it was tied to certain causes of action that were dropped during the litigation. For the testimony to be relevant and admissible, it must align with a specific cause of action, the defendant suggested. The court disagreed. It found this was essentially a contract dispute in which the expert testimony is relevant if the damage calculation has the necessary causal connection to the alleged harm. The defendant's attack on the expert's use of the weighted average cost of capital (WACC) as a discount rate fared no better.

Coal waste arrangement. The plaintiff was a subsidiary of a large energy company active in processing waste coal. The defendant was a major coal mining operation in West Virginia. In 2008, the parties made a five-year agreement under which the plaintiff would perform coal fines recovery operations at the defendant's Pinnacle Mine. The defendant was to provide the plaintiff with access to the material. The plaintiff had the right to terminate the agreement unilaterally if the operations became economically unfeasible.

After coal is mined, it goes through a cleansing process that extracts any waste material. At the same time, the waste material has some small quantities of coal—coal fines—adhering to it. Coal fines have commercial value that the plaintiff hoped to exploit through its recovery work. Specifically, at the defendant's mine, the waste went into an impoundment pool from which the plaintiff would collect the coal fines with a dredge.

The parties fell out when in 2011 the defendant failed to lower the water level of the impoundment such that the plaintiff's dredge could recover coal fines. Also, the defendant upgraded its coal cleansing plant and in so doing reduced the quality of coal fines after the wash. When it was no longer economically feasible for the plaintiff to continue its operations at the mine, it sued the defendant (S.D. W. Va.) alleging breach of the parties' contract and breach of the implied covenant of good faith and fair dealing. The plaintiff also asserted business tort claims, including unjust enrichment. After the defendant won on summary judgment on all counts, the plaintiff appealed the trial court's ruling and the 4th Circuit Court of Appeals overturned.

The case went back to the lower court for trial on the breach of contract and breach of good faith and fair dealing counts. The tort claims, including the unjust enrichment claim, were abandoned.

Liberal admissibility standard. The plaintiff offered expert damages testimony from a CPA, who also was a certified business valuator and financial forensics analyst. He was retained sometime after litigation began to perform three functions: (1) assess the plaintiff's historical financial performance; (2) calculate damages resulting from the harm the plaintiff claimed; and (3) determine the revenue the plaintiff generated for the defendant under the coal fines recovery agreement.

Pretrial, the defendants filed a *Daubert* motion to exclude the expert testimony.

Qualifications. The expert's qualifications were not in dispute, but the court addressed them briefly, "in keeping with the Court's gatekeeping function under Rule 702, *Daubert,* and the subsequent case law."

In reviewing the legal principles underlying the determination of whether expert testimony is admissible in federal court, the court noted the *Daubert* factors: whether the expert's theory or technique can be tested, whether the technique has been subject to peer review and publication, what the known or potential rate of error is, and whether the theory or technique is generally accepted in the scientific or technical community. The court also noted that, under *Kumho Tire,* trial courts have "flexibility in assessing the reliability of expert testimony." Finally, the court noted that, under the applicable 4th Circuit law on expert qualifications, the expert must possess special knowledge, training, or skills "not in possession of the jurors."

Here, it was "indisputable" that the expert had the expertise to testify on issues "germane to this litigation," the court said.

Reliability. To support its argument for excluding the damages testimony, the defendant argued the expert's opinion was neither reliable nor relevant.

As for reliability, the defendant said the expert's method was unreliable because, for one, he used the WACC as a discount rate in calculating future cash flow. Secondly, he "arbitrarily" used the WACC of the plaintiff's parent company even though the plaintiff and the parent company "are not in the same business" and have "distinct risk profiles." The defendant pointed out that, in 2011, in a 10-K filing, the plaintiff's parent company described itself as "operat[ing] in the light and heavy building materials section." In contrast, the defendant noted, the plaintiff was active in the recovery of coal fines. And, at the time of his deposition, the expert did not even know about those differences, the defendant claimed.

The court was not persuaded. To start with, it observed that 4th Circuit law permitted the use of the WACC as a discount rate. Moreover, in his rebuttal report, the expert acknowledged the plaintiff's business was "very low risk," but he said he used the "more conservative" discount rate for the parent company. The expert presented "abundant" evidence that his approach was "analytically sound," the court said. At the same time, the court did not discuss that evidence. It confined itself to saying, "because the Plaintiff was a subsidiary of the parent, it was important for [the expert] to select a discount rate which accurately reflected the Plaintiff's capital structure." The court found that, given *Daubert*'s "liberal" admissibility standards, the expert's methodology was reliable.

The defendant made two other attacks related to reliability. It argued the expert's calculation was flawed because it failed to account for amounts due to the plaintiff from the sale of its assets to a third-party coal refiner.

In deposition testimony, the expert had explained his damages calculation accounted for funds the plaintiff had in fact received from the sale to date. However, he did not take into account funds that were still owed to the plaintiff after a careful investigation showed it was unlikely that the plaintiff would receive future payments from the sale of the assets. According to the expert, "it would be unfair for [the Plaintiff] to accept the risk."

The court said it saw no reason to question the reliability of the expert's method regarding this point. It added the defendant would be able to address "grievances" as to the expert's conclusions in cross-examination.

Finally, the defendant took issue with the expert's analysis of the plaintiff's cash flow and financial performance. It claimed the calculation was unreliable because it was based on "multiple unfounded assumptions." For example, the expert assumed that, but for the alleged misconduct by the defendant, the plaintiff would have continued to operate on the defendant's property until 2023, when that was not at all certain. The defendant also questioned the expert's decision not to account for a $3.4 million impairment charge the plaintiff incurred in 2013.

According to the court, the defendant gave a "litany of examples"—ultimately, none convincing—to preclude the testimony. Instead, the court agreed with the plaintiff that the objections reflected mere disagreements between the defendant and the plaintiff's expert. It was for the trier of fact to decide these and other issues, the court found.

Relevance. The defendant also contended the expert's testimony failed the *Daubert* relevance requirement. Because the posture of the case had changed since the time the expert prepared his opinion—during the appeal and remand, the plaintiff's tort claims were dropped—the expert's opinion no longer "fits" the plaintiff's causes of action, the defendant asserted.

The plaintiff responded that its expert never suggested his calculation was based on the plaintiff's tort claims. Rather, the plaintiff's expert based his calculation on the same assumptions as the defendant's expert. Specifically, because of the defendant's conduct, the plaintiff was unable to access the impoundment pond and recover coal fines—contrary to the parties' five-year agreement. And, the plaintiff said, the defendant confused the concepts of "harm" and "misconduct" and wrongly asserted that, for expert testimony to be admissible, it had to be linked to a specific cause of action.

The court agreed with the plaintiff. The central issue in the case was the alleged breach of contract, the court said. If a jury determines the defendant is liable, the plaintiff will have a right to damages from the breach, the court said. Under case law, an expert's damages opinions must be "causally related to the alleged harm." The plaintiff's expert did not calculate damages based on a particular cause of action but on the harm the alleged misconduct caused.

Finally, the defendant objected that the expert's opinion as to the profits the defendant earned under the agreement were irrelevant since the plaintiff did not pursue disgorgement as a remedy.

The plaintiff responded that the testimony on this point was relevant in connection with many issues, including whether the parties would have extended their agreement beyond the first five years (2013 termination date) and whether the plaintiff's business plan and operation were "failures from the start."

The court again agreed, finding these issues "specifically relate to the Plaintiff's potential damages" under the agreement and, therefore, likely will be issues at trial. Consequently, the plaintiff expert's opinion on the defendant's profits was relevant.

In conclusion, the court found all of the expert testimony admissible and denied the defendant's *Daubert* motion.

Curran v. Curran

Citation: 2016 Conn. Super. LEXIS 77
Date of decision: Jan. 12, 2016
Country: US
State/Jurisdiction: Connecticut
Court: Superior Court
Type of action: Judicial Dissolution (incl. Withdrawal, Buy Out)
Experts: Gordon G. Wisbach (plaintiff and defendant)
Judge: Sheridan
SIC: 5511 Motor Vehicle Dealers (New and Used)
NAICS code: 441110 New Car Dealers

Parties' Valuation Contract Precludes Review of Minority Discount

Another case of seller's remorse. The parties agreed to the buyback of a minority shareholders' interest in a car dealership. Although they stipulated to be bound by the value determination of a mutually agreed upon appraiser, the plaintiff challenged the valuation in court. The sticking point was the appraiser's use of a minority discount, which lowered the value of the plaintiff's interest in the company by about $100,000 when compared to the "full" value of his interest. The court gave several reasons for not interfering with the valuation.

'Final and binding.' The plaintiff held a 30% interest in the defendant, a Volkswagen dealership. After he asked the court for a corporate dissolution, the company asked for permission to buy back his shares. The court urged the parties to take charge of the valuation process by hiring a joint appraiser in order to "avoid a battle of appraisers" or a court-imposed valuation process.

Accordingly, the parties decided to retain a sole appraiser whom they both knew from past appraisals he had done of the company. In a court hearing preceding the formal engagement of the appraiser, both sides raised the issue of whether to apply a minority discount. The court refused to take a position on the issue. But it said the minority discount was "part of the discussion" the parties needed to have to agree on a valuation method.

The parties eventually stipulated in court that the appraiser's valuation "shall be final and binding, with no right of appeal for any party." The appraiser determined that the fair market value of the plaintiff's 30% interest in the company was worth about $385,600. After applying a 25% minority discount, the appraiser valued the plaintiff's 30% interest at $289,200.

The plaintiff did not question the value determination of the company as such. However, he asked the court to decide whether the use of a minority discount was appropriate under the circumstances. Even though the parties had agreed to consider the appraisal final and binding, they "did not agree that [the appraiser] would determine whether or not any discount should be applied to the Plaintiff's shares," the plaintiff contended.

He also pointed out, under the state's statute governing a judicial buyout, the court has the authority to determine the fair value of the contested shares and, in this context, must decide whether or not to use a minority discount. Numerous cases addressing fair value proceedings involving a minority shareholder have found it inappropriate to use a minority discount, the plaintiff maintained.

The defendant countered that the parties' stipulation as to the valuation was binding.

No surprises. The court dismissed the cases the plaintiff cited as "immaterial" to the issue in front of it. It noted that those cases were in a different procedural posture than the case at bar, which did not leave it to the court to determine the value of the plaintiff's shares. Rather, the parties specifically charged their joint valuator with determining the discount issue and stipulated to commit to his valuation. "A stipulation is final, conclusive and binding as to those matters the parties fairly intended to include within its terms," the court said.

The court pointed out that the appraiser was a known quantity to both parties in light of his prior valuation of the company. The plaintiff, therefore, should have anticipated that the appraiser "would apply, or believe it appropriate to apply, a minority discount" as part of the valuation of the plaintiff's shares. In fact, the plaintiff had raised the issue in court prior to formally engaging the appraiser and prior to agreeing to the stipulation, the court observed.

Moreover, the court said, "a range of authorities" suggested the decision as to whether to reduce the value of minority shares is "an integral part of the process of determining the value of those shares to a potential purchaser." Therefore, the parties' appraiser did not exceed the boundaries of his engagement when he applied a minority discount. Citing to case law, the court noted that Step 1 of the valuation typically involves analyzing the value of the corporation, whereas Step 2 involves analyzing the value of the minority shareholder's interest from a buyer's perspective.

And, finally, the language of the stipulation was unequivocal, the court noted. The parties' contract specifically said "final and binding, *with no right of appeal for any party.*" (emphasis in court's opinion) Barring bad faith, fraud, or gross misconduct, "contracts voluntarily and fairly made should be held valid and enforced in the courts," the court in the instant case said.

Here, there was no sign of malfeasance. Accordingly, the court approved the appraiser's value determination.

Editor's note: See PECO Logistics, LLC v. Walnut Inv. Partners, L.P., *2015 Del. Ch. LEXIS 311 (Dec. 30, 2015), for a ruling from the Delaware Court of Chancery that involved similar circumstances—investors trying to walk back their written commitment to a valuation agreement. Like the court in this case, the Chancery refused to unmake the parties' unambiguous agreement.*

Deflecto, LLC v. Dundas Jafine Inc.

Citation: 2015 U.S. Dist. LEXIS 149447
Date of decision: Nov. 4, 2015
Country: US
State/Jurisdiction: Federal/Missouri
Court: United States District Court
Type of action: Intellectual Property
Experts: Marc Vianello (plaintiff); unknown (defendant)
Judge: Smith
SIC: 3564 Industrial and Commercial Fans and Blowers and Air Purification Equipment (fans and blowers)
NAICS code: 333413 Industrial and Commercial Fan and Blower and Air Purification Equipment Manufacturing

Court Decides *Daubert* Attack 'Misses the Mark'

A *Daubert* attack in which the challenger threw every possible objection at the plaintiff expert's damages testimony fizzled. The opponent claimed the expert revealed a lack of understanding of critical aspects of patent law, and it suggested his use of a software program to calculate future damages somehow compromised the calculation. The court rejected those and other arguments. But the case serves as a reminder that any statement an expert makes at any stage in the litigation may be used against him or her.

Competing for major customer. Both parties manufactured and sold dryer vents and competed for Home Depot's business. In fact, Home Depot was the plaintiff's largest customer and accounted for most of its sales. In contrast, the defendant had a number of other major customers. At some unspecified time, the defendant and Home Depot made an agreement that resulted in the defendant's products replacing the plaintiff's products in Home Depot stores in the Northeast. The plaintiff said it lost 30% of its Home Depot sales because of this development.

The plaintiff was aware of the defendant's products for years—one of the defendant's products appeared on the market as early as 2006—but it only filed suit in early 2013. Then it claimed the defendant's vents infringed two of its patents and alleged the defendant engaged in false advertising and unfair competition. The plaintiff unsuccessfully asked for a preliminary injunction to stanch the loss of Home Depot business. It also asked for other remedies, including money damages.

To determine lost profits, the plaintiff retained an experienced CPA and credentialed business valuator, who said he often spent over 50% of his time on patent litigation matters.

'Misdirected' objections. One issue in the case was when damages began to accrue. Under the Patent Act, a patentee may claim damages only for "those acts of infringement that occurred after the patentee gave the alleged infringer 'notice of infringement.'" Notice may be constructive, by marking an article with the patent number, or actual, by communicating to the infringer its belief that the infringer violated its patent(s). The plaintiff acknowledged that it had not marked its patented products and, therefore, had not provided constructive notice. In terms of actual notice, the plaintiff pointed to a cease and desist letter it had sent to the defendant in August 2012 and in which it had mentioned one of its patents.

A related issue was whether the plaintiff had forfeited its right to presuit damages by its delayed filing of a lawsuit. Under the laches defense, if a patentee delays filing suit for more than six years from the time it knew or should have known of the defendant's infringement, there is a presumption of laches—that is, negligence—on the plaintiff's part to act. If the patentee files suit within six years, there is no presumption.

In challenging the expert's damages calculation under *Daubert*, the defendant first asserted that the expert, in his deposition testimony, was confused about the legal limitations applicable to damages and, therefore, produced an unreliable damages calculation. For example, the defendant claimed the expert analyzed damages based on a constructive notice date, when there was no constructive notice. It also alleged the expert mistakenly claimed that actual notice occurred on the date the plaintiff filed suit.

The court called the defendant's arguments "misdirected." The plaintiff's expert was not retained to determine *when* damages began to accrue but to determine the *amount* of damages that have accrued, the court noted with emphasis. It observed that, in effect, the expert, anticipating the plaintiff's problem of showing constructive notice, provided alternate starting dates in his analysis. One calculation was based on constructive notice and the other actual notice.

Similarly, the defendant said the expert, in his deposition, seemed to claim the plaintiff had a right to damages or more than six years prior to filing its suit, when the law only allows damages of up to six years before bringing an action. The court was unconcerned about the expert's deposition statements, noting his report used the correct start date.

Another, but similar, line of objections related to the expert's testimony regarding convoyed sales. Under applicable law from the U.S. Court of Appeals for the Federal Circuit, a patentee may claim damages for profits it would have made on "unpatented components typically sold with a patented item" but for the defendant's infringement. The patentee must show that the unpatented components created a functional unit with the patented components. See *Rite-Hite Corp. v. Kelley Co.*, 56 F.3d 1538 (Fed. Cir. 1995).

The defendant maintained the expert stated the wrong legal standard in his deposition testimony when he said the plaintiff was entitled to convoyed sales damages if "the plaintiff can demonstrate … a reasonable probability that but for the infringement the plaintiff would have made the sales." This was the legal standard for lost profits not for convoyed sales. The legal standard for convoyed sales was in *Rite-Hite*, the defendant argued.

Also, the expert incorrectly designated certain products as convoyed sales when they did not meet the *Rite-Hite* standard.

The court said the defendant's argument "miss[ed] the mark." The lost profits analysis applies to both types of products—sales of unpatented and patented products—said the court. It reminded the defendant that the *Rite-Hite* test did not determine the amount of damages available for recovery, but it determined whether unpatented components qualify for a lost profits analysis. What's more, the defendant's disagreement over whether certain unpatented products were convoyed products went toward the weight of the expert's testimony not its admissibility, the court noted.

Another objection focused on the expert's use of a software program (unnamed) to determine future damages. The defendant also objected to the expert's express disagreements with some of the results the program generated.

The court first noted that the defendant failed to explain what was wrong with the program the expert used. "The mere use of a software program is not fundamentally unreliable," the court said. As to the expert's determination that the software program in this instance did not generate the most accurate projections of future damages, the court found him to be a qualified expert who used his expertise to make this assessment. The defendant's concerns again went toward the weight of the testimony, rather than its admissibility, the court decided.

The court concluded that none of these specific points made the expert testimony unreliable or otherwise excludable under *Daubert* and denied the defendant's motion.

In re DFC Global Corp.

Citation: 2016 Del. Ch. LEXIS 103
Date of decision: July 8, 2016
Country: US
State/Jurisdiction: Delaware
Court: Court of Chancery of Delaware
Type of action: Dissenting Shareholder
Experts: Kevin F. Dages (petitioners); Daniel Beaulne (respondent)
Judge: Bouchard
SIC: 6141 Personal Credit Institutions (except installment sales finance, industrial nondeposit banks, and credit card issuing)
NAICS code: 522291 Consumer Lending

Chancery Achieves Fair Value by Blending Three 'Imperfect Techniques'

The key word in a recent fair value decision from the Delaware Court of Chancery was "uncertainty." A company's uncertain future put into question the reliability of company forecasts and by extension post-transaction discounted cash flow and comparable companies analyses. It also affected the sales process and thus the reliability of the merger price. The Chancery concluded the best indicator of fair value in the situation was an even blend of all three values. This decision by the court's chief judge contains an in-depth discussion of the DCF method. Appraisers interested in beta will find much to contemplate.

Backdrop. The subject of this value dispute was a payday lending company. It was publicly traded and had its headquarters in the United States, but it operated in 10 countries. By mid-2013, it experienced two pressure points: potentially tighter restrictions from regulatory authorities, especially in the U.S. and United Kingdom, and competition. Regulatory uncertainty in the U.K. was a particular concern as this was a key market and a new financial authority there was preparing to tighten restrictions on lenders.

In spring 2013, the company cut earnings projections, fearing the transition might cause liquidity problems for some U.K. clients and lead to higher loan default rates.

In August 2013, management projected EBITDA in the range of $200 million to $240 million. In fall 2013, the company learned that the new regulations in U.K. would take effect on April 1, 2014. They included stricter affordability assessments, a limit on rollovers per loan, and a total cost of credit cap.

In January 2014, the company adjusted EBITDA projections downward to a range of $170 million to $200 million.

The company had some experience with navigating a shifting regulatory landscape in Canada years earlier that proved advantageous as new regulations forced some of the company's competitors to scale back operations or abandon the market. At the same time, some key difference between the Canadian and U.K. regulations made it difficult to gauge the effect of the U.K. changes on the company's future performance.

Two-year sales process. Concerns over regulatory change, management succession, and the company's high leverage caused management to explore a sale to a financial sponsor as early as spring 2012. It retained a financial advisor that contacted six potential contenders. However, by late 2012, the contenders had lost interest. For a year, the financial advisor reached out to more financial sponsors and three strategic buyers. By October 2013, the future buyer, a private equity firm, entered the picture. It knew of the uncertain regulatory environment in which the subject operated and wanted to take advantage of the company's vulnerability. There were two other potential bidders.

In December 2013, the future buyer offered to buy the company for $12.16 per share. This was a preliminary nonbinding indication of interest. Another bidder offered $13.50 per share.

In February 2014, after management provided the two bidders with downward- revised projections, the future buyer lowered its offer to $11.00 per share and requested a 45-day exclusivity period. It said one reason for adjusting its offer was that it had less acquisition financing available because of the company's lowered forecast. The parties entered into an exclusivity agreement.

In late March 2014, the company provided the buyer with another revised EBITDA forecast for 2014 that showed a drop of $24 million compared to the February 2014 projections. A day later, the buyer offered $9.50 per share and gave the company 24 hours to accept its offer. It subsequently extended the deadline to April 1, 2014.

The company's board approved the transaction on that day. The next day, April 2, 2014, the company announced the transaction and a downward EBITDA forecast from $170 million to $200 million to $151 million to $156 million. The merger closed on June 13, 2014.

Starting point DCF. A number of stockholders, owning about $4.6 million shares of common stock, petitioned the Delaware Court of Chancery for a fair value determination under Delaware's appraisal statute's Section 262(h). Chancellor Bouchard handled the proceeding.

Both sides retained eminently qualified valuators to make their case. The petitioners' expert based his valuation on the discounted cash flow analysis alone. The court commended him for also performing a multiples-based comparative company analysis even though he saw no reason to give any weight to it. The expert's DCF analysis yielded a value of $17.90 per share.

The company's (respondent's) expert relied on a DCF analysis that resulted in a $7.81 value per share and a multiples-based comparable company analysis that produced an $8.07 value per share. The expert weighted the results equally and ended up with a fair value of $7.94 per share. During litigation, the company also suggested the transaction price—$9.50 per share—was a reliable indicator of value. Not surprisingly, the petitioners disagreed.

The court, referencing its recent *In re Appraisal of Dell* decision, noted, "the existence of drastic differences between experts' valuations is not an uncommon issue." Studies have shown petitioners' experts on average produce a valuation that is 186% above the deal price, whereas respondents' experts arrive at a price that is 22% below deal price, the court went on to say.

Here, the court decided to do its own DCF analysis by drawing on elements from both experts. For the final valuation, it also considered the result of the multiples-based comparable company analysis and the transaction price.

At the outset of the DCF discussion, the court noted areas of agreements between the experts. For example, they concurred on a 74% debt-to-capital ratio, on a 10% cost of debt estimate, on a 3.14% risk-free rate, and on a 6.18% equity risk premium. The court adopted those inputs.

The primary area of dispute concerned the elements necessary to determine the weighted average cost of capital (WACC)—particularly the beta component. The court made beta-related issues a focal point of the DCF discussion.

Barra beta. The petitioners' expert used Bloomberg LP weekly beta for nine companies for a two-year period. He used raw beta as opposed to smoothed beta. For determining WACC, he estimated three betas: one based on the company's observed beta, one based on all peer companies, and one based on the six of the nine companies that were based in the U.S.

The respondent's expert used two methods to estimate beta and then used the midpoint of the two. He used the same six peer companies that were in the opposing expert's peer set. However, he did not use the subject company's historical beta.

Under the first method, he used Bloomberg data for a five-year period. He smoothed beta. Under the second method, he used beta he had obtained from Barra, a provider of global investment decision-making tools. Barra uses a proprietary model to measure a company's sensitivity to changes in the market or in the industry.

The petitioners' expert objected to the use of Barra betas because, he contended, those cannot be replicated or reverse engineered. As such, it is impossible to determine whether they should be included in a beta estimate or how they should be weighted against Bloomberg betas.

The respondent's expert tried to argue that there were ways to obtain replications of Barra's formulas to perform a quality check on the data's predictive value, but he admitted he had not done this type of analysis in the instant case.

The court rejected the use of the Barra beta in this case. It observed the respondent's expert was not able to re-create the Barra betas he used and he was unable to explain why the company's Barra beta was significantly higher than the Bloomberg beta.

The court relied on Bloomberg betas only.

Beta peer group. Should the peer set include six or nine companies? The experts agreed on six companies that were comparable to the subject. However, the petitioners' expert added three companies that the respondent's expert considered not to be peers. One of the three companies was in credit card services, one offered life insurance products, and a third one specialized in financing to car dealers.

The court agreed that those three companies did not belong in the beta peer group.

But, siding with the petitioners' expert, the court found that it was reasonable to include the subject company's own beta in the analysis by making it a seventh beta in the peer analysis. "[T]he most comparable company to [the subject] is [the subject] itself," the court said.

Beta measurement period. The court noted a five-year period "is the most common for measuring beta and generally results in a more accurate measurement."

The petitioners' expert reasoned the shorter two-year period he used was justifiable because it reflected the regulatory uncertainty in the payday lending market. The respondent's expert countered that none of the factors necessary to justify a shorter period, such as a fundamental change in the market, was present in this case. The court agreed with the respondent's expert and adopted a five-year period.

Beta smoothing. Beta smoothing, the court explained, was an adjustment to "create a forward-looking estimated beta from the historical beta." Here, the respondent's expert made the adjustment by averaging the historical estimate, weighted two-thirds, with the market beta of 1.0, weighted one-third.

The court said smoothing beta was appropriate here—"even if the smoothing methodology appears somewhat crude"—particularly because the court rejected the use of Barra betas, which are forward-looking.

Beta unlevering. The experts used different formulas for beta unlevering. Beta unlevering, the court explained, is a series of adjustments to account for the differences in the capital structures of the peer companies and of the subject company.

The petitioners' expert used the Fernández formula, whereas the respondent's expert used the Hamada formula. The latter, as the petitioners' expert conceded, was the more accepted and commonly used method, although at least one "persuasive" authority has preferred the Fernández formula.

The court said the Fernández formula was not typically used in estimating a public company's WAAC. It decided, in the instant case, given "the lack of observed or even estimated debt betas for each individual company in the peer group," there was no point in using the Fernández formula. Neither method was ideal, the court said, as it accepted the Hamada formula.

Size premium dispute. Besides beta, the experts disputed the magnitude of the size premium.

The petitioners' expert relied on the company's equity market capitalization on the day before the company announced the transaction, April 1, 2014, to conclude the company would fall into the 9th decile in *Duff & Phelps 2014 Valuation Handbook.* Accordingly, he determined a 2.81% size premium.

The respondent's expert used two sources, the *Duff & Phelps 2014 Valuation Handbook* and the *Duff & Phelps Risk Premium Report.* The first source showed a 3.87% rate, and the second a 4.60% rate. Using the midpoint of the two, the expert calculated a final size premium of 4.24%. He noted that a microcap value for the combined 9th and 10th deciles was appropriate because the company's market capitalization was close to the edge of the 9th decile on April 1, the last unaffected trading day, and would have fallen into the 10th decile on April 2, the day the company announced the transaction and the downward EBITDA forecast. The negative financial performance that day was part of the company's intrinsic value, the respondent's expert said. Consequently, it was appropriate to combine the two deciles.

The court found neither expert's approach persuasive. It promptly rejected the use of the *Risk Premium Report.* The court agreed with the respondent's expert that rigid adherence to the April 1 date for the market value meant "missing an important piece of information." The reduced earnings guidance from April 2 was significant, the court said. The announcement lowered 2014 adjusted EBITDA from $170 million to $200 million to $151 million to $156 million and, therefore, "undoubtedly would have affected [the company's] market capitalization, which is the relevant metric for selecting the size premium." The court decided that the market's reaction to the company's announcement would have shifted the company into the 10w decile, which carries a 3.52% size premium. This is the rate the court adopted for its DCF analysis.

Other DCF input disagreements. Both experts based their DCF analyses on the company's March 2014 projections, but the respondent's expert measured net working capital independently, by estimating it at the end of each year as a percentage of total revenue. He said this approach was based on authoritative finance literature. He determined a deficit in working cash and the nonexistence of excess cash.

The court rejected his "recalibration" of working capital based on historical trends, noting both experts otherwise relied on the March projections for their cash flow analysis.

But the court agreed with the respondent's expert that the June 2014 cash balance as estimated in the March projections, rather than the actual March figure, was the most appropriate figure to use "because it estimates [the company's] cash at a point closer to the closing of the Transaction."

The court also found that a two-stage model, rather than a three-stage model, was best suited to value the company's future cash flow. Given the uncertainty surrounding management's projections, the court said, "[I]t is more appropriate to rely on management's projection period and then estimate a terminal value as accurately as possible." The petitioners' three-stage model, which required extrapolating five years of additional projections, added extra risk of speculation.

Comparable company analysis is reasonable. The respondent's expert gave equal weight to the valuation resulting from a comparative company analysis that looked to the same six peer companies he used to calculate beta. He used the median of three multiples: market value of invested capital over estimated 2014 EBITDA, market value of invested capital over estimated 2015 EBITDA, and market value of invested capital over last 12 months' EBITDA. When he averaged the resulting valuations, he arrived at an $8.07-per-share price.

The petitioners' expert suggested multiples-based valuations did not necessarily indicate the intrinsic value of an enterprise, did not allow for the inclusion of factors related to the company's operative reality, and did not fully account for its long-term growth potential.

The court disagreed. It found the respondent's methodology reasonable, and it adopted the value resulting from it.

Merger price has its place. The court found in this case it was proper to consider the deal price as one factor in the overall valuation. The company underwent a lengthy sales process, under the guidance of an independent financial advisor that reached out to dozens of financial sponsors and several potential strategic buyers. There were no obvious conflicts of interests since this was not a management buyout and did not involve discussions to retain existing management, the court observed.

Equal weight to all methods. The court noted that all of the valuation methods proved to be "imperfect techniques." Ultimately, their weakness came back to the same source, "the tumultuous environment" in which the company found itself before and at the time of the sale. Regulatory uncertainty created uncertainty about the company's future performance and "even its viability," the court said.

According to the court, this uncertainty "calls into question" the reliability of the company's projections, particularly the March projections upon which the experts, and the court, based their DCF models. Therefore, it was not appropriate to give special weight to the result of the DCF analysis, the court decided.

The uncertainty also raised doubts related to the sales process, the court found. The buyer was aware of the company's "trough performance and uncertain outlook." These factors, in fact, "were at the core of [the buyer's] investment thesis to obtain assets with potential upside at a favorable price," the court said. It also noted that the buyer was a financial sponsor, rather than a strategic buyer, and as such was guided by achieving a certain internal rate of return rather than fair value.

One of the reasons the buyer gave for reducing its offer to $9.50 per share was that it faced financing constraints based on the subject's downward adjustments in projected EBITDA.

The comparable companies analysis also suffered the impact of the uncertainty because it relied on two years of management's projected EBITDA, the court said. At the same time, unlike the DCF model, this method relied on projections only through 2015, rather than 2018, and one-third of the valuation relied on historical EBITDA data, the court pointed out.

Moreover, the court declared this method less susceptible to firm-specific issues that might interfere with a competitive bidding environment and might raise doubt as to whether the market price reflected fair value.

The differing methods' limitations notwithstanding, they all provided meaningful insight into the company's value, the Chancery said. Consequently, the court weighted the values derived from the different analyses equally to arrive at a $10.21-per-share fair value for the subject company.

Estate of Dieringer v. Commissioner

Citation: 2016 U.S. Tax Ct. LEXIS 9
Date of decision: March 30, 2016
Country: US
State/Jurisdiction: Federal
Court: United States Tax Court
Type of action: Estate and Gift Taxation
Experts: Lewis Olds (appraiser/estate); unknown (IRS)
Judge: Kerrigan
SIC: 6531 Real Estate Agents and Managers (agents and brokers)
NAICS code: 531210 Offices of Real Estate Agents and Brokers

Manipulation of Valuation of Bequeathed Stock Sinks Charitable Contribution Claim

The Internal Revenue Service recently scored a win in a charitable contribution case involving a closely held family business in Oregon. The IRS discovered a significant gap in the date-of-death value of the company stock the decedent had bequeathed to a family foundation and the much lower value assigned to the stock seven months later in the context of a redemption transaction. The decedent's son, who played a number of conflicting roles, instructed an appraiser to value the decedent's majority interest as a minority interest to enable the redemption at a significant discount before transferring a fraction of the bequeathed property to the foundation. The estate not only underpaid federal estate tax, but also was negligent in complying with the law, the Tax Court said. Therefore, an accuracy-related penalty was in order.

Date-of-death valuation. The decedent was the majority shareholder in a closely held real property management company. She also was chair of the board of directors and vice president. One of her sons (Son 1) served as president, and two other sons were directors. Before her death, the decedent owned 81% of the voting shares of the company, and Son 1 owned 19%. In addition, the decedent owned 84% of the nonvoting stock. Son 1 and another son owned the remainder of the nonvoting shares. During the decedent's life and at the time of death, the company was organized as a C corporation.

As part of her estate planning, the decedent set up a trust and foundation. In her will, she left the entire estate to the trust. The trust agreement specified that $600,000 of the estate would go to various charities and the remainder, consisting primarily of the company stock and promissory notes, would be transferred to the foundation. Son 1 was the sole trustee of the trust and foundation.

Shortly before the decedent's death, the directors discussed the possibility of buying some of the decedent's shares in the future. But, at the time of the decedent's unexpected death, in April 2009, no redemption plan was in place.

In November 2009, seven months after the death, the estate procured an independent appraisal of the decedent's stock for estate tax purposes. According to the appraisal, the company's voting and nonvoting shares were worth about $14.1 million on the date of death. Specifically, the appraiser valued the voting stock at $1,824 per share, applying no discounts because these shares represented voting shares and a controlling interest. He valued the nonvoting stock at $1,733 per share, applying a 5% discount for lack of voting power at shareholder meetings. By his calculation, the company's adjusted net asset value as of the date of death was a little less than $17.8 million.

Post-death developments. Also around that time, before the bequeathed interest was transferred to the foundation, the company's executives took a number of measures that changed the way the company operated and the nature and value of the decedent's bequest. Son 1 took the lead role. To avoid built-in capital gains tax on corporate assets, the company elected S corporation status. Son 1, in his role as trustee of the foundation, professed concern that the foundation would have to make an annual distribution of 5% of the value of its assets and would be subject to tax on the value of any excess business holdings the entity had in the company after five years. Eventually, the company's board decided to effect a redemption of shares to freeze the value of the shares into a promissory note, ostensibly to control the risk of a decline in stock value during the ongoing recession.

The final redemption agreement between the trust and the company specified that the company would redeem all of the voting shares and a little more than two-thirds of the nonvoting shares.

The company retained the same appraiser who had valued the shares for estate tax purposes to calculate their value for purposes of the redemption transaction. The appraiser was unaware that after the decedent's death the company had changed to an S corporation, and he treated it as a C corporation. He subsequently testified that he received instructions to value the bequeathed shares as a minority interest. Consequently, for purposes of the November 2009 appraisal, he applied a 15% discount for lack of control and a 35% discount for lack of marketability when valuing the voting shares. By this calculation, the price per voting share dropped from $1,824 to $916.

To value the nonvoting shares, the appraiser added an additional 5% discount for lack of voting power and arrived at a value of $870 per share. The date-at-death value was $1,733 per share.

The appraiser determined that the company's adjusted net asset value was $16.15 million at the date of the redemption agreement.

Also on the same date, Son 1 and another son, acting on behalf of the company, signed a short-term promissory note for $2.25 million and a long-term promissory note for about $3.8 million payable to the trust. The long-term note subsequently was amended to about $3 million.

Around the same time as the redemption, the decedent's three sons bought additional shares in the company, purportedly to inject cash into the company so it could pay off the promissory notes. The result was that the trust was left with zero voting shares and a little over 2,163 of the nonvoting shares. The trust then transferred the nonvoting shares and short-term and long-term promissory notes to the foundation.

Meanwhile, pursuant to three subscription agreements, the decedent's sons obtained 290 of the decedent's 425 voting shares and 3,868 of the 7,736.5 nonvoting shares—all at the highly discounted price. Son 1 received the majority of both types of shares.

IRS discovers disconnect in value. Subsequently, the estate claimed a charitable contribution deduction of $18.8 million, including the date-of-death value of the decedent's majority interest in the company ($14.1 million). The foundation reported receiving a noncash contribution of company stock with a fair market value of $1.86 million, a long-term promissory note with an FMV of $2.9 million, and a short-term promissory note with an FMV of $2.25 million. The trust reported a capital loss of nearly $386,000 related to the sale of the voting stock to the company and a loss of $4.8 million related to the sale the nonvoting shares.

The IRS found the estate's charitable contribution was less than the date-of-death value on the tax return because of the post-death changes to the corporation. It said the charitable deduction could only reflect the value of the promissory notes and the fraction of the nonvoting shares that was transferred to the foundation. The agency determined the estate was liable for a deficiency of over $4.1 million in estate tax and assessed an accuracy-related penalty of nearly $825,000 to reflect the estate's failure to act with reasonable cause and in good faith.

Thwarting decedent's testamentary plan. The estate challenged the agency's findings with the U.S. Tax Court. There was no justification for calculating the charitable contribution deduction based on the value the foundation received. Rather, under the regulations, the date for determining the value of the charitable contribution was the date of death. The estate noted at death the bequest was not subject to a redemption plan or preconditions or contingencies. It claimed that considering the effect of post-death events on the value of the bequeathed interest did not "truly reflect" the fair market value of the decedent's property. And it said the events occurred for valid business reasons.

The IRS maintained that the value of the contribution should take into account the post-death events. The decedent's sons "thwarted decedent's intent to bequeath all of her majority interest in [the company] or the equivalent value of the stock to the foundation," the agency argued. Specifically, the way in which Son 1 obtained the stock appraisals and orchestrated the redemption of the majority interest at a 50% discount made it clear that the sons never intended to carry out the decedent's will.

The Tax Court sided with the IRS. Off the bat, the court noted that the IRS did not disagree that the date of death was the applicable valuation date. However, the events that occurred after the decedent's death and before the transfer of the bequeathed property to the foundation "changed the nature and reduced the value of decedent's charitable contribution," the court found.

The court pointed out that the change in corporate status, the redemption transaction, and the sons' signing of subscription agreements to reflect the purchasing of additional shares in the company all occurred on the same day, some seven months after the decedent's death. The court noted the estate gave business reasons for taking the steps the company's board of directors took, and it found the steps "do appear to have been done for valid business reasons." But, said the Tax Court, there was insufficient evidence "to support the substantial decline" in the company's per-share value. Son 1 explained the drop in value by referring to the poor business climate. This explanation was not persuasive, the court said. It noted that the company's adjusted net asset value was only $1.6 million higher in the date-of-death appraisal. The real reason for the drop in share value, the court found, was Son 1's specific instruction to the appraiser to value the majority interest as a minority interest with a 50% discount.

The court noted that the appraiser credibly testified that he believed the company to be a C corporation and was directed to apply the discounts. The appraisal itself did not explain why the discounts were applied, the court observed.

Intrafamily transactions in a closely held corporation are subject to heightened scrutiny, the Tax Court said. Therefore, the roles Son 1 played within the context of the transactions begged for close examination. The court noted that Son 1 at once served as executor of the estate, as president and director of the company, and as sole trustee of the trust and foundation. He also was a shareholder. In terms of the redemption of the decedent's interest, there was no independent or outside accountability, the court observed. Son 1 gave instructions on how to value the shares, and he and his brothers reduced the value of the assets that eventually were transferred to the foundation "without significant restraints," the court said.

The court concluded that the trust did not transfer the number of shares the decedent had bequeathed or the value of the bequeathed shares. Therefore, the estate had no right to a charitable contribution deduction based on the date-of-death value of the decedent's interest in the company.

Penalty justified. The facts also supported an accuracy-related penalty, the Tax Court found. The IRS showed that the estate failed to inform the appraiser that the redemption was for a majority interest and instead specifically instructed him to value the redeemed stock as a minority interest. These acts represented negligence—the "failure to make a reasonable attempt to comply with the provisions of the internal revenue laws, to exercise due care, or to do what a reasonable and prudent person would do under the circumstances."

The court dismissed the estate's claim that it had acted reasonably because it relied on the advice of counsel. The lawyer, who was a competent professional with sufficient experience to justify reliance, gave advice based on an "errant appraisal," the court said. The estate knew that a significant percentage of the value of the decedent's shares would not be transferred to the foundation and that the sons were acquiring a majority interest in the company at a 50% discount.

None of the cases the estate cited to bolster its arguments allowed for a charitable contribution deduction based on the date-of-death value of assets that are not actually transferred to the charitable organization, the court pointed out.

The estate failed to show that it had reasonable cause or acted in good faith. It was liable for the estate tax deficiency and the penalty, the Tax Court concluded.

In re Discontinuance & Disposition of P.K. Smith Motors, Inc.

Citation: 2016 La. App. LEXIS 475
Date of decision: March 9, 2016
Country: US
State/Jurisdiction: Louisiana
Court: Court of Appeals
Type of action: Judicial Dissolution (incl. Withdrawal, Buy Out)
Experts: David Brewer, real estate appraisal; Ronald Gagnet, business valuation (petitioner); Michael Graham, real estate appraisal; Larry Sikes, business valuation (defendants)
Judge: Calloway
SIC: 5511 Motor Vehicle Dealers (New and Used)
NAICS code: 441110 New Car Dealers

Dodgy Real Estate Valuation Compromises Dependent Business Valuation

In a family dispute over a Chevrolet car dealership, the trial court decided against dissolution and instead held a fair value hearing to determine the price at which the company would buy back the shares of the decedent shareholder. Expert testimony was critical to the outcome, with both sides offering two experts each. Three experts made the cut, but one came up short. The problem was the expert's working on autopilot, submitting a report that was a careless cut-and-paste job and using noncomparable businesses in his analysis. Since this expert's valuation was the basis for another expert's business valuation, it risked upending the dependent analysis.

Request for dissolution. Two brothers each owned 50% of the car dealership their parents had incorporated in 1974. After the father's death, the surviving shareholders—the mother and the two sons—signed an agreement that restricted the transfer of shares in the company during the lifetime and upon the death of a shareholder. Basically, the corporation had an option to buy the shares that were for sale. If the corporation declined to exercise its option, the remaining shareholders had the option to acquire them. Finally, the divesting shareholder had the right to dispose of any shares neither the corporation nor the other shareholders chose to buy.

The agreement included a "Purchase Price" provision that failed to state a value. It said: "The purchase price for each share of stock purchased pursuant to this Agreement shall be $_____."

After the mother's death, the brothers ran the business as equal partners until one of them died in 2009. Discord between the decedent's son, who acted as executor of the estate, and the surviving brother ensued, resulting in a suit in which the estate asked the court to discontinue the business and dispose of its assets. The petition included a plan to hire a third party to value the business for sale as a whole. The surviving brother and the corporation—the defendants—objected and asked the court to enforce the shareholder agreement, which, they said, required a sale of the decedent's shares to the corporation or the surviving shareholder.

Subsequently, the defendants filed their own plan under which the court would determine the value of the decedent's interest in a fair value proceeding. The defendants would either pay it or else agree to liquidation. The defendants specifically pointed to the executor's lack of experience in running a car dealership and the negative effects the dissolution of the business would have on its employees and the local economy. The estate wanted to go forward with the dissolution. It claimed that, since the shareholder agreement failed to state a price, it was an unenforceable contract.

The court agreed to hold a valuation trial in early 2014 during which the executor and the surviving brother as well as their experts testified.

The executor claimed his uncle, the surviving brother, engaged in self-dealing and mismanagement of the company. The latter had acted unilaterally and "kept the estate in the dark" about the company's finances. But the executor also said he never had wanted to shut the company down and did not know what the cost of liquidating it would be. He said he would accept a "fair value" and allow the business to continue operating.

The surviving brother said that he had served as the company's dealer-operator and president since his father's death. The father intended for him to run the car dealership and for his brother to run the oil and gas business the family also owned. The decedent played no real role in the business, the defendant said. At the same time, he admitted the decedent had been the successor dealer in the franchise agreement with General Motors and a guarantor of loans from General Motors Acceptance Corp. (GMAC) and a bank.

The surviving brother noted the point of the shareholder agreement was to ensure the dealership stayed in the family. He explained that the purchase price provision left the actual amount blank because, in 1984, the year the agreement was executed, there was considerable volatility in the oil business and car sales plummeted. The signers of the agreement did not believe they could state a price or per-share value that would be relevant in the future. Instead, the signers intended for a fair market value (FMV) determination when needed.

Two types of valuators at work. Both parties engaged real estate appraisers as well as business valuators to value the dealership and its land.

The real estate appraiser for the surviving brother and the company, the defendants, first valued the company in 2011. He appraised the dealership at $800,000 and the land that went with the dealership at nearly $240,000. He identified the highest and best use of the property and performed an analysis to determine what it would cost to build a similar facility and a comparative study of other dealerships in similar, competing areas. He also looked at comparable sales to value the excess land around the dealership. He explained that his analysis factored in a total depreciation of 75% based on his assessment of the market of comparable sales.

He also performed an appraisal as of 2009, the date of the decedent's death. The resulting value was essentially the same as the 2011 value. Market conditions between 2009 and the time of trial had not changed substantially, the appraiser said.

The defendants also offered the opinion of a CPA who was an expert in valuing closely held companies as to the dealership's value in January 2013, when the request for dissolution was filed.

This expert considered the real estate appraiser's value determination as well as the dealership's monthly financial statements and tax returns from 2007 through 2012, the company's articles of incorporation and other corporate records, and financial statements the dealership submitted to GM through the time of trial. The business valuator said he chose the net asset approach to calculate the company's FMV because it would generate the highest value. Considering the dealership had been in operation for years, he valued the business as a going concern.

Based on the 2009 and 2011 real estate appraisals, the business appraiser first valued the corporation at $1.37 million and $1.4 million. He then applied a 20% discount for lack of marketability (DLOM), which he said was inherent in a closely held corporation. And he applied a 10% discount for lack of control (DLOC) because of GM's control over the dealership. In the final analysis, he concluded the dealership was worth "around a million dollars." This meant the estate's interest was worth about $500,000.

He allowed that the valuations were not based on audited financial information. But he said the detailed financial information GM required from dealers every month "added to his comfort" about the reliability of the financials undergirding the valuations.

Cross-examination exposes flaws. The estate's real estate appraiser said the dealership was worth about $2 million at the time of the decedent's death—double the amount the defendants' real estate appraiser had proposed.

On cross-examination, the estate's real estate appraiser admitted to mistakes and misstatements in his expert report. For example, for his sales comparison, he looked to completely different businesses, including a furniture store and a grocery store, and businesses located in affluent areas in other states. Ultimately, he agreed with opposing counsel that these businesses were not comparable to the subject company. He explained there was a shortage of automotive service buildings in the market, which made it difficult to find a true comparable.

He admitted that as a result of cutting and pasting his report by mistake included items from other documents. He admitted that the report contained a section that purported to be based on discussions with local contractors but was not because the expert had not spoken to any of the contractors.

To value the improvements to the land, he used an effective age of 10 years for the main dealership building even though the structure was built 50 years ago. He used a 33% depreciation compared to the 75% depreciation value the opposing real estate appraiser used. He admitted that, if had he used the same depreciation as the defendants' real estate appraiser, his value determination under the cost approach would be similar to that of the rivaling expert.

The estate also offered testimony from a CPA and certified business valuator. The business valuator based calculations on the problematic real estate appraisal. He explained he rejected the income approach because the dealership was not making enough money, and he concluded the market approach was inappropriate because of the turmoil in the automotive industry in 2009, the valuation date. As a result, he used a net asset approach.

Like the defendants' business valuator, the estate's business appraiser valued the company as a going concern. He said he considered financial statements and tax returns for the five years leading up to the valuation date and, on cross-examination, explained he made adjustments based on the real estate appraisal. He arrived at a total adjusted entity value of over $2.7 million, to which he applied an 18% DLOM but no DLOC. He concluded the estate's 50% interest was worth over $1.1 million.

When he redid his calculation using the real estate appraisals the defendants' expert submitted, the estate's business valuator concluded the 50% interest was worth significantly less, about $673,300.

Trial court seeks 'reasonable price.' The trial court ultimately decided not to dissolve the company but to enforce the shareholder agreement. It noted the agreement reflected a "meeting of the minds" of the signers to keep the business in the family. The agreement did not specify a price or formula for buying back the shares in the company but required a determination of a "reasonable price," the trial court found. It rejected the valuation the estate's real estate appraiser proposed finding "severe flaws in [the expert's] methodology and ultimate conclusions" and instead credited the valuations the defendants' experts offered. The trial court concluded the "fair value" of the company was $1 million and set the purchase price for the estate's interest at $500,000.

Permissible transfer restriction. The estate challenged the trial court's ruling with the state Court of Appeal. In its appeal, it argued the agreement was an unenforceable contract to sell because it lacked a key element: the purchase price. The estate also contended the trial court erred when it permitted valuation expert testimony and when it relied on the defense experts' valuations for its price determination.

The appeals court dismissed the estate's objections. It first decided the shareholder agreement was a valid transfer restriction that specifically aimed "to prevent the type of deadlock that arose here," by requiring the sale of the decedent's shares either to the corporation or the remaining shareholder, the surviving brother. Also, at trial, both the executor and the surviving shareholder testified they would agree to a sale between them at a "fair value." This testimony, in addition to considerations about the negative impact on the local economy, supported the trial court's decision to avoid dissolving the company.

Moreover, prior to trial, both sides filed plans for resolving the deadlock that required valuing the company's shares, the appeals court found. Consequently, "both parties were aware that valuation would be at issue at trial, and both had an opportunity over the several months during which trial was held to get and present expert valuation testimony." Permitting expert testimony was not error, the appeals court said.

As to the trial court's decision not to credit the estate's valuation, the appeals court pointed out the valuation evidence "hinged on" the testimony the estate's real estate appraiser gave and which the trial court found to be severely flawed. "The record supports this factual determination," the appeals court noted. It also observed that the values both sides' business appraisers achieved based on the credited real estate appraisals from the defense real estate appraiser in fact were not that far apart.

Based on the record of the case and the principle of deferring to the trial court's fact and credibility determinations, the Court of Appeal affirmed the trial court's valuing the estate's share at $500,000.

Ericsson, Inc. v. D-Link Sys. (D-Link II)

Citation: 773 F.3d 1201
Date of decision: Dec. 4, 2014
Country: US
State/Jurisdiction: Federal/Federal Circuit
Court: United States Court of Appeals
Type of action: Intellectual Property
Judge: O'Malley
SIC: 7373 Computer Integrated Systems Design
NAICS code: 541512 Computer Systems Design Services

Pivotal Ruling on Damage Calculation for SEP Infringement

Standard essential patents (SEPs) are different and pose special damages challenges. To comply with a standard, devices have to use technology that those patents may cover. Companies worry that this fact exposes them to excessive royalty demands from SEP holders. To alleviate the concern, SEP holders typically commit to granting licenses at a "reasonable and nondiscriminatory" (RAND) rate. The Federal Circuit has made it clear that a royalty calculation in SEP infringement cases has to account for these facts. In a key opinion, the court sets down principles trial courts and experts must follow to ensure damages withstand appeals court scrutiny.

RAND commitment. The plaintiff (two related entities) was a leading telecommunications technology company. Several of its patents covered two features of the 802.11(n) standard, which is the prevailing wireless Internet standard and has become widely adopted. In letters to the Institute of Electrical and Electronics Engineers (IEEE), the organization that published the standard, the plaintiff pledged to "grant a license under reasonable rates to an unrestricted number of applicants on a worldwide basis with reasonable terms and conditions that are demonstrably free of unfair discrimination." The RAND commitment was binding.

In 2010, the plaintiff sued the defendants—a number of networking, electronic, and multinational computer companies—claiming they had infringed several patents that were essential to the 802.11(n) standard. The plaintiff's damages expert examined eight of the plaintiff's previous 802.11 licenses with third parties that involved the claimed patents to determine a per-unit royalty, which he then applied to the defendants' accused products to calculate a reasonable royalty.

In a *Daubert* challenge, the defendants unsuccessfully argued the expert's opinion was inadmissible because his damages model failed to apportion the proposed royalty base between accused and nonaccused features. Moreover, the damages determination "squarely" violated the entire market value rule (EMVR) because the accused features were only part of a chip set that was one of many components in the end product and that did not drive customer demand for the end products. (An extended discussion of the *Daubert* ruling in *Ericsson Inc. v. D-Link Corp. (D-Link I)*, 2013 U.S. Dist. LEXIS 71564 (May 20, 2013), is available at *BVLaw*.)

The case went to trial and the jury found infringement related to three patents and awarded the plaintiff approximately $10 million—roughly 15 cents per infringing device. Post-trial the defendants asked the trial court to set aside the jury verdict and order a new trial. They again attacked the plaintiff's damages model, claiming it relied on licenses that were based on the value of the end products. And they claimed the trial court had failed to provide the jury with adequate instructions on the plaintiffs' RAND obligation.

The trial court denied the defendants' motion. Subsequently, the defendants appealed the damages award with the U.S. Court of Appeals for the Federal Circuit.

No new *Georgia-Pacific* framework. The Federal Circuit considered three damages-related issues:

1. *EMVR violation.* On appeal, the defendants claimed the trial court should have excluded the opinion of the plaintiffs' damages expert. His calculations were based on licenses that were tied to the entire value of the licensed products, even though the protected technology related to only a component of those products.

The plaintiffs countered the award of 15 cents per infringing product aligned with comparable licenses the plaintiffs had. What's more, the Federal Circuit has considered comparable licenses the best evidence of a royalty rate. Also, the plaintiffs' expert carefully apportioned to the value of the patents in suit. He took care to separate the value of the patents at issue from that of other patents covered by the comparable licenses.

The Federal Circuit reviewed some of the principles underlying EMVR. Starting with apportionment, it noted that, when the infringement involves multicomponent products, the reasonable royalty must reflect only the value of the infringing features of an accused product, "and no more." In terms of calculating a royalty base, the starting point must be the smallest salable unit, sometimes "even less," rather than the value of the entire product. The reason is that using the entire market value as a starting point might mislead the jury into overcompensating the patent holder. The exception is a situation in which the patented component drives customer demand.

The Federal Circuit found the testimony the plaintiffs' expert offered did not violate these principles.

As for the defendants' objection to the expert's use of "real world" licenses to value the patented invention, the court noted that licensed-based evidence was acceptable as long as the expert accounted for any facts that distinguished the comparable licenses from factors in play in a given infringement action. According to the Federal Circuit, in admitting expert testimony that "explains to the jury the need to discount reliance on a given license to account only for the value attributed to the licensed technology, as it did here," the trial court did not commit error simply because the expert's analysis referenced licenses based on the value of a multicomponent product.

However, the Federal Circuit went on to say that a trial court should provide the jury with instructions that fully explain the need to apportion the royalty award to the incremental value of the patented feature.

2. *RAND instruction.* Even though the Federal Circuit found the expert's damages model admissible, it struck down the award because of the trial court's failure to instruct the jury on how the plaintiff's RAND promises affected the royalty determination.

Instead of giving the jury a special instruction regarding the plaintiff's obligation to license use of the patents on RAND terms, the trial court gave an instruction on the customary 15 *Georgia-Pacific* factors. In addition, in what amounted to a 16th factor, the court told the jury it "may consider" the plaintiff's RAND obligation.

On appeal, the defendants argued the instructions were improper. Simply to apply the traditional *Georgia* framework meant ignoring the special nature of an infringement action involving SEPs. The defendants suggested there should be a modified version of the *Georgia-Pacific* factors applicable in cases involving RAND encumbered patents.

The Federal Circuit agreed that in SEP infringement cases many of the *Georgia-Pacific* factors were not relevant and some were "even contrary to RAND principles." Factor 4, the Federal Circuit said, was an example. It requires consideration of "[t]he licensor's established policy and marketing program to maintain his patent monopoly by not licensing others to use the invention or by granting licenses under special conditions designed to preserve that monopoly." Here, the plaintiff obligated itself to apply RAND terms in its licensing and, therefore, could not maintain a patent monopoly, the court pointed out. Factor 5 focuses on "[t]he commercial relationship between the licensor and licensee," but this relationship is irrelevant where the plaintiff committed to offer licenses at a *nondiscriminatory* rate, the court said with emphasis. The court also disapproved of the use of Factors 8, 9, and 10 because they were not relevant or were misleading.

"Trial courts should also consider the patentee's actual RAND commitment in crafting the jury instructions," the Federal Circuit went on to say. It is not enough to instruct the jury to consider the patent holder's obligation to license its technology on RAND terms because RAND terms vary from case to case, the Federal Circuit said. Therefore, the jury needs to be aware of the actual RAND promises a patent holder has made, and it needs to know that the promises are an obligation, "not just option," the Federal Court noted.

However, the Federal Circuit refused to go as far as to create a new set of *Georgia-Pacific* factors for RAND-encumbered patents. Instead of providing a bright line rule, the court advised trial courts to consider the facts of the case and "avoid rote reference to any particular damages formula," when instructing the jury.

3. *Apportionment for SEPs.* Finally, the Federal Circuit explained how to apportion damages for SEPs. "Just as we apportion damages for a patent that covers a small part of a device, we must also apportion damages for SEPs that cover only a small part of a standard," it said. The concern is to not reward the holder of an SEP for the patent's incorporation into a standard. According to the Federal Circuit, "technology is not always used because it is the best or the only option; it is used because its use is necessary to comply with the standard." In other words, wide use of a patented technology is not in itself an indication that it is more useful than prior art. It may be the result of a widely adopted standard. Therefore, trial courts and experts must ensure the holder of an SEP only gets compensated for the added value stemming from the superiority of the patented technology, not for the added value of being incorporated into a standard.

The jury "must be told to consider the difference between the added value of the technological invention and the added value of that invention's standardization," the Federal Circuit said.

In sum, the Federal Circuit found the trial court's failure to provide proper jury instructions on the plaintiff's actual RAND commitment, on the *Georgia-Pacific* factors, and on apportionment irreparably compromised the damages determination and struck down the award.

Editor's note: In a ruling that also involved the infringement of patents essential to the 802.11 standard, the Federal Circuit vacated a damages award against Cisco based on the principles set forth in the instant case. A digest of the case, Commonwealth Sci. & Indus. Research Organisation v. Cisco Sys., *2015 U.S. App. LEXIS 20942 (Dec. 3, 2015), appears in this book, and the court's opinion is available at* BVLaw.

Fish v. GreatBanc Trust Co.

Citation: 2016 U.S. Dist. LEXIS 137351
Date of decision: Sept. 1, 2016
Country: US
State/Jurisdiction: Federal/Illinois
Court: United States District Court
Type of action: ESOP
Experts: Robert Reilly (plaintiffs); Jeffrey Risius (defendants); Duff & Phelps (financial advisor to ESOP trustee)
Judge: Alonso
SIC: 5963 Direct Selling Establishments (except mobile food services and food wagons)
NAICS code: 454390 Other Direct Selling Establishments

'Persuasive' Defense Expert Testimony Defeats ESOP Overpayment Claims

A noteworthy ESOP case involving allegations of breach of fiduciary duty and engaging in a prohibited transaction turned on whether the ESOP trustee's financial advisor had performed proper due diligence and issued defensible fairness and valuation analyses. At trial, experts for the parties reached sharply different assessments of the work. The court found the defense expert's testimony validated the advisor's work and that "no more than fair value market value was paid for the non-ESOP shareholders' stock."

Independent financial advisors. The case arose out of a 2003 transaction by which the subject company (Antioch) bought all of the outstanding shares of its stock held outside its employee stock ownership plan. The purchase was part of a tender offer transaction that left the company 100% ESOP-owned.

At the time of the transaction, Antioch was a family business operating as an S corporation. Its core business was direct marketing of scrapbooks and accessories through its subsidiary, Creative Memories (CM). In the late 1990s and early 2000s, the company enjoyed substantial growth. In 1998, EBITDA was $31.9 million; by 2002, it was $85.2 million. In early 2003, the company had over 1,200 employees and over 70,000 consultants.

The individual defendants included family members who then served on the company's board of directors and/or the internal ESOP advisory committee and who held non-ESOP shares.

Concerns over the company's S corp distribution plan prompted the defendants and professionals from Deloitte & Touche in January 2003 to hold an "ESOP Summit" that led to the transaction. Deloitte outlined numerous advantages if the transaction went ahead. It could eliminate corporate income tax, which, in turn, would result in increased cash flow to the company, give the company more flexibility as to how to allocate ESOP contributions, provide non-ESOP shareholders with fair value for their shares, and increase ESOP value in the long run.

Because the transaction involved the issuance of warrants, which only the company could do, it provided for the company, not the ESOP, to purchase the non-ESOP shareholders' stock.

To avoid conflicts of interest, the company removed the defendants from the transaction. It hired an independent trustee, GreatBanc, which then retained independent legal and financial advisors. Specifically, it asked Duff & Phelps (D&P) to analyze whether the transaction was fair to the ESOP from the financial point of view. The company's financial advisor was Houlihan Lokey Howard & Zukin (Houlihan Lokey).

The company provided the advisors with financial forecasts. In the ordinary course of business, it prepared five-year projections, but since the term of the transaction would be 10 years (the waiting period for all the warrants to be exercised) the company also developed 10-year projections. The starting point was taking the individual business unit projections and extending them over the transaction period. To account for the risks of increased competition, uncertainty over the company's ability to expand internationally, and technological threats such as digital photography, the team preparing the projections ratcheted down the revenue and operating margin projections. The 10-year projections assumed revenue growth of between 11% and 13% for the first seven years following the transaction; eventually, growth would slow down to 6% annually. In contrast, in the years prior to the transaction, there was a 26% revenue growth in 2002, a 16% increase in 2001, a 20% increase in 2000, and a 22% increase in 1999.

Both D&P and Houlihan Lokey performed their own due diligence and concluded management's 10-year projections were reasonable and reliable. Lenders committing $170 million to the company for the transaction also found the forecasts reasonable.

During negotiations among the various parties to the transaction, GreatBanc and D&P decided that the proposed package of cash, notes, and warrants would dilute the ESOP's share value. They believed the warrants were worth more than the proposed value and demanded that the number of warrants available to the sellers be fewer than the Deloitte plan envisioned. A lower number meant the ESOP would have a greater stake in the company once the warrants were exercised. Management resisted a cap on warrants. At trial, the defense cited GreatBanc's and D&P's resistance as evidence of an arm's-length negotiation. The court agreed.

GreatBanc and D&P also insisted on a put price protection to help mitigate the dilution of post-transaction stock value. This measure would ensure employees who would leave the company soon after the transaction closed would get as much of the economic benefit of the transaction as those leaving later (who would benefit from the tax savings resulting from the transaction).

In essence, the company offered to pay $850 per share for the non-ESOP shareholders' stock. The sellers had a choice between accepting $850 in cash or accepting a package that consisted of $280 in cash, $280 in the form of a subordinated note, and a warrant worth $290. Assuming the transaction was fair, GreatBanc as the trustee would decline to tender shares of common stock the ESOP owned.

In early December 2003, D&P confirmed to GreatBanc that the deal was fair and reasonable to the ESOP with respect to the consideration the company paid and the terms and conditions attaching to the transaction. The transaction, which did not involve the use of ESOP assets (the company paid), went through.

Post-transaction developments. The company's stock price rose to about $894 per share two weeks after the transaction closed. A year later, an independent valuation firm pegged the price at $943 per share as of December 2004. This, the court noted, meant that employees who had left the company in 2004 received greater value per share than the selling non-ESOP shareholders did in the transaction. However, by the end of 2005, the price began to drop. By the end of 2006, a share was worth about $786.

Immediately after the transaction, the number of employees leaving the company and asking to redeem their shares was greater than anyone had anticipated. However, the court found the unusually large repurchase obligation ($109 million) was unpredictable and not caused by the transaction. On the contrary, the company had used best practices in predicting its repurchase obligation and used the best cash management planning tools available.

In 2006, the company incurred a serious sales decline that continued into 2007. It had, the court found, to do with unpredictable systemic changes in the market and was unrelated to the transaction. The defendants' expert was able to show by way of valuation multiples from comparable companies in the industry that the entire scrapbook industry experienced the decline owing to new digital technology and a change in consumer behavior. He also successfully argued that by late 2007 a global financial crisis was setting in that caused lenders to become jittery and call their loans. In mid-2008, Antioch declared Chapter 11 bankruptcy.

Alleged violations. Subsequently, a number of ESOP participants sued, alleging the defendants' actions ultimately caused the ESOP's shares of Antioch stock to become worthless. Even though there was an independent trustee and the defendants had no control over the decision as to whether or not to approve the transaction, they remained fiduciaries, the plaintiffs claimed. The defendants failed to monitor GreatBanc, the ESOP's trustee, which had a fiduciary duty to the plan and breached it by accepting D&P's fairness opinion and the underlying financial analysis, the plaintiffs maintained.

They further argued that, even though no ESOP assets were in play in the transaction, the defendants engaged in a prohibited transaction by using plan assets—indirectly—to initiate the transaction and selling non-ESOP shares to the company.

D&P's pretransaction analysis. The court decided that, to determine whether the defendants were liable on any of the claims, it had to review the process and analysis by which D&P arrived at its fairness and valuation conclusions.

D&P reviewed aspects specific to the company, including ownership structure, historical share price trend, the state of the company's ESOP, and the company's status as an S corp. It analyzed the company's brand and quality of its products, its culture, its sales network, and potential for international growth. D&P also was aware of vulnerabilities related to competition, technological developments, and potential saturation of the market.

D&P reviewed the company's relevant audited financials and internally prepared latest-12-month period (LTM) tended September 2003. It considered the company's historical revenue compound annual growth rate (CAGR) and EBITDA margins and calculated key financial statement ratios from 1999 through the LTM period.

Projections. Even though D&P found management's projections were reasonable, it decided to develop its own set of projections that were lower than management's projections and the company's past experience.

It projected five-year revenue and EBITDA CAGRs of 10.3% and 5.5%, respectively, compared to the company's actual five-year historical revenue and EBITDA CAGRs of 17.4% and 21.0%, respectively. D&P forecast a five-year average EBITDA margin of 17.8%, compared to Antioch's actual five-year historical average of 19.0%. D&P reduced the growth projections for new ventures and units that it considered largely unproven.

To account for the risk that attaches to projections as they extend further into the future, D&P downward adjusted projected revenues for the transaction and internal company purposes in the later projection years (2007 to 2012).

DCF analysis. D&P performed a discounted cash flow analysis based on its independent, conservative projections. Using the capital asset pricing model (CAPM), it developed a weighted average cost of capital of 12% to 14%. Considering it best to factor risks specific to the company into the projections, it did not apply a company-specific risk premium (CSRP). At trial, D&P's leading analyst explained a CSRP would mean double counting.

Ultimately, D&P determined that the fair market value of the company ranged from $774 to $932 per share ($845 per share using a 13% WACC). Consequently, the transaction's $850-per-share price was within the FMV range.

Comparable company analysis. As a sanity check, D&P also undertook a comparative company analysis, looking to two groups of publicly traded companies: direct sales companies and retail craft/hobby companies. It found that its DCF multiples were generally below the range of valuation multiples for the publicly traded companies. Consequently, the transaction price was fair. If at all, it was unfair to the selling shareholders, not the ESOP, D&P concluded.

Projected repurchase obligation. D&P assumed the company would make a contribution to the ESOP equal to 21% of eligible compensation every year from 2005 to 2013 even though the company agreed to do so only in 2014. Including this expense every year after 2004 lowered D&P's per-share value conclusion.

D&P ran downside scenarios to test the company's ability to handle debt and repurchase obligations going forward if the company's performance fell below expectations. However, its leading analyst explained it did not perform a DCF valuation based solely on a downside scenario because there was "no basis" for using cash flows that were not the expected case. Such an analysis would simply produce a value that was too low, the witness explained.

Trial expert testimony. At trial, both sides presented testimony from valuation experts of great renown on the accuracy and validity of D&P's work.

Plaintiffs' expert. The plaintiffs' expert noted several "flaws" in D&P's analysis related to accounting for industry-related and company-specific risks facing the company at the time of the transaction. A review of industry research from 2003 as well as of selected company consultant sales and productivity figures from that year, and phone calls with a couple of former employees who testified for the plaintiffs at trial, led him to conclude D&P overvalued the company.

The plaintiffs' expert ran five DCF analyses. Four used significantly lower 10-year revenue projections than D&P had used; one analysis used a significantly higher discount rate. As a result, he achieved much lower per-share values, ranging from $315 to $590. He said the most reasonable and reliable value immediately prior to the transaction was $500 per share.

One DCF analysis that used D&P's calculated revenue projections included a 5% CSRP in the 13% WACC, resulting in an 18% discount rate. The addition of the CSRP drastically lowered the per-share value, from $845 to $590. The expert said this was his own estimate, which was not based on a specific formula or quantification of specific risk factors but was "entirely a matter of judgment."

His other four analyses used the 13% WACC but applied that rate to much lower revenue projections. In two analyses, the projections were derived from 10-year sales projections one of the plaintiffs' other experts developed by using ARIMA, a forecasting technique relying on past sales as the only input. As the court noted, "the method essentially uses past performance to forecast future performance."

The plaintiffs' expert admitted he did not remember a single engagement relying on ARIMA projections in valuing a company or its stock, and he said he had not in the past contracted with another professional to use ARIMA to project corporate sales in order to analyze a transaction.

In the other two analyses, the plaintiffs' expert applied the 13% WACC to downside feasibility models Deloitte had prepared for the company in the process leading up to the transaction.

The plaintiffs' expert considered the D&P projections too high but also said: "I don't know that anyone was able to predict 2006 and 2007 because the company's results were a lot lower than any projection, any forecast indicated."

He also faulted D&P for insufficiently considering Antioch's projected repurchase obligation. A post-transaction valuation that factored in the obligation would have resulted in an additional drop in value, resulting in a $468-per-share value. This meant an additional $7.1 million in damages to the ESOP participants, he concluded. Finding there was an $80 million shortfall in the repurchase obligation projection D&P used, he deducted that amount from the company's enterprise value that D&P had determined immediately post-transaction. At the same time, he did not reduce the total number of outstanding shares that were bought with the $80 million.

He allowed that ultimately the difference between his and the D&P analysis could be seen as "two reasonable and skilled analysts" reaching a different conclusion.

He did not perform a comparable company analysis or any other analysis to check his DCF value conclusions.

Defense expert. The defendants' expert was the managing partner of a company witnesses said had "one of the best reputations in the ESOP valuation world." He reviewed both the work D&P had done and critiqued the opposing expert's review of D&P's work.

<u>Opinion of D&P's work.</u> He concluded D&P followed a process that was "methodologically sound and customary" and its fairness and valuation opinions were "reasonable and appropriate." He pointed out that D&P relied on projections that were significantly lower than management's projections, even though a number of advisors at the time of the transaction considered those projections reasonable. D&P's downward adjustments resulted in "a very conservative valuation of Antioch," the defense expert found.

D&P's DCF analysis was proper. Its WACC was conservative from a valuation perspective, the defense expert said. His own analysis showed the appropriate WACC would have been 11.9%, lower than the 12%-to-14% range Duff used. All else equal, the FMV would have been $932 per share, higher than D&P's value conclusion.

The defense expert agreed with D&P that to apply a CSRP of any rate to the lowered revenue projections would be "classic ... double-count of risk," resulting in an undervaluation. Had the opposing expert used the formula for calculating a potential CSRP provided in Shannon Pratt's authoritative treatise, rather than relying on gut feeling, that expert would have achieved a value similar to D&P's value, the defense expert said.

Speaking of being conservative, he noted D&P also added a projected benefit expense of 21% of eligible compensation for years during which the company was not obligated to make it.

He conducted his own independent comparable company analysis, using a broader set of companies, and concluded the EBITDA multiple D&P's DCF analysis implied was at the low end of the range of EBITDA multiples for comparable companies. Consequently, D&P's value conclusions were reasonable and conservative.

The defense expert also agreed with D&P that it was improper to account for the projected repurchase obligation a company incurs when redeeming the shares of employees leaving the company. Share redemption at FMV "inherently has no per share valuation impact," he explained.

Rebuttal to opposing expert. The defense expert found grave flaws with the analysis of the plaintiffs' expert.

For example, he noted that valuators typically account for industry- and company-specific risks by way of conservative financial projections and their WACC, as D&P had done, not by making line-item deductions from the value for each of the risks.

He found four of the opposing analyst's DCF models were wrong because they used improper cash flow projections. Two relied on projections based on the ARIMA statistical forecasting technique, which other witnesses had dismissed as inappropriate for projecting corporate sales 10 years into the future. No other advisors before and after the transaction had used that method in their financial analysis and projections before or after the transaction, the defense expert pointed out. Two of the plaintiffs' expert's DCFs improperly used downside feasibility models.

The fifth analysis included a discount rate that incorporated a "completely subjective and unwarranted 5% CSRP" and applied it to revenue projections D&P had already downward adjusted.

Had the plaintiffs' expert done a comparable company analysis, he would have realized his DCF value conclusions were unsound, the defense expert said.

Court adopts defense expert's opinion. The court credited the defense expert's opinion for its conclusion that there was no overvaluation of the non-ESOP stock in the transaction and no bad-faith conduct. It noted the defense expert's experience, expertise, and independent research and valuation analysis, which it found provided "credible and persuasive support" that D&P followed an appropriate process and used a conservative methodology to arrive at conservative value conclusions. The $850-per-share value was at the "very low end" of the range of values calculated for the company's stock, the court said.

The court said the opposing expert's opinions were "not credible" but seemed to be developed "from the perspective of … hindsight," relying in part on conversations with former company employees who were "sympathetic to the plaintiffs" and who discussed events 10 years after the transaction took place.

Because D&P's opinions withstood scrutiny, no liability was attached to the defendants. The court found for the defendants on all claims. The plaintiffs earlier had made a settlement with GreatBanc, the ESOP trustee.

Gifford v Gifford

Citation: 2015 N.Y. App. Div. LEXIS 7829
Date of decision: Oct. 22, 2015
Country: US
State/Jurisdiction: New York
Court: Court of Appeals
Type of action: Marital Dissolution
Experts: Edward Selig (jointly retained)
Judge: Lynch
SIC: 8711 Engineering Services
NAICS code: 541330 Engineering Services

Service Business Valuation Triggers Double Dip Rule

In a New York divorce case, the owner of a service business appealed a trial court's spousal support order under the jurisdiction's double dip rule. The appeals court agreed that the spousal award payments were based on the wrong earnings determination.

Same income stream. The husband was a geotechnical engineer who owned his own company. Among other things, the success of his business depended on his ability to perform strenuous fieldwork. At divorce, the parties agreed the business was a marital asset and jointly retained an appraiser who valued it at $448,000 based on a capitalized earnings approach, using annual base earnings of $148,000.

The trial court awarded roughly half of the business to the wife by way of a $210,000 payout. Moreover, the court ordered the husband to pay nondurational spousal support under a tiered approach, starting with monthly payments of $6,000 that dropped to $3,000 and ultimately to $800, terminating with one party's death or the wife's remarriage. The court based the spousal support payments on the husband's total average annual income of over $332,400.

The husband contested the trial court's order claiming the awards to the wife amounted to unlawful double counting of his income. The appeals court agreed. It noted that the expert's business valuation methodology, an income approach, triggered the rule against double counting income. "Once a court converts a specific stream of income into an asset, that income may no longer be calculated into the maintenance formula and payout," the court said, citing *Grunfeld v. Grunfeld*, 731 N.E.2d (2000) (available at *BVLaw*).

The appeals court referenced a leading precedential case. "Double counting may occur when marital property includes *intangible* assets such as professional licenses or goodwill or the value of a service business," the court said, citing *Keane v. Keane*, 8 N.Y.3d 115 (2006) (available at *BVLaw*). "It is only where the asset is totally indistinguishable and has no existence separate from the [income stream] from which it is derived that double counting results." Id. (internal quotation marks omitted) The appeals court found that, in the instant case, the husband's solely owned engineering company was a service business for purposes of the double counting rule.

Because the wife obtained an equitable share of the business, it was obligatory for the trial court to base the spousal support award on the husband's baseline earnings of $148,000 instead of his average annual income of $332,400, the appellate court decided.

Pursuant to the reduced income stream available for spousal support, the appeals court downward adjusted the monthly payments starting with an initial sum of $2,700 and declining to $1,350 and ultimately to $360.

Estate of Giustina v. Commissioner (Giustina III)

Citation: 2016 Tax Ct. Memo LEXIS 113
Date of decision: June 13, 2016
Country: US
State/Jurisdiction: Federal
Court: United States Tax Court
Type of action: Federal Taxation
Experts: Robert Reilly (estate/petitioner); John Thomas (IRS/respondent)
Judge: Morrison
SIC: 0811 Timber Tracts (long term timber farms)
NAICS code: 11311 Timber Tract Operations

Tax Court Corrects Prior Valuation of LP Interest to Startling Result

Five years after issuing its original ruling in a tax dispute involving an Oregon timber company, the Tax Court recently revalued the decedent's minority interest in a family partnership. The recalculation became necessary after the 9th Circuit called out the Tax Court for making unjustifiable assumptions and inadequately explained adjustments to an expert's valuation. The recalculation proved a boon to the taxpayer.

First valuation. The flashpoint was the decedent's 41% limited-partner (LP) interest in a partnership that owned a timber company, including almost 48,000 acres of timberland. At the time of the decedent's death, in 2005, the partnership had operated for 15 years. It had two general partners and eight limited partners—all family members or trusts acting on behalf of a family member.

After the Internal Revenue Service (IRS) assessed a deficiency of $12.66 million in estate taxes, the estate petitioned the U.S. Tax Court for review. At the time of trial, the parties were somewhat closer in their positions.

The Tax Court decided to value the LP interest by way of two methods: the discounted cash flow (DCF) approach and the net asset value (NAV) approach. The former accounted for how much the partnership could be expected to earn if it continued timberland operations, and the latter valued the assets as if liquidated. The experts agreed the partnership's timber assets were worth $143 million. They were worth over $150 million if one added assets that were not timberland assets.

The Tax Court gave a 75% weighting to the DCF-derived value. This was the probability, it said, that the partnership would continue. It credited the estate expert's cash flow calculation but decided to make some adjustments to the analysis. The most consequential one for purposes of the appeal was the court's cutting in half the 3.5% company-specific risk premium the estate's expert had proposed. The court decided that a hypothetical buyer could minimize this unique risk by diversifying the portfolio of assets. Therefore, a 1.75% premium was adequate.

The court allowed for a small possibility that the assets would be liquidated and assigned a 25% weight to the value resulting from an NAV calculation. Although it recognized that a buyer of the decedent's interest would face sizable obstacles in forcing a sale of the partnership, it said there was authority that allowed for some degree of speculation as to the future composition of management in valuation. Combining the values resulting from the analyses, the Tax Court concluded the decedent's interest was worth $27.45 million. (A digest of *Estate of Giustina v. Commissioner*, T.C. Memo 2011-141, and the court's opinion are available at *BVLaw*.)

Successful appeal. The estate appealed the ruling with the 9th Circuit Court of Appeals. Although not all of the estate's arguments resonated with the appeals court, it found the Tax Court had made two clear errors that required remanding the case for a new value determination.

The appeals court held the Tax Court had not sufficiently explained its decision to reduce by 50% the company-specific risk premium the estate's expert had developed. The Tax Court did not seem to take into account how much wealth a potential buyer would need to affect diversification, the 9th Circuit observed.

The appeals court made barbed comments about the Tax Court's decision to give a 25% weight to the NAV determination, noting how implausible it was that a buyer of the decedent's LP interest could affect the dissolution of this long-term partnership under the provisions of the partnership agreement.

It ordered the Tax Court "to recalculate the value of the Estate based on the partnership's value as a going concern." (A digest of *Estate of Giustina v. Commissioner*, 2014 U.S. App. LEXIS 22961 (9th Cir., Dec. 5, 2014) (*Giustina II*), and the court's opinion are available at *BVLaw*.)

Consequential corrections. The Tax Court's most recent opinion shows it took the higher court's critique seriously.

"The first revision we make is to change the weight we accorded to the partnership's assets," the Tax Court said. It no longer considered the value of the assets but instead assigned a 100% weight to the cash flows the estate's expert had calculated. Doing so meant the valuation of the decedent's interest was "entirely based on the partnership's value as a 'going concern,'" the Tax Court noted.

Upon order from the 9th Circuit, the Tax Court also explained further its thinking behind the decision to reduce the company-specific risk premium. In the end, the Tax Court decided to disavow its earlier decision to reduce the premium.

The Tax Court said for its original valuation it assumed that diversification of risk was achievable if the buyer was an entity of multiple owners, such as a publicly traded timber company, a real estate investment trust, or a hedge fund. Whether the entity's owners were wealthy or not, there would be diversification because they would have held assets outside their interest in the entity. Also, the entity itself could have diversified the risk related to the LP interest by holding other substantial assets.

The Tax Court emphasized that the one and only reason for halving the 3.5% risk premium was the possibility that a hypothetical buyer could diversify the risk.

The court went on to conclude that its assumption was no longer tenable in light of the 9th Circuit's ruling. The appeals court held that a hypothetical buyer had to be someone who could become an owner under the partnership agreement. Considering all the limited partners were either individuals or trusts for the benefit of individual family members, there was no basis for assuming a multiowner entity could be a buyer. Also, there was no evidence that any of the limited partners had sufficient assets to diversify the risk of owning the 41% LP interest.

Further, the transfer of an LP interest required the approval of the company's two general partners. Considering that by then they had run the partnership for 25 years, it was unlikely they would sell to a party, such as an investment company, whose sole goal was to increase its rate of return on the investment by dissolving the business.

Therefore, the Tax Court conceded there was no rationale for reducing the company-specific risk premium. The Tax Court adopted the estate expert's 3.5% rate, which increased the discount rate for the DCF analysis from 16.25% to 18%. The corrections caused the value of the decedent's interest to drop from almost $27.5 million to about $14 million, the Tax Court found. It ordered the parties to recalculate the deficiency based on the revised valuation.

Grant v. Grant

Citation: 2016 Tenn. App. LEXIS 327
Date of decision: May 12, 2016
Country: US
State/Jurisdiction: Tennessee
Court: Court of Appeals
Type of action: Marital Dissolution
Experts: George Pritchett (appraiser, husband), Michael Wallace (valuation expert, husband); Mark Young, Larry Sharp (appraisers, wife), Scott Womack (valuation expert, wife)
Judge: McBrayer
SIC: 6552 Land Subdividers and Developers, Except Cemeteries
NAICS code: 237210 Land Subdivision

Appeals Court Signs Off on 'Slight' DLOM in Minority Interest Valuation

A recent Tennessee appeals court decision hinged on the issue of whether a marketability discount was appropriate in the valuation of the husband's interests in three real estate development partnerships. The trial court rejected the relatively steep DLOMs the husband's expert proposed, noting an absence of proof that the husband intended to sell his shares in the businesses. Although the appeals court suggested the trial court misunderstood the principle behind DLOM, it deferred to the lower court's findings. By skirting the issue, the appeals court left valuators in a state of uncertainty as to when to apply the discount and at what rate.

Agreement on use of DLOC. The husband was a successful real estate developer who had ownership interests in five businesses. In each of the prior five years, he made well over $600,000 after taxes.

In terms of valuing the marital assets, the parties' dispute focused on three general partnerships in which the husband owned a minority interest. The partnerships bought land, developed it for residential subdivisions, and sold the lots to builders. They paid no realtor commissions when selling the lots.

At trial, both sides offered testimony from real estate appraisers and business valuators.

Husband's experts. The husband's appraiser valued the subdivisions and the undeveloped land belonging to the partnerships. Based on instructions from the client, he used a December 2013 valuation date even though he viewed the properties several months later. He allowed that any improvements to the properties subsequent to the valuation date would increase the appraised values.

He said he used the anticipated use methodology (aka subdivision development method). It assumes that the owner sells all the available lots at fair market value to one hypothetical buyer. The appraiser projected future lot revenues, deducted ownership expenses, and discounted the resulting figure to present value. He said he applied a 7% cost of sale deduction because most owners would incur this type of cost. On cross-examination, he said that if the deduction were eliminated the appraised value would increase by about 4%.

The husband's business valuator used a net asset approach to value the husband's interests in the partnerships based on the real estate appraiser's values. The business valuator conceded that any error in the real estate appraiser's values would have an effect on the business valuations. He explained a minority interest discount was appropriate where the interest holder was not in a position to control the business. This was the case here. The valuator relied on data from a control premium study to determine a base DLOC and compared the results to state case law. (The opinion does not state what rate the valuator decided to use.)

Moreover, even though the husband did not plan to sell his stakes in the partnership, the valuator thought it appropriate to apply a marketability discount. The DLOM, the expert explained, served as "the gauge of a readily available market to turn a particular interest into cash." He also noted the partnership agreements included restrictions on a partner's ability to sell his interest. To determine the DLOM rate, the valuation expert looked to restricted stock studies and state case law on the valuation of closely held businesses. For the three partnerships, he applied an 18% DLOM, a 12% DLOM, and a 30% DLOM, respectively.

Wife's experts. The wife retained two real estate appraisers who both used a March 2014 valuation date to value separate properties. They agreed with the method the husband's appraiser used but made no cost of sale deductions.

The wife's business valuator used the same valuation approach as the opposing valuation expert. The wife's expert agreed it was appropriate to apply a minority discount, but he objected to the use of a DLOM where the husband had no intention of selling his interests.

Other indicators of value. The wife also introduced the husband's personal financial statements for the past five years as evidence that the husband valued the partnership interests much higher than his valuation expert did. Moreover, a partner who also held a minority interest in one of the partnerships said he believed his interest was worth more than the value the husband's expert indicated.

Problematic real estate appraisals. The trial court awarded the husband all of the business interests considering only he had the expertise and ability to operate them. However, the court credited the valuations the wife's experts offered. In terms of all the real estate appraisals, it found the husband's real estate expert was wrong not to use the valuation date closer to the date of the hearing (i.e., the March 2014 date). Further, the court balked at the expert's 7% cost of sale deduction considering the husband never incurred such costs when selling subdivision lots.

The trial also found flaws in the valuations the husband's business appraiser developed. Specifically, the DLOM rates were too high or altogether inappropriate, the trial court said. It noted that, in terms of one of the partnerships, the husband admitted that a large portion of its earlier undeveloped land had been developed and was about to be sold. The sale increased the assets of the partnership, the trial court observed. Also, the husband's partner assigned a higher value to his minority ownership interest than the husband's expert proposed for the husband's minority interest.

At the same time, the court noted that the "Husband might be compelled to sell some portion of his assets [in this partnership] in order to accomplish the property divisions ordered by the Court while still maintaining and supporting the remaining business interests." Consequently, the court reduced the 18% DLOM to a "slight discount for marketability." (The opinion fails to say what "slight" means.)

As for the other two partnerships, the trial court declined to apply a DLOM because the husband had no intention of selling these interests.

Case for generous alimony. The court awarded the wife long-term alimony (alimony in futuro) at an amount of $10,000 per month, finding the husband had had considerable annual earnings and should be able to continue to earn a high standard of living considering he retained ownership of all of his business interests. The wife, in contrast, had no appreciable work history or skills to enable her to earn more than minimum wage.

DLOM dependent on facts. The husband appealed the trial court's findings. In terms of the partnership valuations, he claimed the trial court erred in its DLOM rulings.

The appeals court began its analysis by saying valuing marital property is a fact question and questions of fact are the province of the trial court. Moreover, unless the trial court's findings conflict with the evidence, there is a presumption that the findings are correct.

The appeals court further observed that valuation experts typically use a marketability discount to reflect that there is no ready market for an interest or that provisions in a partnership agreement restrict a partner's ability to liquidate his or her interest.

And it said: "Generally, applicability of the use of a lack of marketability discount depends on the characteristics of the ownership interest being valued, not whether the owner of the interest actually intends to sell the interest."

But even though the owner's intent to sell was the focus of the trial court's DLOM analysis, the appeals court did not explicitly critique or reject the trial court's findings. Rather, it found, "in many instances, the decision to apply the discount is seen as discretionary." In other words, "the decision is discretionary and dependent on the facts of the case," the appeals court noted. "Under the facts of this case," the appeals court went on to say, the trial court did not abuse its discretion in applying a "slight" DLOM for one general partnership and no DLOM in valuing the other two interests.

In terms of factual determinations, the appeals court noted the trial court's objections to the artificially low real estate appraisals proposed by the husband's appraiser and testimony about the effect of those flawed appraisals on the business valuations. The trial court also gave weight to nonexpert evidence that suggested a higher value of the husband's interests than his business valuator proposed. "Resolving this type of factual dispute is uniquely the role of the trial court," the appeals court said in summing up its decision to affirm the trial court's valuations.

The husband also challenged the alimony award. He claimed the trial court erred when it considered his future income from the partnerships to determine his ability to pay alimony because he was awarded these interests in the division of the marital estate.

The appeals court found the applicable provision, Tenn. Code Ann. § 36-4-121(b)(1)(E), expressly provided that, in considering alimony, the court may consider income from assets awarded in the division of the marital estate "to the extent the asset will create additional income after the division."

Consequently, the appeals court also upheld the trial court's alimony ruling.

H.W. Johnson v. Commissioner

Citation: 2016 Tax Court Memo LEXIS 94
Date of decision: May 11, 2016
Country: US
State/Jurisdiction: Federal
Court: United States Tax Court
Type of action: Federal Taxation
Judge: Gale
SIC: 1771 Concrete Work (concrete work except stucco work and asphalt, brick, and paving)
NAICS code: 238110 Poured Concrete Foundation and Structure Contractors

Return on Equity Analysis Undergirds Reasonable Compensation Claim

A taxpayer dispute over executive compensation for purposes of a tax deduction boiled down to whether the taxpayer, after paying the compensation, achieved enough of a return on equity to satisfy an independent investor. If so, there was a strong indication that the compensation was reasonable. The taxpayer met its burden by offering testimony from an expert whose return on equity analysis and data source the Tax Court found more persuasive than the analysis the Internal Revenue Service's expert put forward. The court's opinion serves as a reminder to financial analysts how critical it is to ensure that the chosen comparable companies are in fact sufficiently similar to the subject company in terms of business activity and size of annual sales.

Running a successful concrete business. The case involved a large, very successful concrete contracting business in Arizona that performed curb, gutter, and sidewalk work. Because of its stellar reputation in the industry, the company was able to secure contracts even when it was not the lowest bidder.

In 2003 and 2004, the relevant tax years, the company had over 200 employees, and its contract revenues were over $23.7 million and $38 million, respectively. A husband and wife started the business in 1974, but in 1993 the couple's two sons, who had worked at the company as teenagers, assumed complete control over the company's daily operations. Then the company had contract revenues of about $4 million.

By 1996, the wife owned a 51% interest and the sons each owned 24.5% of the shares.

During the years at issue, the wife was president and chair of the board. The sons were co-vice presidents and, along with their mother, members of the board of directors. In terms of operations, each son was responsible for managing a geographical area. This meant overseeing 100 employees each and working 10 to 12 hours a day, five or six days a week.

The success of the business depended on a reliable supply of concrete. When shortages of concrete kept occurring as a result of Arizona's housing boom, starting in late 2002, the sons proposed to the controlling shareholder, their mother, that the company invest in a concrete supply company. But she rejected the proposal. Consequently, the sons formed a different company that partnered with other investors to operate a concrete supply business. As a majority shareholder, the sons' new entity was able to ensure a steady supply of concrete to the subject company at a discounted price when other contractors temporarily had to suspend operations because they could not procure concrete.

In 1991, the subject company adopted a formal bonus plan, which it amended in 1999. Typically, at year-end, based on the advice of the company's accountant, the board issued bonuses out of a "bonus pool" based on officer performance and the company's ability to pay. Similarly, the company had in place a dividend plan that envisioned paying out dividends when the company's retained earnings were over $2 million.

IRS makes significant concession. In 2003 and 2004, the company paid the sons roughly $4 million and $7.3 million as compensation, claiming these amounts as deductions on its federal income tax returns.

The Internal Revenue Service initially issued a notice of deficiency in which it disallowed over $2.6 million for 2003 and nearly $5.6 million for 2004 of the claimed deductions. The agency subsequently conceded that deductions in the amounts of $3.2 million and $6.5 million were reasonable. Therefore, the amounts in dispute shrunk considerably to about $811,000 for tax year 2003 and $770,000 for tax year 2004.

The company petitioned the U.S. Tax Court for review. At the start of trial, it argued that the IRS's concession meant there no longer was a presumption that the agency's position was correct; in other words, the burden of proof shifted from the petitioner to the IRS. In the end, the petitioner did not pursue this argument. Instead, it claimed that it met its burden of showing the compensation paid to the sons was reasonable.

Five-factor reasonableness test. Under the Internal Revenue Code's Section 162(a)(1), a taxpayer may deduct "a reasonable allowance for salaries or other compensation for personal services actually rendered" as an ordinary and necessary business expense. The crux of the inquiry is whether the executive compensation is reasonable.

The 9th Circuit Court of Appeals, whose law is controlling because this court would handle an appeal in this case, uses the five-factor *Elliots* test to determine reasonableness. Each factor carries the same weight. *See Elliots v. Commissioner,* 716 F.2d 1241 (9th Cir. 1983).

The factors are:

1. The employee's role in the company;
2. A comparison of compensation paid by similar companies for similar services;
3. The character and condition of the company;
4. Potential conflicts of interest; and
5. The internal consistency of compensation arrangements.

In this case, the IRS conceded that four out of the five factors weighed in favor of the petitioner, or at least were neutral. The outcome, the agency contended, hinged on the fourth factor, potential conflicts of interest, which required a determination of whether a hypothetical independent investor would receive an adequate return on equity after paying for the sons' compensation.

Both sides offered expert testimony to support their positions. For completion's sake, the court commented on all five factors.

Regarding Factor 1, the court found the sons were "integral" to the company's success given their "hands-on management style that consistently produced a quality product on schedule." Even if the company benefited from Arizona's housing boom, the dramatic increase in revenues from $4 million in 1993 to over $38 million in 2004 was largely the result of the company's reputation for quality and timely performance, which was a result of the sons' management style, the court found.

In terms of Factor 2, the IRS allowed that, since the company performed so much better than any of the designated comparable companies, making a meaningful compensation comparison impossible. The company's expert determined compensation at the company was 18.4% and 20.9% of gross revenue for 2003 and 2004. The industry average for those two years was 2.2%. The company said the higher compensation rates were justified because it so outperformed the industry average.

The court did not accept the company's argument, saying it lacked the benchmarks necessary to test the company's claim. It found this factor to be neutral.

As for Factor 3, the IRS conceded that the company became a "substantial success" during the relevant years. Accordingly, the court found Factor 3 weighed in favor of the company.

Point of contention. Factor 4 prompted sharp disagreements between the parties' experts. Both experts agreed that the company had pretax returns on equity of 10.2% in 2003 and 9% in 2004. However, they disagreed over what the expected return on equity should have been.

To answer this question, the IRS's expert derived return on equity figures from four data sources, achieving a range from 13.8% to 18.3%. However, the court found the data sources, and by extension the IRS expert's resulting return on equity figures, unreliable when compared with the source used by the company's expert.

The IRS expert's first figure was derived from seven "guideline companies," which the court rejected as not comparable. The problem was the companies were publicly traded, were active in an industry that was different from the subject company's, and had sales that were considerably larger than the subject company's.

The expert's second figure relied on company data gleaned from an annual statement published by Risk Management Association. The court observed that the publication expressly states that the data should serve "only as general guidelines and not as absolute industry norms." Data "may not be fully representative of a given industry," the statement adds.

The expert's third figure drew on the Construction Financial Management Association's annual financial survey. The court noted that many of the companies sampled operated in industries that were dissimilar to the subject company's industry.

The expert's fourth figure was based on data from Ibbotson Associates. The court observed that the data concerned companies operating in the construction industry in general, not the concrete contracting sector in which the subject company operated.

Consequently, none of the data sources on which the IRS's expert based his rate on equity analysis provided meaningful data.

In contrast, the court approved of the analysis the company's expert presented. His figures were based on data from one source, Integra Information, a data service that gathers financial information of privately held companies from government and other sources. Specifically, the expert used Integra data from 33 companies that fell under SIC code 1771 (Construction Special Trade Contractors, Concrete Work). Sales ranged from $25 million to just short of $50 million. He determined the average pretax return on equity was 10.5% for 2003 and 10.9% for 2004. Consequently, the subject company's rate was 0.3% below the Integra average in 2003 and 1.9% below in 2004.

The court dismissed the IRS's objection that the Integra company sample did not show whether any of the companies had independent investors that would be a check on excessive officer compensation. In the court's view, the objection could be made about any privately held company that figured into the IRS expert's analysis. "On balance, we are persuaded that companies which are closest to petitioner with respect to the nature of the business activity and the size of annual sales provide the best index of a reasonable return on equity," the court said.

The IRS further contended that since the company's return on equity (under either expert analysis) fell below the industry average for 2003 and 2004, the sons received excessive compensation in those years. An independent investor would demand a return that was more in line with the company's superior performance.

The company countered its rate of return was close to the industry average and would satisfy an independent investor.

The court said the IRS failed to cite authority to support its claim that under the independent investor test the rate of return on equity must significantly exceed the industry average when the subject company is particularly successful. Case law, in fact, suggests that a 10% return rate would satisfy an independent investor, which means that compensation that leaves that level of rate of return is reasonable. One case found compensation reasonable where the return on equity was only 2.9%, the court noted. See *Multi-Pak Corp. v. Commissioner,* T.C. Memo. 2010-139.

The Tax Court observed that under case law compensation is deemed unreasonable when the resulting return on equity is zero or less than zero. Here, the company's rates of 10.2% and 9% for 2003 and 2004 met the independent investor test and "tend to show" that the compensation payments to the sons were reasonable. Factor 4, therefore, weighed in favor of the company.

Factor 5, which focuses on whether the contested compensation payments were consistent within the company's overall compensation arrangements, also was a win for the company. Here, the court noted, the company had a formal bonus plan.

Based on the applicable *Elliots* analysis, the Tax Court concluded officer compensation for both years was reasonable and, therefore, deductible.

Hanckel v. Campbell (In re Hanckel)

Citation: 2015 Bankr. LEXIS 4202
Date of decision: Dec. 11, 2015
Country: US
State/Jurisdiction: Federal/South Carolina
Court: United States Bankruptcy Court
Type of action: Bankruptcy
Experts: W. Ellison Thomas (Family); Matthew Bernstein (Trustee)
Judge: Duncan
SIC: 3732 Boat Building and Repairing (boat building)
NAICS code: 336612 Boat Building

Bankruptcy Court Favors DCF to Value Dissociated Interest

Prior to filing for Chapter 7 bankruptcy, the debtor, who owned a stake in a family business, transferred his share to his father, the co-owner. Subsequently, the Chapter 7 trustee proved the transfer was a fraudulent conveyance, and the court declared it a dissociated interest belonging to the estate. Litigation followed as to the trustee's authority over the interest and as to its value. Recently, the Bankruptcy Court ruled on the best valuation methodology, the parties' challenges to expert testimony, and the appropriate valuation date.

Transferred interest sparks suit. In 2000, the debtor and his father formed a company that sold and repaired boats. Each man owned 50%. An operating agreement restricted membership and the transferability of membership in the company; it provided that certain events, including bankruptcy, could terminate the interest holder's membership. If that occurred, the dissociated member would receive the distributions to which he was entitled prior to the event, as well as the fair market value of the interest as of the date of the dissociating event. Although the mother was not an owner of the business, she in effect directed it. The father and mother owned the land and buildings the company used and leased them to the business.

During the financial crisis, the company struggled. Its problems were compounded by the debtor's financial problems with other investments. The mother made substantial loans to keep the company afloat. The father and debtor received salaries, but the company never made sufficient profit to make distributions to its owners.

In fall 2010, the family decided to "take [the debtor] out of [the company]." In summer 2012, two months after signing a dissociation agreement that made the father the sole owner of the company, the debtor filed for Chapter 7 bankruptcy. A former business partner then sued the debtor, alleging the transfer of his interest in the boat business was fraudulent. Ultimately, the Chapter 7 bankruptcy trustee, who was substituted as the plaintiff in that suit, won on the fraud claim.

Litigation between the family and the trustee ensued. The family claimed it was "impracticable" to operate the business without a nonfamily member. It asked the court to dissolve the company, distribute its assets, and assign zero ($0) fair market value to the debtor's interest. The trustee objected to the dissolution of the company and the zero valuation. He argued that Section 363(h) of the Bankruptcy Code authorized him to sell the estate's and family's interests in the company.

Throughout the company kept operating as before.

The court ultimately found the estate held the debtor's dissociated interest. In October 2015, a trial as to its valuation took place. Both sides presented expert testimony and claimed the opposing expert's opinion was inadmissible under *Daubert*.

Calculation report v. conclusion of value. The family's expert, an experienced CPA who stated he had 20 years of experience advising clients on whether to buy businesses, said there was "no template for valuing a boat dealership."

He decided to value the contested interest on the date the debtor filed for bankruptcy (2012) and based on the expert's understanding of the operating agreement. He also spoke with the family's lawyers and accountants and reviewed relevant financial statements. Moreover, he reviewed and critiqued the opposing expert's report.

He explained he typically conducted two types of valuations. One was a calculation report, which represented a less formal valuation for which the appraiser and the client decided on the methodology. The other kind of valuation was a conclusion of value, which was more comprehensive and typically used multiple valuation approaches. Given the company's financial condition here, he decided to perform a calculation of book value only, which required him to total the company's assets and liabilities and subtract the latter from the former. Based on the available financial information, he found that the full value of the company not including repayment of the mother's loans in full was -$195,000. If there were repayment of the loans, the value would be -$580,000, the expert said. Under either scenario, the dissociated interest, which was held by the estate, was worthless.

The expert pointed to multiple risks related to the informal way in which the business was run. They made it unlikely that a hypothetical buyer would purchase the debtor's interest in the company, the expert said. For example, the company had no employment contracts and no noncompete agreements; it also did not have a formal lease. The debtor could leave the business and set up a competing business, the expert noted. He pointed out that the father's salary was considerably below market value. And, he said, the only reason the mother had not asked for repayment of the loans was because the company was a family business.

DCF 'nonsensical'? The trustee's expert, an experienced CPA and business valuator, submitted two expert reports. One was based on a valuation as of the date of the transfer of the interest to the father (prebankruptcy). The other valuation was based on values as of March 2015—about six months prior to the valuation trial. The expert testified as to the most recent report only. He relied on the company's business records and on information resulting from consultation with the trustee only.

He noted that the company's performance and prospects were not as dire as the opposing expert portrayed them. After the debtor's transfer of his interest, the business in fact showed improved sales. The most accurate way to value a going concern was to use a discounted cash flow (DCF) analysis, he said. To calculate cash flow, he assumed that the company's operating costs, salaries, rent, and debt would remain constant or vary at a predictable rate. He developed the discount rate by combining the standard 20-year Treasury yield, a common stock equity premium, and by accounting for risk factors specific to the company's being a family business that was closely held and not publicly traded.

He furnished the court with a table illustrating how changes in the growth rate and discount rate affected the company's value:

		Discounted Cash Flow				
		21%	23%	25%	27%	29%
Rate of Growth	21.0%	$167,000	$148,000	$133,000	$120,000	$109,000
	21.5%	$347,000	$310,000	$279,000	$253,000	$232,000
	22.0%	$500,000	$447,000	$403,000	$367,000	$336,000
	22.5%	$650,000	$582,000	$525,000	$479,000	$439,000
	23.0%	$801,000	$717,000	$648,000	$590,000	$542,000

The trustee's expert concluded the company was worth $403,000 assuming a 22% growth rate and discounting cash flow by 25%. Therefore, the dissociated interest belonging to the estate was worth $201,500.

The trustee's expert admitted on cross-examination that he had not been aware of other risk factors specific to the company, which, he allowed, could lower the valuation. For example, he did not know about the company's lack of a formal lease, threats from floor plan lenders to leave (one had already left), and the loss of a boat manufacturer. His valuation also did not factor in the repayment of the mother's loans even though they appeared as debt on the books. He decided that, since the loans were no longer accruing interest, they did not "act" like debt and for purposes of the valuation should not be treated as debt that was due immediately.

The family's expert critiqued the use of the DCF analysis in this instance. The company was in financial distress, he claimed. In this situation, it was "nonsensical" to use a valuation approach that envisioned payments to equity holders.

Multiple valuation issues. At different stages in the trial, the trustee challenged the court's authority to value the interest, arguing the value should be based on the trustee's sale of the asset. At that time, the court dismissed the objection. After trial, the trustee filed a motion for a new trial or to reopen the record based on new information that, he said, could affect the value of the company. Specifically, the family had filed a malpractice suit against the attorney who had advised the debtor to transfer his interest in the company. The trustee claimed the lawsuit was an asset of the company, and the family had an obligation to disclose it as part of the valuation process. The family countered the interest held by the estate did not entail any managerial rights.

In ruling on the trustee's motion, the Bankruptcy Court resolved the following valuation issues.

Authority to value debtor's interest. The court reminded the parties that the interest held by the estate was that of a dissociated member. It became dissociated as a result of the bankruptcy filing, but it was recovered by the trustee after the bankruptcy filing. State and bankruptcy law provided for the court to value the interest, the Bankruptcy Court decided. Among other provisions, it pointed to the state's LLC Act, which requires the LLC to purchase or "cause" the purchase of the dissociated interest. "Valuing that interest is part of causing the purchase," the court said. The family had a right to a determination of the value of the LLC interest that it had to purchase.

Challenges to expert testimony. The Bankruptcy Court rebuffed both sides' *Daubert* challenges. The family claimed the trustee's expert did not use the most recent financial information and did not interview the family members; therefore, his valuation was unreliable and irrelevant. The trustee contended the valuation the family's expert provided was inadmissible because he used an improper methodology and the wrong valuation date.

The court said both witnesses were experts in business valuation and their testimony was helpful to the court. Both appraisers supported their analysis with financial documents, and both used widely accepted methods. Both also explained why they chose the method they used and explained what was wrong with the other expert's approach. Their testimony was admissible.

Valuation date. The court observed that the facts of the case presented a conundrum in terms of the valuation date. What's more, there was no state case law on point, the court noted. Under the company's operating agreement, the dissociated member had a right to distributions and the fair market value of his interest in the company as of the date of the dissociating event, the court observed. The value of the distributions was zero ($0). The company's liquidity problems prevented it from making distributions in the past, and the trustee did not even argue that the estate was owed outstanding distributions.

Determining the fair market value of the interest at dissociation was problematic because the dissociation occurred through bankruptcy, the court explained. However, at the time of bankruptcy, the interest was not part of the debtor's estate owing to the transfer two months before bankruptcy. Only when the interest was recovered by way of the trustee's litigation did it become part of the estate, either at the time the court ordered the recovery or at the time the court's order became final.

The court noted that the parties were litigating since the court's earlier ruling that the debtor's membership was a dissociated interest. However, the company kept operating as if the dissociating event never occurred. There was evidence that its business actually was improving. Since neither the state's LLC statute nor case law considered this sort of dissociation event, the court looked to a Montana case with a somewhat similar fact pattern for guidance. Based on that case, the court in the instant case decided the most sensible approach was to designate the trial date as the date of dissociation and valuation.

Valuation methodology. Using the trial date as the valuation date, the court found the DCF analysis the trustee's expert proposed was the better approach for valuing the contested interest. For one, the trustee expert's valuation was nearer to the date of trial. Also, the expert valued the company as a going concern, which made sense considering the business continued to operate and improve.

The family expert's valuation was based on data that were over four years old, the court observed. The expert failed to provide the court with any evidence of how that data could or would change over time. Also, valuing the interest at a fixed point in the past was "inconsistent with the ongoing actions of the members of [the company]," the court pointed out.

But the court gave a nod to the family expert when it made adjustments to the trustee expert's valuation. It noted the failure of the trustee's expert to consider certain risk factors specific to the company, which, by the expert's own admission, might decrease the anticipated profits. Consequently, the court decided to discount cash flow by 30%, one percentage point over the highest rate the trustee's expert used, and to lower the growth rate to 21.5%, as opposed to the 22% rate the expert had assumed for his valuation. The adjustment resulted in a value of $210,000 for the company and a value of $105,000 for the dissociated interest.

In conclusion, the Bankruptcy Court ordered the company to purchase the dissociated interest for $105,000. Payment of that amount to the estate would extinguish the interest, the court said.

Healthcare v. Orr

Citation: 2016 Cal. App. Unpub. LEXIS 440
Date of decision: Jan. 20, 2016
Country: US
State/Jurisdiction: California
Court: Court of Appeals
Type of action: Contract
Judge: Fybel
SIC: 8011 Offices and Clinics of Doctors of Medicine (except mental health specialists, HMO medical centers, and ambulatory surgical and emergency centers)
NAICS code: 621111 Offices of Physicians (except Mental Health Specialists)

Buyer's Failure to Assign Value to Practice Goodwill Nullifies Noncompete

Plenty of cases explore the connection of goodwill valuation and noncompete clauses. But a recent California case centering on the sale of a solo practitioner's medical practice to a large healthcare provider adds a noteworthy twist. The issue was the enforceability of the parties' noncompete/nonsolicitation agreements where the asset purchase agreement failed to specify a value for the goodwill of the seller's practice.

Seller reactivates sold practice. In late 2009, a California-based solo practitioner who was looking to sell her medical practice entered into negotiations with Monarch Healthcare, a large healthcare provider. The potential buyer offered $1.7 million for the building, which the doctor owned, but informed the doctor her medical practice had no monetary or goodwill value. The doctor responded she was not "comfortable with the concept that my business/practice has no value" and that she planned to continue her current practice.

Negotiations continued and the parties eventually agreed to a sale of the building (for $1.7 million) and the medical practice. As part of the sale, the doctor began to work for the buyer. The healthcare provider agreed to pay the seller a $100,000 signing bonus after 30 days of employment. Under the employment agreement, the doctor received an annual salary of $165,000 and an annual bonus of up to $25,000 as well as benefits for her services to the buyer.

The parties' sales agreements included an asset purchase agreement that specified a price of about $34,700 for the medical practice. The contract provided that the assets being sold included "[a]ll of the goodwill of 'The Medical Practice," but it allocated 100% of the purchase price to "[f]urniture, fixtures, equipment and supplies."

Moreover, it included a covenant not to compete and a nonsolicitation clause. In essence, the seller-doctor agreed that, for a three-year period following her leaving her employment with the buyer, she would not perform medical services within a designated area and would not solicit patients or former patients of the practice.

Less than three years after the sale, the doctor left the buyer's employment and announced her plans to continue practicing medicine "in another capacity." She said she had transferred her patients "to other physicians." Subsequently, she reactivated her practice in a different form and set up her new medical office within the forbidden zone.

The buyer filed a complaint alleging a number of violations, including breach of contract, interference with contract, and unfair business practices. It asked the trial court for a temporary restraining order against the doctor. The court granted the injunction as it related to the solicitation of patients but did not prohibit the doctor from starting up a new practice.

No 'clear indication' of goodwill value. The doctor subsequently challenged the nonsolicitation clause injunction with the California Court of Appeal, arguing the trial court's ruling was an abuse of discretion.

The appeals court began its analysis by noting that, under California's Business and Professions Code (Section 16600), noncompete and nonsolicitation clauses are generally not enforceable. Public policy wants to "ensure that every citizen shall retain the right to pursue any lawful employment and enterprise of their choice." However, case law interpreting the statute allows for a narrow exception under Section 16601. Specifically, "in certain defined circumstances, persons who sell the goodwill of a business may agree to refrain from carrying on a similar business." The point is that it would be "unfair" to allow the seller to compete in a way that diminishes the value of the asset he or she sold to the buyer.

Under controlling case law, for the exception to apply and the noncompete or nonsolicitation clause to be enforceable, "there must be a clear indication that in the sales transaction, the parties valued or considered goodwill as a component of the sales price."

Here, the Court of Appeal found the exception did not apply because there was no clear indication that the parties assigned any value to goodwill. The court noted that the parties' asset purchase agreement indeed stated that the goodwill of the seller's medical practice was one of the assets the buyer bought. However, that agreement allocated no portion of the $34,700 purchase price to goodwill. Instead, it assigned 100% of the price to furniture, fixtures, equipment, and supplies. The court observed that an exhibit to the agreement explained the total cost for each category (furniture, fixtures, equipment, and supplies), multiplied by a percentage valuation. The total cost times the respective valuation percentages resulted in $34,700. With no indication that the buyer paid for the seller's goodwill, the court said the noncompete and nonsolicitation clauses "were neither necessary nor enforceable to protect the value of the goodwill because the parties agreed the goodwill had no value."

The buyer argued that whenever a noncompete was part of the sales agreement there was an inference that the business had goodwill that was being sold. This claim carried no weight with the court. The Court of Appeal observed: "The issue here is not whether goodwill was among the assets being sold to Monarch. The issue is the value placed on that goodwill." Here, the parties' asset purchase agreement "plainly" showed the buyer gave no consideration for goodwill. Also, the doctor's declaration in opposition to the buyer's request for an injunction stated that the buyer "never increased its offer for my practice, and never moved off its position that there was no goodwill value to the practice."

Because the nonsolicitation clause was unenforceable, the trial court abused its discretion in prohibiting the seller-doctor from soliciting patients identified in the asset purchase agreement, the California Court of Appeal decided.

In re Horsehead Holding Corp.

Citation: 2016 Bankr. LEXIS 3187
Date of decision: May 2, 2016
Country: US
State/Jurisdiction: Federal/Delaware
Court: United States Bankruptcy Court
Type of action: Bankruptcy
Experts: Lazard Freres (debtors); none (equity holders)
Judge: Sontchi
SIC: 1031 Lead and Zinc Ores
NAICS code: 212231 Lead Ore and Zinc Ore Mining

'Dramatic' Valuation Adjustment Justifies Equity Committee

Recently, in *In re Sunedison*, a complex bankruptcy case involving renewable energy businesses, we reported how unusual it is for courts to appoint an equity committee that represents the shareholders' interests in reorganization discussions. But, as the instant case shows, it is not impossible. After hearing testimony from shareholders, as well as lawyers for the debtors and creditors, the court concluded that "something doesn't smell right" about the valuations of the subject company and ordered the formation of an equity committee. Upon our request, Lexis has made available a transcript of the hearing leading to the court's ruling.

Suddenly bankruptcy. Horsehead is a leading producer of zinc and manufacturer of value-added zinc products. Two of its subsidiaries, Zochem and INMETCO, are profitable businesses that recycle metals-bearing waste. The focal point of the valuation dispute in Bankruptcy Court was the company's state-of-the-art North Carolina plant, which had run into production problems.

With zinc prices declining, the company experienced difficulties in 2015 and 2016. However, as late as December 2015, management, in numerous public statements, including filings with the Securities and Exchange Commission and investor earnings calls, represented the company had sufficient liquidity to continue operating and to proceed with the building of the plant. An unqualified audit opinion by a major accounting firm seemed to back up the company's representations.

The company's year-end SEC 10-K report, filed March 2016 for 2015, said the company was solvent with $970 million in total assets and about $435 million in total debt. A KPMG valuation report suggested the company was worth $1.1 billion.

However, in January 2016, the company skipped a $1.8 million payment on a $30 million line of credit. In February 2016, the company filed for Chapter 11 bankruptcy. In terms of the skipped payment, shareholders later noted that the company had represented to them that there would be no problem making payment within the grace period.

In a valuation analysis Lazard Frères prepared on behalf of the debtors, the firm suggested a valuation range of approximately $255 million to $305 million for the company, assuming the North Carolina plant remained idle. The report essentially assigned zero value to the plant, in which the company had invested somewhere between $500 million and $550 million. The entire value was with the two subsidiaries the Lazard valuation suggested.

Shareholders in the company challenged the debtors' post-petition valuation. In their motions, two investors in particular, Guy Spier and Phil Town, argued for a hearing on the formation of an equity committee under the Bankruptcy Code's Section 1102(a)(2). The debtors, as well as an official committee of unsecured creditors and the U.S. Trustee, objected to the appointment of such a committee.

Value in plant? Besides Spier and Town, a number of other personal investors expressed concerns to the court about the speed with which the bankruptcy proceedings moved and the fate of their investment.

The gist of the equity holders' argument was that the company's CEO and CFO were under pressure given the volatility of the market and problems with getting the plant up and running. They surrendered control to "a savvy hedge fund which specialized in distressed debt and who's extremely knowledgeable of the bankruptcy court rules." That hedge fund tried to control the proceedings in an effort to take over the company's assets for less than adequate consideration.

Spier, the primary spokesman for the shareholders, said the KPMG valuation made sense. He dismissed as baseless objections from the debtors and the U.S. Trustee that the valuation was outdated and that its EBITDA multiples were "too rich."

The company, Spier explained, operated in a cyclical industry. Investment analysts know that cyclical industries show their highest EBITDA multiples at cyclical lows. Markets and rational actors tend not to focus on current conditions but look forward. As Spier put it: "The fact that the company is going through difficulties is in itself quite the most bullish sign you can possibly have." The debtors, he suggested, wrongly convinced the U.S. Trustee that at cyclical lows the multiples had to be low, "when it is the exact opposite," he said.

He also challenged the claims by debtors and creditors that the North Carolina plant was absolutely impaired. If that was the case, why didn't the company take a write-down, he asked. He noted that there were strict accounting rules on recognizing an impairment loss, yet the company's accountants "didn't say anything; the company didn't say anything; their filings didn't say anything. SFAS 144 is very specific."

Both Spier and Town maintained that the debtors did not write down the value of the plant because they believed there was value in it.

According to Town:

> The company has spent over 550 million dollars building a state-of-the-art plant. It will take approximately 80 million, maybe 112 million dollars to get the thing running to top level. And the real value, we think, is pretty obviously, when you do that, in a year-and-a-half to three years, something in the neighborhood of 1.1, 1.2 billion. And for that reason, there is equity, and therefore we deserve an equity committee to defend our interest in this business.

Creditors have a right to full recovery but "not to swallow the company or the whole of the company," the shareholders said.

No legal basis for committee? The debtors and their supporters argued case law did not provide for the formation of an equity committee in the instant case.

Parties seeking an equity committee first had to show "a substantial likelihood of recovery to equity." If they could do so, the next question was whether a committee was necessary to adequately represent the interests of the equity holders. In other words, the debtors said, shareholders had no right to form a committee "where its only purpose would be to challenge valuation."

There was no substantial likelihood of recovery, the debtors explained. Notwithstanding statements in late 2015 that the company had liquidity, in January 2016, the price of zinc started to drop considerably, the plant did not perform as expected, and there was a "very real run on the bank," counsel for the debtors said. Although the debtors talked to nearly 30 different financial institutions, they did not receive financing other than on a priming basis.

In terms of the KPMG valuation, counsel first dismissed it as inadmissible hearsay. There also were substantive problems with the report, he said. KPMG assumed 2017 EBITDA of approximately $150 million, which was based on the assumption that the plant would restart at no cost to the Chapter 11 cases. That was an inappropriate assumption. Even if the plant were to restart, EBITDA for 2017 would only be about $30 million, the debtors' attorney said. Also, the time necessary to fix the plant was not one year or 18 months as assumed earlier, but three years.

A high-end valuation of the company was $305 million, whereas prepetition funded debt was more than $400 million, not counting another $60 million allocable to general unsecured claims, he stated.

In other words, the company was hopelessly insolvent. Forcing creditors to shoulder the financial burden of paying for the professionals working on behalf of the equity committee when there was a substantial likelihood that the creditors would not get paid in full was improper, the debtors contended.

'Going out on a limb.' The court sided with the shareholders. It acknowledged it was "going, frankly, out on a limb" in terms of the legal requirement that shareholders show a substantial likelihood of recovery to equity. And it cautioned that its decision to allow an equity committee was not a decision on the likelihood of recovery. Rather, the court's ruling was prompted by a series of inconsistent actions. "But there was a certain valuation scenario that existed pre-petition and there's a radically different valuation scenario that exists post-petition, and there's a sufficient amount of ambiguity as to what's right and who's right." All of these factors justified the formation of an equity committee in this case, the court concluded.

The court cautioned shareholders it would "aggressively" monitor the professional fees spent on the equity committee and would not allow for an extended discovery process.

In re ISN Software Corp. Appraisal Litig.

Citation: 2016 Del. Ch. LEXIS 125
Date of decision: Aug. 11, 2016
Country: US
State/Jurisdiction: Delaware
Court: Court of Chancery of Delaware
Type of action: Dissenting Shareholder
Experts: Bruce B. Bingham (petitioner); David G. Clarke (petitioner); Daniel Beaulne (respondent)
Judge: Glasscock III
SIC: 7371 Computer Programming Services
NAICS code: 541511 Custom Computer Programming Services

Chancery Relies on 'Simple and Powerful' DCF for Fair Value

In a statutory appraisal action, Vice Chancellor Glasscock of the Delaware Court of Chancery recently joined the chorus of colleagues who have decried the astounding gaps in values the opposing experts routinely propose. This case, more than any other, generated judicial skepticism regarding valuation. Where it is now routine for the petitioner's expert to propose a DCF value double that of the respondent's expert, here a petitioner expert claimed the fair value was eight times the value the DCF analysis of the company's expert implied. The court declined to adopt any of the three expert opinions in its entirety and performed its own DCF analysis.

Family feud. At the heart of the dispute was a festering disagreement between two brothers. They had "a long and contentious history in [the Delaware Court of Chancery]."

The flashpoint this time was ISN, a company that provided a subscription-based online contractor database assisting users with record keeping and compliance. It operated in some 70 countries and had experienced substantial growth in the period leading up to the merger. The company was privately held and controlled by one brother, Bill Addy. The other brother, Brian Addy, controlled one of the two petitioners, which were minority stockholders in ISN.

ISN completed the merger on Jan. 9, 2013. Bill Addy decided that certain minority shareholders were entitled to receive $38,317 per share in cash. Other shares remained unchanged and outstanding.

The two petitioners asked the Chancery for appraisal under 8 Del. C. § 262. For trial, all parties offered expert testimony on the company's fair value as of the date of the merger. The experts used a variety of valuation methods and weighted them "as they saw fit."

The court described the value gap as "alarmingly" wide. An expert for one petitioner arrived at a fair value of $230,000 per share. The other petitioner's expert said it was $222,414 per share. In contrast, the company's expert said it was $29,360 per share.

Methods in play. The court relied exclusively on the DCF method but discussed the other approaches the experts used.

Guideline public companies method. All three experts used the guideline public companies method and factored the results into their value conclusions. (The court's opinion does not explain the specific weighting.) The experts disagreed over the makeup of the public companies set and how to compare the companies. They also disagreed over the applicable size premium.

The court rejected this methodology because the subject company had no "direct" public competitors. It found unconvincing the petitioners' argument that the company belonged to the "software as a service" (SaaS) industry, which included a variety of business applications such as applications to manage accounting and customer relations as well as contractors.

DCCF method. The company's expert gave a 50% weighting to the result of the direct capitalization of cash flow analysis.

The court noted the DCCF was appropriate where a company "has reached a steady state" or if there were no other feasible valuation approaches. As neither condition applied in the instant case, this method was inappropriate.

Past-transaction analysis. The company's expert also analyzed two precedent transactions for value and assigned a 12.5% weight to each result.

The first transaction occurred three months before the merger when one of the petitioner companies sold its shares of INS stock to the other petitioner for $29,783 per share. The transaction included other, nonstock compensation.

The second transaction occurred three weeks before the merger when one of the petitioners sold stock to a third ISN stockholder. As part of the consideration, the seller received parcels of "ranch" land in a Colorado resort housing development.

The court rejected this valuation approach. It noted again that ISN was a privately held company; its stock was not regularly traded and as such was "illiquid." It pointed out that the seller, Brian Addy (the dissenting brother), in one transaction was not necessarily motivated by achieving the highest sales price, but by liquidity and other factors. The transactions lacked certain hallmarks of an arm's-length deal such as multiple buyers and reliance on complete and accurate financial information, the court said. Also, both transactions included "complex and incompatible forms of consideration."

Comparable transactions analysis. An expert for one of the petitioners assigned 5% of the total value to the value resulting from a comparative transactions analysis all the while admitting the number of comparable transactions was limited.

The court declined to consider this analysis, noting the petitioner had failed to explain it sufficiently.

DCF-related disagreements. The surest way to arrive at fair value in this case was the DCF, the court decided. Although complex, the DCF "relies on a simple and powerful concept," the court explained. Specifically, it estimates the fair value of a company "by summing up the company's future cash flows, discounted to present value."

An accurate DCF valuation depends on accurate projections, the court went on to say. And using the appropriate projection period is "integral" to a DCF analysis. Here, the experts disagreed over whether to use a five-year period (company's expert), a six-year period, or even a 10-year period (petitioners' experts).

The company did not create long-term projections in the course of business. Therefore, the experts had to develop their own, making different assumptions as to growth and efficiency. In doing so, the court noted, the experts were able to look to the company's subscription-based business model, customer retention, and the inelastic demand for the company's product.

All experts agreed the company was growing, but they disagreed over the remaining length of the growth stage.

The court decided five-year projections were the safest. Projections out more than that "owe more to hope than reason," the Chancery said.

The court hinted at disagreements among the experts on many other assumptions and inputs. (For no apparent reason, the court decided to discuss them mostly in footnotes.)

Adjustments. Ultimately, the court used the company expert's DCF model as a framework for its DCF, making a series of adjustments. These were:

- No change in working capital adjustment.

  The company's expert determined the company's working capital requirements were 12% of its projected revenue. He arrived at this conclusion by analyzing the needs of a set of guideline companies in the IT sector, which, he said, had similar subscription billing practices.

  Since the court had rejected the use of the GPC method, it rejected the working capital analysis that gave rise to the adjustment. Instead, the court adopted the reasoning of one of the petitioner experts: No adjustment to working capital was necessary since the company historically operated with a negative working capital balance.

- Separate annual cash flow adjustment for change in deferred revenue.

  The court noted the company typically recorded part of its cash receipts as deferred revenue rather than revenue earned. Normally, this practice would result in a cash flow adjustment for the change in working capital. Because the court rejected such a change, it included a separate adjustment.

- Separate cash flow adjustment in 2014 for expected tax refund.

  The company expected a $16.5 million tax refund based on its change of accounting methods, which it factored into its working capital calculation. Since the court rejected a change in working capital adjustment, it included a separate adjustment.

- Addition of cash reserve.

  The court noted the company used part of its cash to create a separate "Buyout and Litigation Reserve" account. Since the balance of the account, $34 million, was not necessary for ongoing operations, the court added that amount to the company's discounted cash flows.

- Use of 2.46% size premium.

  The court said its size premium was based on Ibbotson's 8th decile and aligned with the experts' use of Ibbotson for determining the size premium.

- Use of capital asset pricing model (CAPM) to arrive at 10.46% cost of equity.

  All the experts decided the weighted average cost of capital was equal to the company's cost of equity because the company did not have long-term debt at the time of the merger, the court noted. The court agreed.

Conclusion. As a result of the specific adjustments, the court arrived at a fair value of $98,783 per share. The number of outstanding shares, which was itself a sticking point during the proceedings, was 3,614, the court decided.

Jafar v. Mohammed

Citation: 2016 Tex. App. LEXIS 3706
Date of decision: April 12, 2016
Country: US
State/Jurisdiction: Texas
Court: Court of Appeals
Type of action: Judicial Dissolution (incl. Withdrawal, Buy Out)
Experts: Jeffrey Jones (plaintiff/appellee); N/A (defendants/appellants)
Judge: Busby
SIC: 4899 Communications Services, NEC (ship to shore broadcasting carriers)
NAICS code: 517212 Cellular and Other Wireless Telecommunications

In Buyout, Income-Based Expert Appraisal Beats Other Value Indicators

In a Texas partnership dispute, the defendants were left high and dry when the trial court excluded their expert because of a missed deadline. They then launched an unsuccessful attack on the plaintiff's expert under the state version of *Daubert*. After the trial court not only admitted but adopted the expert's valuation, the defendants appealed, arguing, among other things, the valuation was unreliable because the valuator prepared the appraisal three years after the valuation date. The appeals court found historical data enabled the appraiser to re-create the worth of the partnership during the earlier period. The defendants' other reliability arguments were similarly unsuccessful.

Disqualified expert. Three partners operated a cellular phone and accessory store. Under a partnership agreement, the plaintiff acquired a 50% share for $20,000. As the manager of the store, he was responsible for its day-to-day operations.

In May 2010, the plaintiff sent notice to the two other partners—the defendants—that he intended to withdraw from the partnership. They decided to continue the business. When the plaintiff demanded payment of the redemption value of his partnership interest under Texas business law, the defendants offered to buy him out for $8,000. They also offered to retain an appraiser to calculate the value of the plaintiff's interest but did not actually do so.

Subsequently, the plaintiff sued for redemption and raised a number of other claims, including breach of contract. The defendants counterclaimed.

The trial court ultimately found for the plaintiff on the statutory claim for redemption and held a bench trial to determine the worth of the partnership and any additional recovery owed to the plaintiff.

The defendants missed the deadline for designating their expert and proceeded to trial with no expert valuation testimony. The indicators of value they were able to present were a $12,800 appraisal of the partnership's personal property from the country and the $20,000 payment the plaintiff paid to buy into the partnership. One of the defendants testified that he sold a similar store for about $15,000 in 2013. Therefore, the partnership was worth that much.

Expert favors multiple-of-earnings method. In contrast, the plaintiff's expert was an experienced business valuator. He used the plaintiff's date of withdrawal from the partnership as the valuation date. For his calculation, he reviewed weekly sales reports for 2008 through 2010, sales tax reports for five consecutive quarters in 2009 and 2010, and the building's lease and operating expense reports. He performed research on the cellular phone industry through IBISWorld, a database providing business intelligence on various industries.

He also considered interest rates controlling at the time of the assignment and national, regional, and local information on the economy from the Federal Reserve Bank. Moreover, he consulted a national guide on the value of cellular phone businesses.

To calculate the business's fair market value, he used all three valuation approaches.

Under the asset approach, he used the asset-accumulation method to determine the business was worth $150,000.

Under the market approach, he used the direct market data method to conclude the business's price-to-gross value was $210,000 and its price-to-earnings value was $175,000.

Under the income approach, he used the multiple of discretionary earnings method. He found that a 1.75 multiplier reflected the rate of return an investor would require given the risk associated with the business. He determined the partnership's discretionary earnings by subtracting operating expenses from the gross income. He did not deduct salary to owners, depreciation, interest expense, or any personal expenses running through the business. Applying the multiplier to the earnings and adding the net value of certain assets, the plaintiff's expert concluded the business was worth $171,000.

He said his experience as a broker selling similar stores told him that buyers favor the income approach over other approaches. His expert report included spreadsheets, income statements, and balance sheets to show the raw data and applicable formulas.

At trial, the defendants unsuccessfully tried to exclude the testimony under the state's Rule of Evidence 702 and *Daubert*. *See E.I. du Pont de Nemours & Co. v. Robinson*, 923 S.W.2d 549 (Tex. 1995).

The trial court admitted and adopted the plaintiff's expert opinion. It found the fair value of the partnership was $171,000, which meant the plaintiff's 50% interest was worth $85,500. In addition, the court awarded the plaintiff $6,000 in expert witness fees.

The defendants appealed the exclusion of their expert and the trial court's crediting the opposing expert's valuation at the state Court of Appeals. (They did not contest the expert fee award.)

NAICS code inconsequential. The appeals court provided a detailed pretrial timeline that showed that counsel for the defendants did not follow the trial court's docket order carefully and failed to identify the valuation expert in a timely manner. (This oversight may well be grounds for a malpractice suit.) Since the defendants were unable to show good cause for the late designation or lack of unfair surprise to the plaintiff, the appeals court upheld the exclusion of the defendants' expert.

The defendants' challenge to the plaintiff expert's valuation also fared poorly. They tried to argue the expert should have been excluded based on his lack of qualifications and the unreliability of his opinion. The Court of Appeals promptly dismissed the qualifications argument because the defendants had not raised it during trial and, therefore, failed to preserve it.

The defendants gave a number of reasons why the testimony was unreliable, which the appeals court considered in turn.

(1) The report was unreliable because it was based on information related to businesses grouped under NAICS code 51332, which encompasses stores such as Sprint, T-Mobile, Verizon, and Cricket—all much larger and more complex than the contested business, the defendants claimed.

The appeals court found that, if the analysis were flawed as a result of using this specific code, the flaw would only affect the value determination under the market approach. But the market-based valuation ultimately was inconsequential to the outcome of the case because the expert decided to rely on the value derived from the income approach. The latter was the value the court adopted. It was $171,000.

(2) The report was unreliable because the expert prepared it three years after the plaintiff withdrew from the partnership. There was "absolutely no way to simulate the worth of a business three years later," the defendants contended. They also claimed the business went downhill after the plaintiff's withdrawal.

The appeals court disagreed. The expert used historical economic data to calculate the partnership's value as of the valuation day, May 2010, the court said. He was not constrained to calculating the present value of the business. Also, the defendants did not show how any deterioration in the business subsequent to the plaintiff's departure affected the reliability of the expert's determination of value on the date of the plaintiff's withdrawal from the partnership.

(3) The report was fatally flawed because the expert failed to review the business's bank records and "subjectively adopt[ed] the unreliable and unscientific valuation method" the plaintiff's counsel used.

This argument also had no traction with the court. Even though the expert did not have access to the bank records, he had enough other relevant data (weekly sales reports, quarterly sales tax report, and operating expense reports) to perform an appraisal, the court said.

The court noted that, under the expert's multiple of discretionary earnings method, he calculated discretionary earnings by subtracting operating expenses "and this calculation would not be affected by how much of the remaining earnings the partners chose to accumulate as cash or to withdraw." The court pointed out that any additional cash on hand would have been treated as an asset in the expert's analysis and would have led to a higher value than the one the expert proposed.

The appeals court concluded that the plaintiff's expert relied on the type of data others in the field of business valuation rely on. His report explained why he preferred the income approach and supplied the raw data on which his valuation was based. In admitting the expert's opinion, the trial court did not abuse its discretion, the Court of Appeals decided.

Moreover, the trial court had discretion to reject other indicators of value and base its redemption award on the valuation of the plaintiff's expert. This testimony provided sufficient evidence to support the redemption the trial court ordered, the appeals court concluded.

In re Marriage of Johnson

Citation: 2015 Ill. App. Unpub. LEXIS 2673
Date of decision: Dec. 2, 2015
Country: US
State/Jurisdiction: Illinois
Court: Appellate Court of Illinois
Type of action: Marital Dissolution
Experts: Melissa A. Gragg, Kevin S. Carlie (wife); Brent D. Maschhoff (husband); FP Transitions (husband)
Judge: Stewart
SIC: 6282 Investment Advice (except portfolio managers)
NAICS code: 523930 Investment Advice

Comparable Transaction Exposes Error in Court's Enterprise Goodwill Ruling

In an Illinois divorce case, the flashpoint was the value of the enterprise goodwill of the husband's financial services business. The trial court credited the income-based valuation of the husband's expert and awarded the business to the husband at a relatively low value. The appeals court ordered a new trial on valuation, questioning the methodology underlying the valuation and finding the goodwill value was in obvious conflict with reliable market data.

Two components to business. The husband owned a financial services business that operated as an S corporation. He managed clients' investment accounts, gave portfolio-related advice, and provided estate and tax planning services. Since the principal place of business was in Centralia, Ill., the accounts were called the "Centralia accounts" for purposes of valuation and litigation. The accounts were primarily fee-based. At the time of trial, the husband had 265 clients and managed over $75 million in assets.

Nine months after filing for divorce, in August 2012, the husband bought client accounts from the estate of an Indiana financial advisor who was killed in an accident (the "Indiana accounts"). The initial purchase price for those accounts was $460,000. But after a six-month "look back" period, accounts worth about $12 million had left. As a result, the husband received a downward adjustment of the purchase price to $366,255. The husband explained that the Indiana accounts were commission-based because the prior owner had conducted business that way. This meant the advisor had to make a transaction to generate revenue, the husband explained. He characterized the value of the Indiana accounts as "exceptionally lower than [the] Centralia business" and said he sought to change the Indiana accounts to a fee-based system. Ultimately, he hoped to increase business earnings, but he could not be sure of the size of the increase considering the Indiana accounts were transaction-based.

The Indiana purchase also included a consulting fee agreement under which the husband paid the deceased advisor's son, who was licensed, $115,000 to work with the husband and introduce him to clients to develop relationships and retain as many clients as possible.

In 2012, the business showed a gross income of $478,000. This amount included income from August 2012 through December 2012 stemming from the Indiana accounts.

In October 2012, the husband retained FP Transitions, a firm that specializes in building and valuing financial services businesses. By its own account, the firm operates the largest open market for buying and selling financial practices. Under the market approach, it valued the husband's company at $1.11 million considering only the Centralia assets under management. The same firm subsequently valued the business at $1.24 million as of July 2013, considering both the Centralia and Indiana assets under management. For purposes of the litigation, the valuation date was August 2013.

Sway of multiattribute utility theory. At trial, the wife asked the court to order the sale of the company and the division of the proceeds. Or, if the court were to award the business to the husband, it should order him to pay the wife one-half of its value, excluding personal goodwill attributable to the husband.

Both parties presented expert testimony of the company's fair market value as of August 2013. Because the husband learned shortly before trial that the FP Transitions appraisers did not testify in divorce matters, he retained a different appraiser. This expert acknowledged FP Transitions' leading role in the financial services sector. But he decided to value the husband's company under a capitalization of earnings approach. He calculated that, as of the valuation date, the company's 110% value was $785,000. He decided to apply a 75% discount to account for the husband's personal goodwill and concluded the company's enterprise goodwill was $196,250.

The wife engaged two valuation analysts, who concluded the 100% value of the company was nearly $1.5 million as of August 2013. Discounting this amount by 67% to account for the husband's personal goodwill, they arrived at a fair market value of the company's enterprise goodwill of $495,000.

The wife's appraisers used a market approach. Specifically, they looked to the husband's acquisition of the Indiana accounts, which occurred 14 months before the valuation date. In addition, they considered the FP Transitions valuations, which were based on a similar methodology.

The trial court noted the enterprise goodwill was the parties' most substantial asset. Under state law, enterprise goodwill is a marital asset, whereas personal goodwill is not. In crediting the husband's trial expert, the trial court found it significant that this expert used the multiattribute utility theory to determine what portion of the business represented enterprise goodwill and what part was personal goodwill. The trial court awarded the business to the husband at a value of $196,250.

Financial evidence belies court's valuation. The wife challenged the judgment at the state's appellate court. She contended the valuation of the company was "against the manifest weight of the evidence." Moreover, the allocation of marital property represented an abuse of discretion by the trial court.

The appellate court agreed with the wife. It noted at the start of its analysis that valuing a closely held corporation "is not unlike determining the fair market value of a professional corporation." One of the best ways to do so was to view a similar transaction, which is what the wife's experts did, the appeals court observed. It noted that the trial court had the benefit of a recent transaction—the husband's purchase of the Indiana accounts a year earlier—but chose to ignore it.

According to the appellate court, by crediting the husband's expert, the trial court valued the company's enterprise goodwill at $196,250—at a time when the company managed assets worth more than $75 million. The figure the trial court assigned to enterprise goodwill was less than the amount the husband had paid a year earlier for the Indiana accounts, which had only approximately $35 million in assets under management and which, by the husband's own testimony, were less valuable than the fee-based Centralia accounts. The trial court's adopted figure was even less than the difference between the purchase price for the Indiana accounts and the $115,000 consulting fee the husband had agreed to pay the deceased Indiana advisor's son for purposes of working with him on retaining clients.

"Even if we assume the $115,000 consulting fee was for personal goodwill and subtract it from the purchase price of $366,255, this still leaves a value of $251,255 for the enterprise goodwill of the Indiana accounts," the appellate court determined. Under these calculations, the trial court's enterprise goodwill value, at $196,250, conflicted with the manifest weight of the evidence.

The appellate court dismissed the significance of the multiattribute utility theory to the valuation issue in front of the court. This theory seeks to determine what is enterprise and what is personal goodwill, but "it does not address the overall fair market value of the business before the discount for personal goodwill," the reviewing court said.

Finally, it pointed out that the trial court's erroneous valuation of the company's enterprise goodwill improperly decreased the value of the assets awarded to the husband. As a consequence, the valuation skewed the distribution of assets to the parties. Therefore, the appeals court also ordered a new trial on the distribution of property.

In re Marriage of Kerkhoff

Citation: 2016 Iowa App. LEXIS 905
Date of decision: Aug. 31, 2016
Country: US
State/Jurisdiction: Iowa
Court: Court of Appeals
Type of action: Marital Dissolution
Judge: Potterfield
SIC: 8361 Residential Care (homes for the elderly)
NAICS code: 623312 Assisted Living Facilities for the Elderly

Divided Court Addresses Issue of Appreciation of Gifted Property

In a divorce case, the most noteworthy issue was the appreciation of separate gifted property. In his dissent, the chief judge of the Iowa Court of Appeals called it "a troublesome issue throughout the country." Different states handle it differently, and the results have been "chaotic and inconsistent." The judge was especially alert to the way in which different courts have analyzed one factor: the contributions each party made toward the appreciation. In the instant case, the court's majority found the nonowner spouse made no meaningful contribution to the gifted property and did not deserve any part of the appreciation. The dissenting judge said she should have received half of it.

Sizable appreciation in value. The husband owned a minority interest in a series of business entities that his father, an accomplished businessman, completely controlled. The parties stipulated the total value of the husband's interest was about $6.3 million, including a 30% discount for lack of marketability and lack of control.

The husband and the wife were co-owners of one of the corporations, which built and ran senior living centers. The husband administered the centers. He was paid a very low salary but received management fees and distributions at the discretion of the father. The result was a considerable discrepancy in the couple's W-2 income and adjusted gross income.

The wife was not involved in the decision-making related to the senior living centers and did not attend corporate meetings. But at times she had assisted the husband with tasks related to the facilities. Most of the time, she took care of the family.

Also, beginning in the 1970s, the father gave shares of stock in the family corporations to the husband and the husband's siblings. The trial court said these gifts were part of "a complex tax avoidance scheme." The father testified at trial that, in giving the corporate stock, he only intended to make gifts to his children, not their spouses.

The dispute at trial focused on the treatment of the gifted stock and the determination of the husband's income for spousal and child support. Both parties relied on expert testimony to bolster their positions.

In terms of the stock, at the time of divorce, the couple had been married for 23 years. The gifted stock had appreciated by almost $5 million. Importantly, the wife did not claim a right to the gifted stock, but she asked the trial court to award her half of the appreciated amount: $2.5 million.

In terms of calculating child and spousal support, the wife's expert determined the husband's net annual income was about $170,000. He arrived at that figure by averaging income figures for three years and, as he admitted on cross-examination, by assuming the husband realized the total income related to the percentage interests he held in the various family businesses, as opposed to the actual distributions he received at the discretion of his father.

The husband's expert found the gross annual income was about $165,300. He averaged five years of annual income and only considered the actual distributions to the husband.

As for the gifted stock, the trial court declined to award the wife any portion of the appreciation in value. The trial court's analysis focused on the right to the gifted stock, as opposed to the appreciation in the value of that stock.

The court noted the donor's/father's intent was clear: The gift was to the husband only. Other considerations were that the wife did not contribute to the care, preservation, or improvement of the gifted property. She had no close independent relationship with the donor/father. She did not make separate contributions to the parties' economic welfare that assisted the preservation of the gifted property.

Also, the trial court said, the gifted corporate stock provided "minimal support" to the parties during the marriage. The businesses provided income and distributions to the husband, at the sole discretion of his father. The "real" value of the gifted stock was "the establishment of a standard of living for the parties," the court found. It concluded the stock was primarily relevant in determining spousal support.

The trial court concluded it was not inequitable to set aside the gifted interests—and, it seems, by extension the appreciation in their value—to the husband.

As for the income determination, the trial court credited the husband's expert and as a result awarded the wife $3,300 in alimony per month and child support of about $662.

No inequity, majority says. The wife unsuccessfully appealed both findings with the state's Court of Appeals.

The majority of the appeals court began its review by noting that Iowa state law provides that property that is gifted or inherited by one spouse is not "generally" subject to division regardless of when the property was gifted or inherited. However, a division is permissible "upon a finding that refusal to divide the property is inequitable to the other party or to the children of the marriage." *See* Iowa Code § 598.21(5), (6).

In making an equity decision related to the gifted or inherited property, state courts have considered a number of factors such as: (1) what contributions the parties made to the property, its care, preservation or improvement; (2) whether there was an "independent close" relationship between the donor and the spouse of the donee; (3) what contributions either party made to "their economic welfare to whatever extent those contributions preserve the property for either of them"; (4) whether either party has special needs; and (5) whether there is anything else that would make it "plainly unfair" to the nonowner spouse to set the property aside for the exclusive enjoyment of the donee spouse.

Further, the state Supreme Court previously noted that the length of the marriage "may be an important factor" in the determination.

The appeals court majority found the trial court undertook the proper analysis. The majority did not seem to find it relevant to the outcome of the case that the wife did not ask for a portion of the gifted stock but for the stock's appreciation in value.

Noting the need to give "significant deference" to the trial court's credibility determinations, the majority also affirmed the trial court's income determination. The trial court simply found the husband's expert's income valuation more reliable, the majority said. The majority noted the wife did not argue the spousal and child support awards were per se inadequate but asked for an upward adjustment of the support awards only if the appeals court decided the income attributed to the husband was too low. Since this was not the case, an upward adjustment was not appropriate.

Different analysis needed. The majority's and trial court's conclusion sparked a strong dissent from the chief judge of the Court of Appeals. He said he believed the outcome was contrary to case law, the principles underlying the applicable statute, and inequitable.

The dissent thought it "significant to realize" the dispute was not over the original gift but over the appreciation of the gifted corporate stock. The wife only wanted a share of the appreciation that arose during the marriage, the dissent pointed out.

For its part, the dissent looked to case law dealing specifically with the question of appreciated stock value. The dissent noted that courts have divided the appreciated value of assets "even when separately held where the increase resulted from the talent, time and effort of the marital partners." *See In re Marriage of Friedman*, 466 N.W.2d 689 (Iowa 1991) (available at *BVLaw*).

The dissent also found that a case dealing with the treatment of the appreciation of premarital property, rather than gifted or inherited property, was instructive. The court in that case specifically addressed the contributions factor and noted it was not "useful to analyze the exact duties performed by the marriage partners." In a longtime marriage, as long as neither party "shirked his or her duties," there was no reason to treat the parties differently in terms of property distribution. Further, in a long marriage, there was no need to consider "how each asset appreciated—fortuitously versus laboriously." *See In re Marriage of Fennelly*, 737 N.W.2d 97 (Iowa 2007).

Both *Friedman* and *Fennelly* provided principles that should apply when dealing with the appreciation of any asset, premarital, marital, or separate gifted or inherited property in a long-term marriage, the dissent said. The proposition in *Fennelly* that in a long-term marriage there should be a division of the appreciated value as long as neither party "shirked their duties" was not only equitable, but also a way to avoid the difficulties of having to weigh the parties' contributions, the dissent found.

It went on to say that even if the court in the instant case were to "tread into the deep waters of weighing the contributions," it should find in favor of a distribution to the wife. The husband was actively involved in the business, and the family relied on the income and dividends from the corporation. At the same time, the wife contributed in other ways to the marriage by being a stay-at-home mom. Moreover, for one of the businesses, she "assisted in running errands, entertaining residents, and promotion work."

The dissent also questioned the trial court's and majority's finding that the gifts never significantly improved the couple's lifestyle—a factor that militated against a division of the gifted property. The fact that the couple chose to live a conservative lifestyle that did not match its net worth "should not impact the division of their property," the dissent said.

It concluded the appreciation in stock should be divided equally. Doing so would make an alimony award to the wife unnecessary because she would receive either the same amount of dividends as the husband or an equalization payment that would allow her to support herself, the dissent noted.

Kminek-Nierenberg v. Kenneth Nierenberg

Citation: 2016 N.J. Super. Unpub. LEXIS 2051
Date of decision: Sept. 8, 2016
Country: US
State/Jurisdiction: New Jersey
Court: Superior Court, Appellate Division
Type of action: Marital Dissolution
Judge: Per Curiam
SIC: 4581 Airports, Flying Fields, and Airport Terminal Services (air freight handling at airports, hangar operations, airport terminal services, aircraft storage, airports, and flying fields)
NAICS code: 4881119 Other Airport Operations

Court Digs Through Appreciation Issues in Complex Divorce Case

In a drawn-out New Jersey divorce litigation with multiple defendants, including the owner-spouse's parents and several family businesses, a recurring theme was how to deal with separate corporate assets and any appreciation related to them. The dispute was complicated in part because critical assets at times changed status. The case illustrates the challenges facing an expert asked to propose a reasonable value determination for equitable distribution purposes and the applicable legal principles.

Backstory. Several years before his marriage, the husband and his parents established a number of corporations related to operating Princeton Airport in New Jersey. Initially, all three partners each held a one-third interest in the companies.

One of the contested assets was "DKN," a company that owned and later sold land adjacent to the airport. The husband borrowed almost $130,000 from his parents to buy his interest. In a "like-kind" exchange under Section 1031 of the Internal Revenue Code, the company later acquired an apartment complex in Philadelphia. To enable the transaction, the husband and his parents used some personal funds. Besides the funding, the husband had no meaningful role in managing and arranging for the sale of the Philadelphia property.

The majority of the additional funding for the Section 1031 exchange came from the "A-20" account whose ownership became another flashpoint in the litigation.

Other subjects in the divorce proceedings were Princeton Air, which operated the day-to-day affairs of the airport, and Princeton Aero, which acquired the airport.

In fall 1992, the husband and wife married. In 1999, the husband's parents executed an estate plan under which each parent gifted his and her one-third ownership interest in three of the companies to the husband, making him the sole owner of those corporations. But the parents maintained their combined two-thirds ownership in Princeton Aero and retained control of the airport. In connection with the transfers, the parties also executed a new shareholder agreement that required shares in Princeton Aero to be sold back for "book value" in the event of the death, divorce, disability, or bankruptcy of a shareholder.

The husband and wife separated in summer 2003, and the wife filed for divorce in early 2005. The parents invoked the "divorce provision" in the shareholder agreement in 2007. It required the husband to sell his shares back to Princeton Aero for their book value, $125,000.

Equitable distribution rulings. The divorce trial was bifurcated and went on between 2012 and 2013. The wife subsequently challenged most of the trial court's rulings with the New Jersey Superior Court, Appellate Division.

Estate plan. In trial court, the wife initially contested the validity of the estate plan, especially the new shareholder agreement and its buyback provision. She alleged the plan was an attempt to defraud her of her equitable distribution.

The trial court found the wife had failed to show the parents knew of any marital difficulties when they made the estate plan. The parents had gifted their two-thirds interest in DKN and the other two corporations to the husband as part of a legitimate plan to transfer value out of the estate without giving up control of the airport. There was no improper purpose or conspiracy to deprive the wife of a share of any asset to which she had a right, the trial court found. The applicable statute allows for "reasonable restrictions on the transfer of shares," the trial court said.

DKN. The wife also claimed that a loan to the husband to buy DKN was commingled with marital funds, which exposed the asset to equitable distribution. The court said the husband's interest in DKN remained separate at all times.

What's more, credible witness testimony showed DKN was a passive premarital asset for purposes of equitable distribution. Neither the husband nor the wife made any meaningful contributions to DKN's investment property. From 1999 to 2004, the land the company owned was farmland and, as such, passive until the last portion of it was sold in connection with the Section 1031 exchange.

Even though in 2004 the husband and the wife listed DKN as a nonpassive asset on their joint tax return, the IRS designation was not controlling for purposes of ruling on equitable distribution, the trial court decided.

Moreover, the husband's role in the Section 1031 exchange and his subsequent involvement with the Philadelphia property were "minimal and passive," the trial court found.

Finally, the court concluded the company's value did not increase during the marriage. Therefore, there was no appreciation subject to equitable distribution.

However, because the husband used over $63,000 in marital funds to affect the Section 1031 exchange, the wife was entitled to half of that amount, plus reimbursement for taxes because the company was an exempt and passive entity.

On appeal, the court's appellate division upheld all of the findings related to the estate plan and DKN.

The appellate panel affirmed that DKN was a passive asset. It noted: "Passive immune assets can be defined as those assets whose value fluctuations are based exclusively on market conditions." *See Valentino v. Valentino,* 309 N.J. Super. 334 (1998) (available at *BVLaw*). DKN, therefore, was not subject to equitable distribution unless the husband used marital funds to help effect the Section 1031 exchange. The trial court correctly had decided to award the wife half of the marital funds the husband had used in connection with the like-kind exchange, the appellate division said.

The appellate panel also agreed with the trial court's finding that a designation for tax purposes did not determine the asset's status for purposes of marital distribution.

Princeton Air. The trial court decided that Princeton Air, which was a premarital asset as well as a gifted asset, was an active asset for equitable distribution purposes.

The court said the wife was entitled to the company's appreciation in value from 1992, when the parties were married, to 2000, when the company was gifted to the husband by his parents, and then to 2005, when the wife filed for divorce.

The court further found that the wife's expert analysis contained "major flaws" because it failed to consider the court's early ruling that a two-third interest had been gifted to the husband and made immune from equitable distribution.

To calculate the amount subject to marital distribution, the trial court used the 1992 valuation of the wife's expert, a valuation for year 2000 that was based on reported earnings from 1999, and a year 2005 valuation based on adjusted earnings as determined by the wife's expert. Over $200,000 was available for marital distribution, the court found. It awarded the wife half of that amount.

The appellate panel explained that, under case law, an "active immune asset involves contributions and efforts by one or both spouses toward the asset's growth and development which directly increase its value." When the increase is the result of the owner spouse alone, it is not subject to distribution. But "to the extent that it may be attributable to the expenditures or the efforts of the non-owner spouse ... a determination must be made regarding the extent the original investment has been enhanced by contributions of either spouse." *See Valentino.*

The appellate panel concluded the valuation methodology the trial court used was within the lower court's discretion.

Princeton Aero. For Princeton Aero, which the husband's parents still controlled, the trial court found the wife had a right to one-sixth of the appreciation during the marriage: about $58,200. The percentage reflected one-half of the husband's one-third interest.

The court rejected the valuation the wife's real estate expert performed, finding he used the wrong valuation date: 2008 instead of 2005, the date the wife filed for divorce. The court rejected the wife's proposition to extrapolate back to 2005 from the expert's 2008 valuation.

It found the wife's expert's 1992 valuation, which showed the company was worth about $1.9 million, was "a workable baseline for the value of the real estate asset at the time." It compared well with the tax-assessed value. The court compared the figure with an adjusted valuation for 2005 of about $2.2 million and decided the difference was "a supportable appreciation" figure.

The appellate panel concluded the trial court carefully had considered the valuation evidence. In rejecting the wife's expert's valuation as inflated, the trial court properly considered profit margins, an FAA lien, restrictions on the land affecting marketability, lack of inflation evidence, and the actual rental values, the appellate panel found. "The trial court was not required to simply restrict its analysis to the book value, but was to arrive at a fair value for its appreciation," the appellate division said.

A-20 account. One major unresolved issue in the appeal was the status of the A-20 account that was used in connection with the Section 1031 transaction as well as to advance money needed to buy and sell airplanes.

The trial court found the account was jointly titled to the husband's father and Princeton Air, but the father was the sole owner. As such, the asset was exempt from equitable distribution.

The appellate division disagreed, noting the A-20 account contained funds from the father, Princeton Air, and other business entities. Also, the account used Princeton Air's tax identification. It was not gifted as part of the estate plan, the appellate panel said. And the account did not appear to be funded solely by corporate monies. All of these open questions required a remand to the trial court to determine the appropriate percentages of ownership concerning the account.

In concluding, the appellate panel pointed out that a resolution of the A-20 account ownership issue might affect the valuations of Princeton Air and Princeton Aero and by extension the equitable distribution findings.

Lacoste v. Lacoste

Citation: 2016 Miss. App. LEXIS 460
Date of decision: July 19, 2016
Country: US
State/Jurisdiction: Mississippi
Court: Court of Appeals
Type of action: Marital Dissolution
Judge: Barnes
SIC: 7299 Miscellaneous Personal Services, NEC (except diet and weight reducing services, personal care services, valet parking services, babysitting bureaus, debt and credit counseling, consumer bartering services, and formal wear and costume rental)
NAICS code: 812990 All Other Personal Services

Court Disapproves of Nonexpert Valuation of Key Marital Asset

It takes an expert to prepare a reliable business valuation. That's the message from a recent Mississippi divorce case in which the couple's main asset and source of income was the husband's fitness company. Neither party retained an expert, leaving the trial court to do its own valuation. Although the appeals court appreciated the trial court's predicament, it found the latter's methodology and resulting valuation unacceptable. Remanding, the appeals court suggested the trial court appoint an independent expert should the parties fail to offer professional valuations.

Flawed income approach. Just before the marriage, the husband set up a fitness training company as a single-member LLC. The business model was that the husband would travel to various facilities to conduct group or individual training sessions. Consequently, other than a company car and some transportable training equipment, the company had no assets. The husband's income fluctuated depending on his ability to obtain sponsorships from medical insurance companies or medical centers. In 2010, the business showed a net profit of about $190,100; in 2011, profit rose considerably, to over $462,000; and, in 2012, it was over $223,000.

The trial court classified the business as marital property because the wife, who was a personal trainer, contributed substantially to building the company. The husband did not challenge the classification. At the same time, the court decided to award the entire asset to the husband and compensate the wife through equitable distribution of other marital property.

The parties relied solely on the trial court to value the business. The court considered the three common valuation approaches but rejected two. Because of the way in which the business operated, the asset approach made no sense, the court found. It also ruled out the market approach for lack of sales data for comparable companies. The court noted that, since the company's success depended on the husband's reputation and his ability to market himself, it would be difficult to achieve an accurate comparison.

The best approach to value the company was the income approach, the court found. At the same time, it noted: "To properly value the company under an income-based approach, the Court would need a valuation expert to review the historic earnings, and after adjusting the income to reflect normalized earnings, multiply the normalized earnings by a capitalization factor."

However, there was no expert testimony. An accountant who prepared the company's taxes testified to the business's net profit in 2012-2013, but she was not qualified as an expert. Neither party even provided sufficient financial data to apply the income approach, the court observed.

The trial court decided to base the entire valuation on the profit/loss statement for the previous year, 2013, which showed a net profit of nearly $359,000. The trial court added the value of the car the husband used to transport himself and his equipment to client sites. It subtracted the amount the husband owed on the car, as well as fees he owed to the company's accounting firm for tax-related work. Based on this simple calculation, the trial court decided the business was worth about $347,400.

Bona fide goodwill problem. On appeal, the husband contended the trial court's valuation was "incorrect." For one, the trial court failed to determine the business's future income stream. Also, the trial court's statement that the company relied on the husband's "reputation, work ethic, and positive results for his clients" suggested the court erroneously included the husband's personal goodwill in the valuation.

At the beginning of its analysis, the state Court of Appeals noted that the husband "failed to suggest a valuation or present any testimony or other evidence on valuation."

But, regardless of the parties' neglectful behavior, the appeals court ultimately agreed with the husband that the lower court's valuation was untenable.

The appeals court pointed out that the trial court itself recognized how important an accurate business valuation was to its achieving an equitable distribution of assets and how complex the task of valuing this business was. However, instead of requiring the parties to produce expert testimony or additional financial evidence, the trial court tried to do the best it could with the information available, the appeals court observed.

The appeals court disapproved of the trial court's approach. It noted that the business valuation was "such an important aspect of the [trial court's] ruling that further testimony was essential to establish a proper valuation to divide the marital property fairly and correctly." There was no support for the trial court's decision to base the value on one year's financial statement, particularly when there was evidence that the income fluctuated drastically from year to year.

Also, the reviewing court said, it was likely that the business was "intertwined with goodwill, as [it] hinges on [the husband's] reputation and personal efforts." State law required the exclusion of all goodwill in valuing a business for purposes of marital distribution in a divorce case.

The appeals court said it was not confident that the lower court's approach produced a "correct" business valuation, and it remanded. It noted the parties either could produce their own valuations or offer expert testimony. If they failed to do so, the trial court had the authority to appoint an independent valuation expert. "Such valuation must exclude goodwill," the appeals court emphasized.

Failed double-dip argument. The husband also tried to claim that the mistaken business valuation raised a double-dip problem in that the trial court used the 2013 profit/loss figure to calculate both the value of the business and to set alimony and child support.

The appeals court declined to explore this issue. Considering the remand, it was not necessary to determine whether the trial court's valuation included goodwill for purposes of a double-dipping argument, the Court of Appeals said. Further, in this case, the award to the wife was "rehabilitative," not permanent, alimony. Because rehabilitative alimony served a unique purpose, it was not related to equitable distribution, the appeals court said. The trial court was not required to revisit the rehabilitative award to the wife on remand.

Editor's Note: BVR's "Charting Goodwill Jurisprudence" (January 2016) provides a state-by-state breakdown of goodwill jurisprudence. It is available at bvresources.com under "Free Resources."

Lane v. Lampkin (Lampkin II)

Citation: 2015 Miss. LEXIS 503
Date of decision: Oct. 8, 2015
Country: US
State/Jurisdiction: Mississippi
Court: Supreme Court
Type of action: Damages (incl. Lost Profits)
Experts: James Koerber (estate/petitioner); Brent Saunders (surviving shareholder/respondent)
Judge: Kitchens
SIC: 5211 Lumber and Other Building Materials Dealers (except home center stores)
NAICS code: 444190 Other Building Material Dealers

High Court Finds Trial Court's Damages Assessment Unsound

A knotty shareholder suit involving a rock-selling business triggered a challenge to the trial court's damages calculation at the state Supreme Court. The trial court found the surviving partner violated his duty to the business when he unilaterally set up another company that took over the old company's operations. The court fashioned a remedy that combined a business valuation with a lost profits analysis. The decedent partner's estate appealed, claiming the trial court used an improper method for calculating damages. In a cursory opinion, a divided appeals court affirmed, but the Supreme Court, siding with the estate, overturned.

Usurpation of business opportunity. Two partners set up a business that bought and sold rocks on land they owned jointly. Each partner owned a 50% interest in the company, which operated on a line of credit that both partners personally guaranteed. The line of credit was the primary source of funds for buying inventory. The defendant (surviving partner) also owned a construction business that was one of the rock company's major clients. One partner died in 2006, and his stock in the company and the land transferred to the plaintiff estate.

The company's line of credit was to expire within months of the death. Unable to obtain a timely loan guarantee from the estate's executors, the defendant formed a new company that performed the same services as the subject company, sold to the same customers, and used the same premises. With the new company, he completed the old company's contracts and paid its debts. He asked the court for a declaratory judgment that he had the right to invest in and operate his own rock-supplying business; had not breached a fiduciary duty to the old company; and had the authority to sell the old company's existing inventory, collect its accounts receivable, and use incoming money to pay its debts. The estate sued, alleging the defendant breached his fiduciary duty to the old company by usurping a business opportunity. It sought present and future lost profits resulting from the defendant's actions.

A two-step trial followed. The court first found the defendant liable for breach of a fiduciary duty.

Lost profits v. 'net book value.' In the damages phase, both parties presented experts who disagreed as to the proper way to determine damages.

The estate's expert testified that the defendant's construction company bought rock from the subject company but failed to make timely payments. As a result, the subject company's line of credit kept growing, which, in turn, prevented it from paying its bills and from remaining viable. The expert determined that, from 2000 to 2007, the company's net income was about $21,000.

The estate's expert also found that between 2003 and 2011 nearly 650,000 tons of rock remained unreported and diverted from the subject company. He said that, after the decedent's death, the unreported rock went to the defendant's new company. This diversion of rock resulted in nearly $1.1 million in lost profits to the old company. The expert further determined the old company suffered nearly $271,000 in lost profits from 2011 through 2012 based on the average of lost profits from 2007 through 2010. In terms of past profits, he explained that rock prices prior to the defendant's breach were significantly lower than rock prices after the breach. In 2003, one ton cost $4.00 and sold for $11.24. In 2009, after the defendant had started a new company, a ton cost about $6.50, but the defendant sold it for about $36. Therefore, past profits were not indicative of future lost profits.

Moreover, the estate's expert found that there was a loss of assets of nearly $170,000. He concluded that the total loss stemming from the defendant's misconduct was over $1.5 million.

The defendant's expert disputed there was unreported rock. Rather, he said, the defendant "moved the tons" from the old company to the defendant's new company because he "kept on running the thing just like he was doing before." To calculate damages, this expert performed a valuation of the "net book value" of the subject company. He found, in the year the decedent died, 2006, the company was worth $165,000. A year later, in 2007, it was worth $156,000. The expert made deductions to this figure and then added the value of the corporation's existing assets. The result was a net book value of over $125,000.

The trial court independently assessed damages. It found the defendant's expert had accounted for the unreported rock. For the years 2008 through 2012, the court used the estate expert's calculation of net income of about $21,000 to arrive at "historical lost profits" of nearly $105,000.

The court added this amount to the defendant expert's net book value of $125,000 to find that the subject company was entitled to total damages of about $230,000. The court ordered the defendant to pay this amount "as a result of his usurpation of corporate opportunity." Alternatively, if the parties decided to dissolve the old company, the defendant was to pay $115,000, the trial court decided.

'Illogical' approach? The estate appealed. The Court of Appeals affirmed, finding the trial court had not abused its discretion in terms of how it calculated damages and in deciding the unreported rock claim in favor of the defendant.

Four judges on the appeals court dissented, finding the trial court had committed reversible error. The law required the use of a lost profits analysis in cases involving liability for a breach of fiduciary duty or usurpation of a corporate opportunity, the dissent said. The trial court's use of a business-valuation analysis in this case had no support in authority. "'Net book value' is simply an accounting term that is not directly related to the actual value of the corporation's assets," the dissent said. To include a net book value calculation in a damages calculation, as the trial court had done, was "illogical."

'Misleading' lost profits analysis. The estate subsequently appealed the prior rulings to the state Supreme Court. The appeal included two major damages issues:

1. *Methodology.* The estate called the trial court's "purported lost profits analysis" flawed and contended the trial court had used a business valuation as opposed to the required lost profits analysis.

The Supreme Court agreed. It said the trial court's "historical lost net profits" determination failed to account for the post-breach increase in the price of rock the estate's expert had pointed out in testimony. Moreover, the trial court did not explain why it awarded lost profits damages for 2008 through 2012, but not 2007, the year after the decedent's death, when the defendant's new company started to operate. The trial court's "historical net book value" was "misleading," the high court said.

Further, the state Supreme Court found the trial court ignored precedent by injecting a business valuation into its damages calculation. Prior case law applicable to shareholder derivative suits that allege a breach of fiduciary duty requires the use of a lost profits analysis, the high court explained. The principle is that the party breaching a fiduciary duty "is responsible for the *entire loss suffered* by the corporation as a result of the breach," the high court said with emphasis.

The Supreme Court clarified that a business valuation analysis was appropriate in divorce and eminent domain cases as well as in dissenting shareholder disputes but not in the instant case. It disapproved of the trial court's comment that the experts were "just splitting hairs" when they disagreed over how to calculate damages. The state Supreme Court agreed with the dissenters on the Court of Appeals that the experts in fact were "testifying about detailed and important accounting terminology."

2. *Rock inventory.* The estate also argued that the trial court's failure to account for the unreported rock inventory in its damages calculation was reversible error.

The Supreme Court also found this argument persuasive. It noted that, even though the defendant's expert admitted that the subject company's inventory was diverted to the defendant's new company, the trial court refused to "take into consideration any purported 'unreported product.'" Under the law, the defendant was responsible for "*the entire loss suffered* by the corporation as a result of the breach," the Supreme Court noted again with emphasis. Here, the entire loss included the inventory the defendant diverted from the old company to his new company. Contrary to the trial court's finding, it was "clear" that the rock was not accounted for and that it was sent to the defendant's company, the Supreme Court said. This diversion was an improper transfer of corporate assets for which the defendant should be held accountable, the high court concluded.

The trial court's damages assessment was arbitrary, the Supreme Court summed up in its findings. Therefore, it remanded for a new damages determination.

Editor's note: An extended discussion of Lane v. Lampkin, *2014 Miss. App. LEXIS 497 (Miss Ct. App., Sept. 16, 2014), as well as the appeals court's opinion, is available at* BVLaw.

Luminara Worldwide, LLC v. Liown Elecs. Co.

Citation: 2016 U.S. Dist. LEXIS 93348
Date of decision: May 18, 2016
Country: US
State/Jurisdiction: Federal/Minnesota
Court: United States District Court
Type of action: Intellectual Property
Experts: Donald Gorowsky (plaintiff); unknown (defendants)
Judge: Noel
SIC: 3999 Manufacturing Industries, NEC (other miscellaneous products not specially provided for previously)
NAICS code: 339999 All Other Miscellaneous Manufacturing

Court Clarifies Rule 26 Protection for 'Reporting' and 'Non-Reporting' Experts

In a patent infringement case, the defendants claimed sections of the plaintiff expert's damages report that gave background on the contested technology were inadmissible because the expert lacked expertise on the issues. The court not only disagreed, but also found Rule 26 required this kind of information in an expert report. The court also discussed how the amended Rule 26 rule treats communication with a "reporting expert" differently from communication with a "non-reporting expert."

Background information. The plaintiff had an exclusive license from Disney to use inventions related to flameless candles. The primary defendants were Chinese companies with whom the plaintiff had entered into a nondisclosure agreement to manufacture the unique candles. During the negotiations, the plaintiff showed the defendants a prototype candle and shared technical details about the design. The defendants subsequently obtained a patent in China as well as the United States for artificial flame technology and began selling flameless candles in the U.S. in 2012.

The plaintiff sued, claiming the defendants' products infringed its patents. In addition, the plaintiff added as defendants a host of stores that sold flameless candles the Chinese companies manufactured. The Chinese companies countersued, contending the plaintiff wrongfully interfered with existing and prospective business relationships.

The plaintiff sought lost profits and retained an expert "to review the facts of this case, perform analysis and develop opinions regarding damages suffered by [the plaintiff] as a result of the patent infringement and alleged wrongful conduct of Defendants."

The expert's report included three distinct sections in which: (1) the expert provided some history of the development of flameless candle technology; (2) discussed the defendants' infringement of the patents-in-suit; and (3) discussed the absence of noninfringing alternatives in the market. Each section included a footnote in which the expert stated that he had been asked to assume the facts in the section, "which I understand are supported by evidence from various [plaintiff] and [defense] witnesses ... as well as documents that have been produced in discovery by both parties."

Moreover, the report included a section, "Scope of Engagement," in which the expert expressly stated that he had not been asked to analyze liability issues and had not arrived at any conclusions regarding liability. His analysis proceeded from the belief the plaintiff would be able to prove liability.

The defendants objected to the three sections in two ways. First, they said the expert discussed matters for which he lacked the technical knowledge and qualifications—e.g., the history of the development of flameless candle technology. Second, the footnotes that went with the three sections "are a complete abdication" of the expert's responsibility to show the "complete" basis for his opinions.

The court declined to strike the sections. It observed that Federal Rule of Evidence 703 provides that an expert "may base an opinion on facts or data in the case that the expert has been made aware of or personally observed." Here, the expert made it clear that these sections were not his expert opinion but were relevant background facts of which he was apprised. "It is common for experts to rely on information outside of their field of expertise in rendering expert opinions," the court said.

The court went further. It found that the information the defendants sought to strike was exactly the kind of information Federal Rule of Civil Procedure 26(a)(2)(B)(ii) "contemplates" when it says an expert report should include "the facts or data considered by the witness" in forming his opinion.

Lost profits calculation flawed. The defendants were more successful in their attack on the expert's lost profits calculation under the four-part *Panduit* test.

To show lost profits, a patent holder must show that, "but for" the defendant's infringement, the patent holder would have made the additional profits flowing to the defendant as a result of the wrongdoing. Here, the plaintiff's expert used the *Panduit* test to show "but for" causation.

Panduit requires that the patent holder show: (1) demand for the patented product; (2) the absence of acceptable noninfringing substitutes; (3) a manufacturing and marketing capability to exploit the demand; and (4) the amount of profit that would have been made.

To establish the plaintiff had the manufacturing and marketing capability (Factor 3), the expert compared the maximum quantity of units the plaintiff's existing contract manufacturers could produce with the combined quantity of units the plaintiff and the defendants shipped. He reduced the analysis to a graph that showed that, excepting one month, the plaintiff had sufficient capacity. He cited a number of documents that he said supported the data the graph displayed. One of them was an Excel spreadsheet that included manufacturing capacity data.

The defendants claimed they did not receive the spreadsheet until late in the litigation and the plaintiff withheld the documents underlying the data in the spreadsheet. Consequently, they were unable to know how the spreadsheet data were gathered, summarized, and produced. The defendants asked the court to impose a discovery sanction on the plaintiff and to forbid the plaintiff's expert from relying on the spreadsheet or any information included in it. They also wanted the court to strike "this aspect" from the expert's testimony.

The plaintiff tried to argue there were no underlying data for the spreadsheet. The court dismissed that argument swiftly, noting the data "must have originated somewhere, whether in concrete form or within the knowledge of a relevant witness." Sanctions were in order, the court found. They included producing all documents supporting the spreadsheet data on manufacturing capacity, making a witness with knowledge of the plaintiff's manufacturing capacity available for deposition, allowing the defendants to amend their expert report, if necessary, and requiring the plaintiff to pay reasonable expenses related to the defendants' motion to strike.

The court declined to strike the spreadsheet and related information from the expert's testimony.

Protection for nonreporting expert. Besides challenging the opinion of the plaintiff's damages expert, the defendants also asked the court for an order requiring the plaintiff to disclose material plaintiff counsel provided to a named inventor on the patents-in-suit, including communication between the two. The court earlier had found the inventor was a fact witness for the plaintiff, that is, a "non-reporting" expert.

The plaintiff claimed that this communication was privileged under the amended Federal Rule of Civil Procedure 26.

The court disagreed. It noted that, prior to 2010, "courts generally held that all documents and information disclosed to any testifying expert in connection with his testimony, including any communications with attorneys, were discoverable by the opposing party."

One effect of the 2010 amendments was that it separated experts into reporting and nonreporting experts, the court explained. Reporting experts are "experts retained or specially employed to provide expert testimony, who are required to provide a full expert report under Rule 26(a)(2)(B)." Nonreporting experts are "other individuals with specialized knowledge, skill, experience, training, or education, who are only required to provide a written disclosure under Rule 26(a)(2)(C)."

According to the court, the amended rule expressly protects communication between counsel and the reporting expert but "is silent as to whether communication between a party's attorney and a non-reporting expert are also protected." The court said this omission was intentional. It pointed to the advisory committee notes for Rule 26, which, it said, clarified that the amended Rule 26 did not protect communications between nonreporting experts and counsel.

In other words, the 2010 amendments did not change the law as to privilege waiver of nonreporting experts. Therefore, any documents and information the plaintiff's non-reporting expert considered in connection with his expert testimony, including communication with plaintiff counsel, were discoverable.

The court added that the amended Rule 26 did not exclude the possibility of protecting the information under another doctrine, including the work product doctrine.

Marten Transp., Ltd. v. Plattform Adver., Inc.

Citation: 2016 U.S. Dist. LEXIS 97754
Date of decision: July 26, 2016
Country: US
State/Jurisdiction: Federal/Kansas
Court: United States District Court
Type of action: Damages (incl. Lost Profits)
Judge: Lungstrum
SIC: 4213 Trucking, Except Local (general freight, truckload)
NAICS code: 484121 General Freight Trucking, Long-Distance, Truckload

Court Distinguishes Between Proving Fact of Damage and Amount

An economic damages case about the unauthorized use of a company's name and trademarks by the defendant's websites explains the different standard of proof that applies in tort actions when it comes to showing the plaintiff sustained lost profits as opposed to quantifying the loss. The defendant argued the plaintiff could not show it lost specific jobs as a result of the defendant's wrongdoing and, therefore, incurred no economic harm. The court found there was sufficient evidence to support a reasonable inference that the plaintiff lost potential workers and, by extension, profit and upheld the damages theory and award.

One measure of damages. The plaintiff was a transportation company, and the defendant operated websites advertising open driver positions on behalf of commercial trucking companies. For two years, the plaintiff paid the defendant to advertise its job opportunities; in so doing, it authorized the defendant to use the plaintiff's identifying information and registered trademarks. Then it terminated its relationship with the defendant. However, the defendant continued to display the plaintiff's information and accept applications that kept being addressed to the plaintiff. It also left eight other companies on the websites and ultimately discarded the applications.

When caught, the defendant initially said it left the company information up only while it tried to "figure out" how to avoid a negative effect on its search engine ranking and how to protect its site's integrity. In actuality, the defendant kept using some of the plaintiff's marks even after the plaintiff had sent a cease-and-desist letter and started litigation.

The plaintiff made a number of claims against the defendant, including federal trademark infringement and unfair competition in violation of the Lanham Act and unauthorized use of identifying information, trademark infringement, and tortious interference with prospective contractual relationships under state law.

The jury awarded different amounts for four different claims, totaling $1.25 million in actual damages as well as $2 million in punitive damages. The court decided the damages for the four claims were duplicative: For each claim, the plaintiff asked for the same measure of damages, lost profits. Therefore, the court only entered judgment for $500,000, the highest award on a claim by the jury in terms of actual damages. It allowed the entire punitive damages award.

In post-trial motions with the same court, the defendant, among other things, asked the court for judgment as a matter of law on the lost profits claim, whereas the plaintiff wanted the court to increase the actual damages amount to $1.25 million. The court denied both motions.

Drivers equal jobs and profit. At trial, the plaintiff's overarching damages theory was that the defendant withheld applications from drivers and made it impossible for the plaintiff to learn about job seekers at a time of industry driver shortage. As a result, the plaintiff had to turn down jobs that it could have performed with additional drivers.

An employee of the defendant said in an internal email exchange that the number of applications generated for the plaintiff was over 5,000. At trial, the plaintiff asked the jury to calculate lost profits based on that number of applications. The plaintiff added that historically 4% of applications resulted in hires, the average driver worked 52 weeks for the plaintiff, the plaintiff averaged about $3,500 per week per driver in revenue, and the average profit margin on such revenue was 10.79%.

After trial, the defendant attacked all components of the damages theory, concluding it was too speculative under the law.

The court began its discussion by pointing out that, in tort actions, the applicable case law distinguished "between proving the fact of damage and the amount." The fact of damage must be proved to a certainty, whereas the amount need only be a "reasonable approximation."

The court said the inconsistent language in the defendant's briefs made it hard to discern whether the defendant argued the plaintiff had failed to prove it suffered any lost profits or whether the defendant argued the plaintiff had not established the amount of damages with reasonable certainty.

The court decided the claim was that the plaintiff had not shown it had suffered any losses. The court disagreed with the defendant's argument.

For example, the defendant said it was inappropriate under the law for the plaintiff to determine lost revenue and profits based on "overall company performance indicators," i.e., historical averages for its hiring rate. Without evidence that the plaintiff would have hired a particular applicant, there was no basis for claiming actual damages, the defendant contended.

The court rejected this argument. Case law simply required that lost profits be shown by sufficient evidence, the court said. Besides company hiring averages, the plaintiff offered other evidence of actual damages.

The defendant claimed the 5,000-plus applications number included time outside the infringement period. Because the actual number of withheld applications could not be determined, there was no evidence that the defendant withheld any applications during the infringement period, the defendant argued.

The court disagreed. "The number of applications bears on the amount of damages, not the fact of damages, and as [the defendant] agrees, some speculation and approximation with respect to the amount is permitted," the court explained.

The defendant also contended the plaintiff did not show it suffered actual loss from the defendant's withholding of applications. The plaintiff failed to show it would have received the applications but for the defendant's infringement, the defendant said. Moreover, it was unlikely that the unauthorized use of the plaintiff's name and marks or the infringement affected applicants who used the defendant's sites to apply to all companies represented there.

This argument, too, had no traction with the court. There was evidence that users of the website were confused about whether the plaintiff would receive their applications, the court noted. Many applicants attempted to apply to a group of specific companies, including the plaintiff, and some only sought to apply to the plaintiff. It was reasonable to infer that, if the plaintiff had not been listed on the defendant's websites, some of the applicants would have contacted the plaintiff directly or through some other internet job board. Although it is "not necessarily believable that *all* 5,157 applicants in fact would have applied to [the plaintiff] in some other way," this figure only set the upper range for possible damages, "which may be determined by approximation and some degree of speculation," the court explained.

What was clear was that, but for the defendant's misconduct, the plaintiff would have received at least some additional applications, the court said.

The defendant then claimed the plaintiff failed to provide any analysis that it would have hired particular applicants from among the applicants to the defendant's websites.

The court dismissed this argument. There was evidence that there was a driver shortage and the plaintiff was constantly hiring; that the plaintiff had the capability and wish to hire up to thousands more during the damage period; that the plaintiff turned down work because of a lack of drivers; and that, prior to the defendant's misconduct, the plaintiff did hire internet job applicants. Therefore, it was not simply conjecture to assume the plaintiff would have hired some of the applicants.

Finally, the defendant contended the plaintiff failed to identify specific jobs it lost resulting from the defendant's misconduct. Therefore, the damages claim was improperly speculative.

Not so, the court said. "One could reasonably equate drivers with jobs and profit," the court said. The plaintiff's damages theory explained that it would have hired many more drivers had it known about the applicants and turned down jobs because of the lack of drivers. It showed it generally made a profit on those jobs. Therefore, the plaintiff showed it lost profitable business as a result of the defendant's conduct.

In sum, the court found the plaintiff showed the fact of damage with the degree of certainty the law required. Given the defendant's failure to articulate its objections to the amount of damages the jury awarded to the plaintiff, the court did not address the damages calculation.

No additional damages. The plaintiff argued, under its damages theory, lost profits exceeded $4 million and the defendant offered no alternative calculation. It was likely that the jury intended to award $1.25 million (the sum of the damages for the four claims) in actual damages and $2 million in punitive damages. Therefore, the court should increase the actual damages to $1.25 million.

The court adhered to its earlier ruling that the separate awards were duplicative. Also, the amounts the jury did award showed it "clearly intended to award less than the amount claimed," the court noted. Further, there was evidence challenging the plaintiff's argument it would have made hires from 4% of the withheld applications. The defendant showed the plaintiff in effect hired at a far lower rate from internet job board applications, including the defendant's websites. Consequently, "the Court cannot interpret the jury's verdict" in the way in which the plaintiff proposed, the court decided.

At the same time, the court rejected the defendant's attack on the punitive damages award, noting a jury could have found the defendant's conduct was "sufficiently aggravated to warrant punishment."

Mattress Closeout Ctr. IV, LLC v. Panera, LLC

Citation: 2016 U.S. Dist. LEXIS 91881
Date of decision: July 15, 2016
Country: US
State/Jurisdiction: Federal/Michigan
Court: United States District Court
Type of action: Damages (incl. Lost Profits)
Experts: John Zerbo (plaintiff); unknown (defendant)
Judge: Rosen
SIC: 5712 Furniture Stores (except custom furniture and cabinets)
NAICS code: 442110 Furniture Stores

Court Deems Future Lost Profits Formula an Exercise in Speculation

Most litigators making or defending against damages claims related to business losses know to hire an expert to support their positions. But an expert who accepts the information a litigant supplies at face value and who develops his own "formula" for computing future lost profits based on plainly unsustainable assumptions does the case a disservice. Such was the situation recently when a court decided to dismiss most of the plaintiff's damages claims on summary judgment. Expert deposition testimony showed the plaintiff "cannot show lost future profits beyond speculation," the court said.

No basis for exemplary damages. The plaintiff was "the Marshalls or TJ Maxx of the mattress world." It had four outlets. The defendant was a leading restaurant brand with over 1,700 bakery-cafés throughout the U.S. and in Canada.

One of the plaintiff's businesses and the defendant shared a wall. In April 2013, the plaintiff noticed water leaking into its storeroom and notified the defendant. It took the defendant three months to investigate the problem. In August 2013, the defendant hired a contractor to fix the leak and remove any mold. By December 2013, the remediation work was done.

The plaintiff admitted it suffered no damage to its inventory and did not incur repair costs. However, it wanted compensation from the defendant for "lost business income," "lost employee time," "lost principal's time," and "lost future income." When negotiations with the defendant failed, the plaintiff sued, alleging negligence and nuisance. It sought compensatory damages in excess of $100,000 and "exemplary damages" totaling $50,000. The latter were based on the defendant's "selfish and obnoxious conduct" and "repeated attempts at delay and its harassment of [the plaintiff]." The plaintiff retained an expert to calculate damages.

The court found for the plaintiff on liability, principally because the defendant took no steps to oppose the plaintiff's liability motions for summary judgment.

The court swiftly dismissed the demand for exemplary damages, explaining they usually were a remedy where the loss to a business was unquantifiable, as might be the case with loss of reputation or goodwill. Future lost profits and lost time of employees did not fit the category. Here, there was no "hard" evidence that any damage to the plaintiff's showroom had a long-lasting effect on the plaintiff's customers, the court noted.

In fact, the opposite was true, the court observed. The plaintiff's damages expert testified that sales records showed an increase in sales and profits for the year immediately following the damages period (April 2013 to August 2013). What's more, the court explained, the plaintiff's claims related to lost business were quantifiable and compensable by money.

No actual loss. In calculating compensatory damages, the plaintiff's damages expert allocated $2,405.00 to lost employee time. He said the company's owner told him employees spent about 10 hours per week for 12 weeks (the damages period) "shuffling things around, doing different things" because of water leaking into the storeroom. The expert did not know whether this was time the employees spent in excess of their regular hours, and he admitted he did not review employee time cards or payroll schedules to verify the number of hours.

The expert also determined damages in the range of $39,150 to $41,250 related to the time the owner allegedly wasted on handling the water leak issue. The expert admitted he lacked hard proof in the form of payroll records or hourly billing sheets to support the 150-hour claim. He said the owner told him to use this number.

In terms of the two hourly rates underlying the calculation, the expert explained the owner also practiced law and told the expert he generally billed between $250 and $300 per hour for legal work. The expert decided to average those figures and arrived at a $275 hourly rate—the rate he used to calculate the upper range of damages. The expert did not review legal bills or invoices to verify that those were the rates the owner charged for legal services.

The expert based the lower range of damages on a lower hourly rate. The starting point to calculate the lower hourly rate was the annual income the owner stated for income tax purposes. The expert assumed the owner would work about 2,000 hours a year (40 hours per week for 50 weeks) and decided to allocate 1,000 hours to time the owner spent in the mattress business and 1,000 spent on the law practice. When the expert divided the income amount stated on the owner's tax return by 1,000 hours, he arrived at a $261 hourly rate.

During his deposition, the expert admitted that the 150 hours he assigned to the owner's lost time was time that actually was included in the 1,000 hours. He conceded that in actuality the company incurred no additional costs for the 150 hours the owner claimed to have spent on the water leak.

Other wrinkles in the expert's calculation were that the income reported for tax purposes included income resulting from all of the four outlets, not just the store that experienced the water leak. The expert did not apportion income to the damaged store. And there was no documentation to support the expert's assumption that the owner spent 1,000 hours on the mattress business.

There was no reasonable basis for the computation of lost employee or lost principal's time, the court said. Moreover, since the expert "categorically testified that no loss was actually incurred" related to these two damages categories, the court dismissed the claims.

Attempt to extend lost profits fails. The defendant did not dispute loss of business during the damages period, but it said the plaintiff's claim of "future lost profits" for five years beyond the damages period was based "on nothing more than speculation and conjecture."

In his deposition, the plaintiff's expert explained future losses were based on a formula he had developed. He started with the "actual" number of customers the company lost during the damages period (35) and the "historical" percentage of repeat/referral customers of the company's four outlets (15.2%). According to the expert, the formula showed the company would lose five repeat customers it would have had but for the water leak damage. Next, the expert totaled the sales the damaged store had recorded in the three months before the damages period and divided it by the total number of customers. The result was an average transaction amount of about $770. Next, he multiplied the transaction amount by five (the lost customers) to arrive at future lost income for 2014. In determining lost income for the following years, he compounded the number of lost customers and multiplied the number by the average transaction amount.

He admitted there was no certainty as to the projected increase in lost customers. "I mean there is no way of actually knowing that." He said it was just a "theory." He also admitted that it was impossible to know whether a person would decide not to buy a mattress in the future because of a water leak in one showroom in 2013.

The court agreed with the defendant that the lost future profits claim was "speculative, at best." There was no way of knowing whether there would be any loss to the plaintiff in the future from decreased sales or lost customers because of the water leak, the court said. It noted the expert's basis for the "formula" to project future losses was "questionable." He based the repeat/referral customer figures on all of the company's outlets, not just the damaged store. And he admitted he did not know whether the proposed 15.2% repeat/referral rate actually represented the rate for the damaged store alone.

In dismissing the plaintiff's future lost profits claim, the court ruled that at trial the plaintiff was only allowed to pursue recovery of damages for ordinary negligence and nuisance during the damages period.

Editor's note: Sitting for a deposition can be a trying experience for an expert (and the retaining attorney) because much is at stake. The testimony can set the course for the rest of the litigation. A recent article in Business Valuation Update *provides seven surprising insights from attorneys on expert deposition testimony. Find it at sub.bvresources.com/defaulttextonly.asp?f=downloads.*

In re Mercury Cos. (In re Mercury II)

Citation: 2015 Bank. LEXIS 3443
Date of decision: Oct. 9, 2015
Country: US
State/Jurisdiction: Federal/Colorado
Court: United States Bankruptcy Court
Type of action: Bankruptcy
Experts: Neil H. Demchick (plaintiff); Scott P. Peltz (defendants)
Judge: Romero
SIC: 6361 Title Insurance (title insurers-direct)
NAICS code: 524127 Direct Title Insurance Carriers

'Reasonably Equivalent Value' Analysis Meets FMV Standard, Court Says

After filing for Chapter 11 bankruptcy, the plaintiff claimed the sale of certain subsidiaries to the defendant entities was an avoidable fraudulent transfer. The Bankruptcy Court considered the valuations the parties' experts presented at trial for the subsidiaries "useful but not determinative." Without ascribing a value to the subsidiaries, the court found the sales price met the "reasonably equivalent value" requirement. The appeals court ordered the Bankruptcy Court to revisit the issue adopting an "objective creditor's perspective" rather than the subjective view of the debtor's management.

Quick sale. The plaintiff was a title agency with operations in Colorado, California, Arizona, and several other states. It experienced serious financial trouble when the housing market buckled. In April 2008, the plaintiff executed a credit agreement, as part of a $45 million loan, that was secured by most of its own and its subsidiaries' assets, including accounts receivable. In July 2008, the lead creditor swept $40 million from the plaintiff's accounts. Based on this event and other considerations, the plaintiff's management stopped doing business in 161 locations and closed many subsidiaries.

Management believed that four successful Colorado-based subsidiaries would make a great target for a swift acquisition. But when it proposed a sale to their largest underwriter, First American Title, the latter declined the offer. By contract, the plaintiff had an obligation to obtain First America's consent to a sale of the subsidiaries to a third party. Management subsequently proposed a quick sale of stock in the subsidiaries to the defendant entities. Within days, the parties executed a purchase agreement that specified a purchase price of $5 million to be paid in cash. The defendants immediately wired $1 million of the amount and took control of the Colorado subsidiaries that same day. A day later, they wired an additional $1.48 million toward the purchase price. But slightly over $2.5 million of the purchase price remained outstanding. Twenty-three days after the sale, the plaintiff filed for Chapter 11 bankruptcy.

Subsequently, the plaintiff sued the defendants in Bankruptcy Court on various grounds. One of the claims was that the plaintiff should be able to recover the value of the Colorado subsidiaries because it received less than the "reasonable equivalent" value for the businesses and was insolvent on the date of transfer. Since both parties agreed on the insolvency issue, the court focused its ruling on the "reasonably equivalent value" issue.

Debtor's subjective beliefs. At trial, the parties' experts adopted a similar valuation approach (discounted cash flow analysis), but their conclusions were "vastly different." In a nutshell, the plaintiff's expert assumed there was no need to conduct an immediate sale. The Colorado subsidiaries could have stayed in business for 30 to 60 days to get to a sale, the expert said. In contrast, the defendant's expert built his valuation on the immediacy of the sale and the plaintiff's financial distress on the transfer date. The plaintiff's expert found the subsidiaries' stock had a positive value of nearly $15 million, whereas the defendants' expert concluded it had "negative value."

In its original decision, the court found neither expert report was "wholly determinative." The plaintiff's expert failed to show that a less rushed sale would have yielded an additional $10 million; the defendants' expert improperly excluded certain revenue from his calculation and failed to consider that the defendants were willing to pay $5 million for the subsidiaries and indeed considered the deal a good one. According to the Bankruptcy Court, one valuation appeared "excessive" and the other "too low."

The court noted that, without a doubt, the debtor received some value, in the form of the payments from the defendant. The circumstances of the sales suggested the plaintiff's officers held the mistaken belief that they had to sell the subsidiaries immediately, when, in reality, the plaintiff had access to sufficient cash to cover impending liabilities such as payroll so as to avoid punitive actions from the state's department of insurance. According to the Bankruptcy Court, the company's president panicked, but he also "desired an immediate sale." Management received what it asked for, the court said. It concluded that the sale produced reasonably equivalent value and, therefore, was not avoidable.

Both sides appealed the decision with the district court based on various grounds. One of the issues the appellate court ordered the Bankruptcy Court to reconsider was whether the company had received reasonably equivalent value for the subsidiaries under the fair market value standard of value—thus excluding subjective factors such as management's view of the state of the company at the time of the transfers.

Emphasis on objective value-related factors. On remand, the plaintiff contended its expert was the only one who proposed a fair market value calculation. Accordingly, the court should credit this expert's $15 million valuation.

The Bankruptcy Court was not persuaded. The plaintiff's expert failed to consider negative factors in his analysis that affected the fair market value analysis, the court noted. They included the cash sweep and the resulting closure of non-Colorado subsidiaries. Also, at least 27 major lender customers stopped doing business with the Colorado subsidiaries. And, at the time of transfer, there was a real risk of a "mass exodus" of employees of the Colorado subsidiaries if there was no quick sale. Moreover, First America, the largest underwriter, had the ability to block a sale to a third party. And the plaintiff's expert failed to explain a key assumption: that the company could have continued to operate another 30 to 60 days.

On remand, the defendants claimed the fair market value was $2.5 million, the amount the defendants actually had paid toward the agreed-upon price. Revisiting the defendant expert's valuation, the court noted his analysis, too, was defective. The expert assumed an immediate sale was necessary when there was evidence that it was not.

The court noted two factors that guided its modification of the plaintiff expert's $15 million valuation:

1. *DLOM.* The plaintiff's expert applied a 10% discount for lack of marketability (DLOM), which he described as "net of control premium." He started from the premise that the plaintiff was selling 100% ownership of its shares in the Colorado subsidiaries. "The more control one has, the more marketable the shares are," the plaintiff's expert said. Moreover, the company was able to continue as a going concern for "30 to 60 days."

On remand, the plaintiff suggested that, if the court took issue with its expert's assumption on timing, it should apply the 30% DLOM the opposing expert had used.

The court did just that. It found a 10% DLOM was too low. The company did not have as much control as the plaintiff's expert assumed, considering its contractual obligation to obtain First America's consent to a sale. The use of a 30% DLOM lowered the valuation to a little over $11.7 million.

2. *Capital structure.* On remand, the plaintiff allowed that its expert had developed a capital structure based on "what a hypothetical buyer would hold, not what the [subsidiaries] or the [parent company] historically held." For purposes of valuation, the plaintiff admitted, "any comparative analysis should be considered together with a review of the company's specific and relative financial situation."

Specifically, the plaintiff's expert used a 30.28% debt structure, which he said was the middle ground between the 6.38% then-current year mean and the five-year average of 36.83% stated in the *Ibbotson Cost of Capital Yearbook.* He said the title companies historically carried debt of between 25% and 30%, in the form of intercompany payables. At the same time, he clarified that the title companies themselves did not hold debt; rather, the debt was held at the parent company level.

The defendants' expert found the Colorado subsidiaries did not have a lot of long-term debt and the industry itself did not require a lot of it. He found the weight of the debt should be 6.38% based on Ibbotson's yearbook.

The court adopted the defendant expert's analysis because he adhered more closely to the applicable legal standard and considered the unique circumstances of the Colorado subsidiaries and the title industry as a whole, instead of using only book values, as the plaintiff's expert had done. The experts' different capital structures resulted in a $3.2 million difference in value. In adjusting the plaintiff expert's valuation, the court subtracted that figure from the $11.7 million to arrive at an $8.5 million valuation. This amount represented the maximum value the court was able to ascribe to the Colorado subsidiaries, the court said. In other words, the evidence showed a range of value between $5 million and $8.5 million for the subsidiaries.

The final issue was whether the sales price, $5 million, was within the range of "reasonably equivalent value." The court found it was. Jurisprudence addressing the "reasonably equivalent value" issue allows for a buyer to "get a good deal, even a great deal, but not an obscene deal at the expense of the debtor's creditors," the Bankruptcy Court explained.

Considering all the factors in play—fair market value, an arm's-length transaction, and the parties' good faith—there was no reason to undo the sale of the Colorado subsidiaries, the court concluded. Even if the applicable value of the subsidiaries were $8.5 million, the defendants simply got a good deal, the Bankruptcy Court added.

Editor's note: An extended discussion of the Bankruptcy Court's original decision, Mercury Companies, Inc. v. FNF Security Acquisition, Inc. (In re Mercury Companies, Inc.), *2014 Bank. LEXIS 1230 (March 31, 2014), along with the court's opinion, is available at* BVLaw.

Merion Capital LP & Merion Capital II LP v. BMC Software

Citation: 2015 Del. Ch. LEXIS 268
Date of decision: Oct. 21, 2015
Country: US
State/Jurisdiction: Delaware
Court: Court of Chancery
Type of action: Dissenting Shareholder
Experts: Borris J. Steffen (petitioners); Richard S. Ruback (company/respondent)
Judge: Glasscock
SIC: 7372 Prepackaged Software (software publishing)
NAICS code: 511210 Software Publishers

Uncertainty Over Key Inputs Compromises DCF, Chancery Says

Following the M&A playbook, arbitrageurs petitioned the Delaware Court of Chancery for a statutory appraisal of their shares, alleging an activist investor forced the subject company to sell itself below its value. Experts for both sides agreed that the discounted cash flow analysis was the best method of valuation. But the court ultimately decided the merger price was the more reliable indicator of value based on irreducible uncertainties surrounding key DCF inputs, including the equity risk premium.

Two auctions. BMC Software was one of the largest software companies in the world. Its portfolio included products for simplifying and automating the management of IT processes as well as applications and databases. The company also provided consulting services related to its products. In recent years, as mainframe computing declined and technology shifted, it experienced stunted growth. Even its enterprise service management unit, which drove most of the growth by licensing software, saw increasingly lower profit margins as a result of relentless competition from established and startup companies. For the relevant years—2011, 2012, and 2013—the company's revenue rose from $2.07 billion to $2.17 billion to $2.20 billion; net earnings, on the other hand, dropped from $456.20 million to $401 million to $331 million. License bookings fell as well.

In mid-2012, the company's performance problems prompted a team of activist investors to increase its equity stake in the company in order to compel a sale. The investors began a proxy fight, which hurt the company's reputation in the marketplace. Following a settlement of the dispute, in July 2012, the company formed a strategic review committee and retained a financial advisor to explore options to increase shareholder value, including a sale. Two potential financial buyers gave nonbinding indications of interest: One was $45 to $47 per share; the other was $48 per share. But in October 2012, in the wake of positive second-quarter financials, the company decided to abandon the sales process, believing it could continue to do well as a stand-alone company. However, by year-end, the financial results were sluggish again and management projections proved overly optimistic. The activist investors resumed their campaign to force a sale. The company began by re-engaging the earlier potential buyers and received nonbinding offers from three financial sponsors: $42 to $44 per share, $46 to $47 per share, and $48 per share. Then, the $48-per-share potential buyer decided it could no longer pursue a bid that veered too far from the then-current trading price of $43.75 per share. Meanwhile, the eventual buyer adjusted its offer to $45.25 per share. After more negotiations, the company and the eventual buyer agreed on a merger price of $46.25. The agreement included a 30-day market check, i.e., a go-shop period. Despite the company's contacting 16 potential bidders during that period, it received no alternative offers.

Also, during the go-shop period, a group of shareholders filed suit for breach of fiduciary duty in the Delaware Court of Chancery, contesting the sales process. The merger proceeded and closed in September 2013. In April 2014, the court approved a settlement between the litigants finding the sales process had been fair.

Subsequently, two groups of shareholders, whom the court described as "arbitrageurs who bought, not into a going concern, but instead into this lawsuit," petitioned the court for a fair value determination of their shares under the state's appraisal statute, 8 Del. C. § 262.

Regular projections. Management, in the ordinary course of business, created several types of projections. They included forecasts for an annual plan for the upcoming fiscal year. The annual plan was for internal use only and reflected optimistic goals. The projections were both "a stretch" and attainable, management believed. In the past, the company repeatedly had failed to reach the goals.

Also, in October, the company typically prepared high-level three-year forecasts that were less detailed than the annual plan. And, separately, the company's finance group prepared detailed three-year projections that went to ratings agencies. Unlike the high-level projections, the ratings agencies projections were not subject to top-down scrutiny.

Based on the 2013 annual plan, the company developed several sets of projections leading up to the merger. The final set served as the basis for the financial advisor's fairness opinion and for use in the final data pack to potential buyers. The financial projections factored in two critical aspects of doing business: ongoing smaller-scale M&A activities to ensure the company remained competitive and stock-based compensation (SBC) for its employees.

In terms of the M&A activity, the projections mostly were concerned with forecasting so called "tuck-in" transactions by which the company would habitually buy individual products or technology that it could incorporate into an existing business unit. Large-scale acquisitions, including buying a new business unit, were relatively rare. In the years leading up to the merger, the company undertook over a dozen tuck-in transactions, and, at trial, its CEO and CFO explained that, if the company had remained public, it would have continued to pursue tuck-in acquisitions in the future.

According to the company, stock-based compensation was vital to attracting and retaining talent in the technology sector. The company expensed the fair value of the stock options, less expected amount of forfeitures, on a straight-line basis over the vesting period. Its SBC expenses increased significantly over the years and represented about 7% of revenue in 2013, the merger year. Management said it would have continued to issue SBC had the business remained a public company.

To avoid diluting the company's shares, each time the company issued stock in connection with SBC, it bought company stock in the open market.

'Wildly divergent' DCF valuations. The parties retained valuation experts who both relied on the DCF method to determine the company's fair value at the time of the merger. The same method produced vastly different outcomes. In a nutshell, the petitioners' expert contended the fair value of the company per share was $67.08, i.e., 145% of the merger price. Other valuation methods were not appropriate under the facts of the case, the petitioners' expert claimed.

The company expert's DCF analysis resulted in a $37.88-per-share price, which was just a bit more than half of the value the opposing expert proposed. The company's expert performed two sanity checks. First he conducted a DCF analysis that used projections from various Wall Street analysts that had followed the company, and second he performed a comparable companies analysis based on trading multiples from select publicly traded software companies.

Key inputs in court's analysis. The court began its fair value determination by performing its own DCF calculation. It decided to use the company expert's analysis as a framework because it found he better explained and defended his positions as to some key inputs that accounted for the value gap.

Financial projections. Both experts relied on the same management projections, but the company's expert decided to reduce the projected revenue by 5% to account for the fact that in the past the company had missed its revenue goals.

The court allowed that the projections revealed "a bias toward optimism" but overall found them to be reliable. It called the company expert's approach "too speculative to accurately account for that bias."

But, when in the final analysis the Chancery adopted the merger price rather than the DCF value, it expressly mentioned the company's history of "problematic" projections, such that the figures "could distort value." Judging from the record, there was no reliable method to adjust the projections, the court concluded.

Discount rate. The expert's difference in discount rate came down to the equity risk premium (ERP). The petitioners' expert used a supply-side ERP, reasoning that valuation calculations were forward looking. In contrast, the company's expert used a historical ERP, calling it "the most generally accepted ERP" and saying "any model that attempts to estimate future ERP is subject to intolerable estimation errors. "

The court agreed the calculation was forward looking, and it noted that recent decisions from the Chancery, including *In re Orchard Enterprises*, 2012 WL 2923305 (available at *BVLaw*), favored using a supply-side ERP.

At the same time, the Chancery acknowledged that the question as to which ERP to use was "a vigorously debated topic, not just between these two experts, but in the financial community at large." It added "scholarship may dictate other approaches in the future." Using a supply-side ERP, the court determined a discount rate of 10.5%.

As to the larger issue of which valuation method to use, the Chancery noted that the continuing debate over what type of ERP to use represented another uncertainty that ultimately caused it to choose the merger price over the DCF value in this case.

Terminal growth rate. The petitioners' expert developed a range of rates between the long-run inflation and nominal GDP rate. He then added 50 basis points to the midpoint between inflation and GDP to arrive at a long-term growth rate of 3.75%.

The company's expert performed an analysis of implied EBITDA growth rates for comparable companies, which he found averaged -1.7%. He ultimately adopted the 2.3% inflation rate as the long-term growth rate, saying the real cash flows of the business would remain constant in the long run.

The court rejected both determinations. It noted that the evidence as to the company's prospects for growth was inconclusive. Based on precedent, the court applied a terminal growth rate that was the midpoint of inflation and GDP, 3.25%. It said the midpoint approach was "sound," but the petitioner expert's decision to add 50 basis points to the midpoint was arbitrary. The court added that the rate of inflation generally was the floor for a terminal value. The accepted notion was that, once an industry had matured, a company would have steady growth roughly equal to the rate of nominal GDP growth. It also found that there was insufficient evidence that the companies the company's expert considered for his implied EBITDA growth rates analysis were comparable.

Ultimately, the uncertainty surrounding the growth rate was another factor in the court's decision to look to the merger price instead of the DCF value. The court said it did not have "complete confidence in the reliability of taking the midpoint between inflation and DGP as the Company's expected growth rate."

SBC. Both experts considered stock-based compensation, but in different ways. The petitioners' expert calculated shares outstanding based on the treasury stock method. The company's expert included SBC as a cash expense, which decreased the free cash flow projections.

The court adopted the calculation the company's expert proposed. It stressed that only the company expert's analysis accounted for *future* stock-based compensation. In contrast, the petitioner expert's treatment only accounted for stock-based compensation that had been awarded at the time of his report. Treating stock-based compensation as an expense was reasonable, the court said, considering the company historically bought back stock awarded to employees to avoid dilution; "in that sense, it is clearly in line with a cash expense," the court noted.

M&A expense. The experts also disagreed over whether it was appropriate to deduct tuck-in M&A expenses from the cash flows. The court observed that they were a line item in the management projections the company used during the sales process and were the basis for the fairness opinion. There was credible testimony that the company planned to continue using this strategy to ensure growth had it remained a public company. If a valuation did not account for M&A activity and the related expenses, the projections would be inflated, the court said. Therefore, it was necessary to deduct M&A expenses from income to calculate cash flow.

Based on the various inputs, the court's DCF analysis yielded a $48.00-per-share price.

Sale yields more reliable value. Several reasons caused the court to use the merger price as the indicator of value. Besides the irreducible uncertainty over critical DCF inputs, there was the huge value gap resulting from the expert's DCF calculations. Further, the company pursued a "robust, arm's-length" sales process. It undertook two auctions over a period of several months to test the market and evaluated numerous bids before settling on the final price, $46.25. It shopped itself around again during the go-shop period it negotiated with the buyer group. A shareholder class action suit, which preceded the statutory appraisal action and which claimed the sales process was compromised because of the board's breach of fiduciary duty, ended in a settlement in which the court described the process as fair. There was no evidence that any pressure the activist investors exerted on the company led to a rushed, ineffective sale, the court here concluded.

Two-part synergy test. The final step in the court's fair value determination was deciding whether or not it was necessary to adjust the merger price for synergies. Under the common law interpretation of the appraisal statute, the court must deduct any value not attributable to the company as an independent going concern. It is easy to understand that the sales price may capture synergies where the buyer is a strategic acquirer, the court said. But here the acquisition was financial, not strategic.

The company pointed to testimony from a representative of the buyer stating the buyer expected to benefit from tax reductions and other cost savings as a result of taking the acquired company private. Without the prospect of those savings, the buyer would have been willing to pay only $36 per share, that representative said. This figure, the court observed, was close to the going-concern value the company's expert proposed. Simply pointing to an internal valuation as proof that synergies informed the merger price, as the petitioners did in litigation, was insufficient, the court concluded. The company's expert had not performed a valuation based on the "deal-price-less-synergies" approach. Therefore, it was unclear "whether the purported going-private savings outweighed the Buyer Group's rate of return that was required to justify the leverage presumably used to generate those savings."

The court explained there was a two-part test for deciding whether to adjust the market value to fair value. First, it is necessary to determine whether the deal generated synergies. If so, the next question is whether the sellers captured the value of the synergies in the deal price. Here, neither party quantified what additional value to ascribe to the acquisition besides the going-concern value, and neither party determined what portion, if any, the buyer shared with the stockholders. Therefore, in this case, it was not necessary to reduce the merger price for synergies, the court concluded.

The court adopted the merger price—$46.25 per share—as the fair value of the company's stock.

Moore v. Moore

Citation: 2016 Ark. LEXIS 82
Date of decision: March 10, 2016
Country: US
State/Jurisdiction: Arkansas
Court: Supreme Court
Type of action: Marital Dissolution
Judge: Wood
SIC: 4311 United States Postal Service
NAICS code: 491110 Postal Service

In Controversial Move, High Court Strikes Active Appreciation Rule

Under Arkansas statutory law, the increase in the value of nonmarital property is nonmarital property. But, in a line of decisions going back nearly 30 years, the Arkansas Supreme Court created an exception to the statutory rule by way of the active appreciation doctrine. Recently, however, a divided court reversed itself when it disavowed the doctrine and overruled its prior decisions. What adds to the controversy is that the court did so of its own volition. In petitioning the court for review, neither of the parties advocated for a change in case law.

Trial court follows precedent. Prior to marriage, the husband formed a U.S. mail contractor company. At divorce, some eight years later, the trial court found that the company was separate property and not subject to marital distribution. But, based on controlling case law, the court used the active appreciation doctrine—which considers the appreciation of separate property to be marital property if it is the result of the owner spouse's efforts during the marriage—to award the wife half of the company's growth in value. The court found the appreciation was the result of the husband's significant effort during the marriage to grow the business. It also said the company's stock value increased as a result of the wife's contribution to the business. The total appreciation amounted to over $556,000.

The husband appealed this and another finding with the state Court of Appeals, which dismissed the appeal based on procedural grounds. The parties then petitioned the state Supreme Court for a review of the appeals court's procedural ruling. The state's high court, in turn, decided to use the opportunity to address the substantive issues in the case, including the issue of appreciation.

In contesting the trial court's ruling on appreciation, the husband argued that, under the applicable state statute, any increase in the value of a nonmarital business remained nonmarital property. But he also acknowledged that there was a line of cases in which the state Supreme Court had used the active appreciation analysis to carve out an exception to the statutory law. Rather than arguing the controlling cases were wrong as a matter of law, the husband contended the exception was inapplicable to the facts of this case. Therefore, the trial court in this instance erred in awarding the wife half of the appreciation, he said.

High court overrules precedent. A majority of the state Supreme Court performed an altogether different analysis. The majority began by noting that the applicable statutory provision (Ark. Code Ann. § 9-12-315(b)(5)) defines marital property as "all property acquired by either spouse subsequent to the marriage except ... the increase in value of property acquired prior to marriage." Therefore, the court's majority said, "[T]he increase in value of property during a marriage is nonmarital, without exception, and should be returned to the owning party."

The high court then went on to "expressly overrule" all prior cases in which the Supreme Court once had "redefined marital property through the 'active appreciation' rule." These cases, and the active appreciation rule, "clearly conflict with the statutory scheme," the court's majority said. How to define marital property and how to divide property at divorce is "a matter of policy with which the legislature, not this court, is almost exclusively tasked," it added.

It noted that some lower courts have confused the issue even more when, in deciding whether or not to reclassify nonmarital property as marital property, they have weighed the efforts of both spouses instead of simply assessing the efforts of the owner spouse. This is what the trial court did in the instant case.

A majority of the Supreme Court decided it was time to stop the confusion and return to the plain language of the statute, notwithstanding the legal doctrine of stare decisis, which cautions against overruling precedent. In creating the active appreciation doctrine, the judiciary moved the law "too far from the statute," the court's majority said. To correct this "palpable error," it was necessary to overturn the prior case law.

It decided that, in the instant case, under the governing statutory provision, the growth in value of the husband's separate company was nonmarital property. The trial court erred in awarding the wife half of the appreciation.

The Supreme Court did note that a related provision of the statute (Ark. Code Ann. § 9-12-315(a)(2)) allowed for the division of nonmarital property under an analysis that considered a series of factors, including the length of the marriage, the parties' age, health, and station in life, the amount and sources of income, employability, and more. However, an award under this provision required specific findings by the trial court to justify the distribution of nonmarital property. The trial court in the instant case did not perform this type of analysis, the Supreme Court's majority pointed out.

New ruling's broad and narrow implications. Accordingly, with this decision, the state Supreme Court: (1) disavowed its earlier rulings permitting a division of nonmarital property under the active appreciation analysis; and (2) remanded the instant case to the trial court to award any appreciation in the value of the husband's business to the husband as nonmarital property "absent a specific statutory finding to justify any distribution to [the wife]."

Dissent. Two judges dissented on this issue. Their principal contention was that, almost 30 years ago, the court construed the statute to allow for an exception. During all of this time, the legislature failed to amend the statute "in any way to express its disagreement with" the court's 1987 decision in *Layman v. Layman*, 731 S.W.2d 771 (1987), or in the court's subsequent decisions in *Farrell v. Farrell*, 231 S.W.3d 619 (2006), and *Brown v. Brown*, 284 S.W.3d 17 (2008).

In light of the legislature's failure to act, there arguably was a presumption that the legislature acquiesced or passively approved of the high court's interpretation of the statue, the dissent said. Moreover, it was troubling that the majority found it necessary to overrule precedent where neither party asked for the three cases to be overruled. In the instant case, the question of whether to overrule the active appreciation rule was not in front of the court, and it should be reserved for another day, the dissent stated.

Editor's note. The majority's phrase "absent a specific statutory finding to justify any distribution to [the wife]" can be read in two ways: (1) the award to the wife of the appreciated value is invalid because the trial court failed to make the required statutory finding; or (2) the award is salvageable if the trial court on remand makes the required statutory finding.

MSKP Oak Grove, LLC v. Venuto

Citation: 2016 U.S. Dist. LEXIS 84950
Date of decision: June 29, 2016
Country: US
State/Jurisdiction: Federal/New Jersey
Court: United States District Court
Type of action: Fraud
Experts: Shelley Brown (plaintiff); unknown (defendants)
Judge: Simandle
SIC: 7299 Miscellaneous Personal Services, NEC (except diet and weight reducing services, personal care services, valet parking services, babysitting bureaus, debt and credit counseling, consumer bartering services, and formal wear and costume rental)
NAICS code: 812990 All Other Personal Services

Expert Prevails by Documenting Adherence to Valuation Standards

A recent *Daubert* case illustrates how a thorough expert report can help an embattled valuator stay afloat in the maelstrom of litigation. The plaintiff retained an expert to show the defendants committed fraud, but she received incomplete documents. Next, the defendants attacked the expert opinion in a *Daubert* motion contending the expert used hindsight to value the subject company.

The court found she sufficiently documented how the many assumptions, estimates, and adjustments that went into her re-creation of missing information aligned with valuation standards and the authoritative literature.

Contested shareholder distributions. The four defendants owned a company, Hollywood Tanning Systems (HTS), which operated tanning salons and sold franchises and tanning equipment to other tanning salons. HTS had a lease agreement with the plaintiff's predecessor in interest that allowed HTS to sublease the space to a franchisee. Ultimately, the franchisee sublettor defaulted on the lease.

In spring 2007, HTS made a purchase asset agreement with a third-party buyer in which the latter agreed to acquire most of HTS's assets and assume most of the company's debts in exchange for $40 million. As part of the deal, the defendants also were to receive a 25% interest in the buyer and contingency payments based on the buyer's future earnings. The day the transaction closed, the four defendant shareholders each received over $5.8 million of the $40 million sales payment. Other sales proceeds went toward settling the company's debts. HTS retained a few small receivables but essentially stopped operations in June 2007. Following the sale, the buyer went into bankruptcy.

A year after the asset sale, the plaintiff sued the defendants over the sublettor's default on the lease and won a judgment for over $411,000, which remained unpaid. The plaintiff then sued the defendants claiming HTS fraudulently distributed over $23.8 million to its shareholders, leaving the company unable to pay creditors, including the plaintiff.

After five years of litigation taken up with motions to dismiss and discovery, the main issue boiled down to whether the $23.8 million payment to the shareholders was a proper shareholder distribution or an illegal diversion of the buyer's assets.

Reverse engineering financial situation. To bolster its legal theories of intentional and constructive fraudulent transfer of assets, the plaintiff hired an expert. She was a CPA and accredited valuation and financial forensics analyst with extensive experience. Within the span of a few days, she prepared two reports. The first report was a "fraudulent conveyance report" and the second report a "valuation report." In the reports, she explained that she had not been provided with many of the documents "normally maintained by companies of this size for tax and management purposes." Also, the documents that were made available to her came in a PDF version rather than the native file format. As such, they excluded critical underlying information. She found that, in terms of the valuation date (the date of the distributions), HTS's general ledger showed only deposits of about $4.3 million as proceeds from the transaction and about $128,000 from the transfer of "other accounts" but did not show the $23.8 million disbursed to the defendant shareholders.

For the expert to provide an opinion as to whether the company received reasonably equivalent value for the shareholder distributions or whether it was insolvent or became insolvent at the time of the transfer, she had to reverse engineer the company's financial situation from the incomplete records. Part of the process, she explained (in her report and in a *Daubert* hearing) was re-creating income statements and balance sheets. This meant making "normalization adjustments" pursuant to the AICPA's Statements on Standards for Valuation Services Section 100 (VS-100), treatises by intellectual leaders in valuation (Pratt and Hitchner), and generally accepted accounting principles.

She explained VS-100.41 advised using discounts to account for nonoperating assets and excess operating assets in a business valuation. Here, she discounted the value of the company's assets related to "investment in stores held for resale" that had not reopened for over a year. She said that a review of certain losses the company booked on its tax filings made it clear that those stores should not have been considered functioning stores. She concluded the company overstated its net income accounts receivable by $3 million. Similarly, based on the Pratt treatise, she adjusted projections as to the buyer's ability to generate income in the future. She attached copies of the sources guiding her analysis to her reports.

In terms of the company's fair market value as of the valuation date, she concluded that HTS did not receive reasonably equivalent value from the defendants for the distributions. The assets left to the company after the distributions and diversion of cash to the defendants were unreasonably small in relation to the business or transaction. At the time of the distributions, the company knew or should have known that it would incur debt beyond its ability to pay as the debt became due. The distributions left the company insolvent. There was evidence of post-transaction insolvency in the company's 2007 year-end financial statements.

The defendants tried to exclude the expert opinion under *Daubert*. They claimed the reports were stand-alones, and since the expert did not attach a summary of methodology to the "fraudulent conveyance" report, it was per se inadmissible. They said the reconstruction of the company's financial health was based on an unreliable methodology (hindsight) and the valuation report was not helpful to the trier of fact.

The plaintiff countered that the two reports formed part of one expert opinion and the discussion of principles and methodologies that appeared in the valuation report covered the fraudulent conveyance report as well.

The court agreed with the plaintiff. In discussing Federal Rule of Evidence 702 and *Daubert*, the court referred to "a trilogy of restrictions on expert testimony: qualification, reliability, and fit."

Here, there was no dispute that the testimony met the first two requirements, the court said. The expert was well qualified to offer an opinion on the fair market value of the seller, HTS, and the buyer on the valuation date. The "fit requirement," the court explained "goes primarily to relevance," that is, the testimony must be relevant to the legal issues in the case and assist the trier of fact in resolving the legal questions. In this case, the expert reports were "certainly relevant" to the resolution of the plaintiff's fraud and concealment claims, the court found.

Opinion heavy on assumptions. The issue was reliability of the methodology the expert used. The court rejected the defendants' proposition that the reports were separate and that one was missing a section on methodology considering the expert produced the reports within a few days of each other. At the *Daubert* hearing, the expert convincingly explained she prepared a two-part report to facilitate and expedite discovery in the case. She also explained that she intended the methodologies and approaches sections appearing in the valuation report, as well as the attached copies of the AICPA standards and treatise pages, to apply to both parts of the report.

In terms of substance, the court found the methodology the expert used to re-create HTS's financial situation and value the business accorded with accepted business valuation principles. "In short, she described her application of reliable, recognized principles of accounting and valuation analysis," the court said. It noted that determining how much weight to give a report that relied "so heavily on assumptions and is subject to so many scope limitations" was a question for the jury. As for the expert's performance during the *Daubert* hearing, the court said, while it "may have detected some confusion or non-responsiveness to several cross-examination questions, those hesitations are relevant to the witness's demeanor … on the witness stand," and, therefore, go toward the weight of the testimony, not its admissibility. The testimony was admissible in its entirety, the court found.

The plaintiff tried to use the expert testimony to have the court decide the case in its favor on summary judgment. But the court declined to go that far, finding there were too many factual disputes as to the fraud claims to resolve the case "at this juncture."

Nieman v. Nieman

Citation: 2015 Ohio App. LEXIS 5021
Date of decision: Dec. 14, 2015
Country: US
State/Jurisdiction: Ohio
Court: Court of Appeals
Type of action: Marital Dissolution
Judge: Shaw
SIC: 8011 Offices and Clinics of Doctors of Medicine (except mental health specialists, HMO medical centers, and ambulatory surgical and emergency centers)
NAICS code: 621111 Offices of Physicians (except Mental Health Specialists)

Ohio Appeals Court Clarifies Provision on Tax Affecting at Divorce

An Ohio divorce statute requires a court to consider the tax consequences of the property division. But case law says that taxes are only a proper consideration in valuing a business when they are not "speculative." Recently, the Ohio Court of Appeals reviewed a trial court's decision to tax affect even though the owner spouse did not contemplate a sale anytime soon and the distribution of assets did not require him to sell his business interests. This decision provides valuators with a test of what "too speculative" means.

Similar pretax valuations. The husband, an orthopedic surgeon, held a minority interest in four companies related to his practice. At divorce, the parties' assets were substantial, and for trial both spouses retained financial experts to determine the value of the husband's ownership stake.

The husband was 44 years old when he filed for divorce. He indicated he planned to remain in the community in which he was working at the time. He did not indicate he planned to sell his ownership stake in any of the businesses anytime soon or at any time before retiring. The record suggested he might have to sell his interest in one of the businesses when he retired. But it was unclear as to whether he would need to sell his interest in the other businesses at retirement or ever.

The appraisers' pretax valuations were close. The husband's expert calculated that the husband's interest in the four businesses before accounting for taxes was about $4.74 million. The wife's expert arrived at an aggregate value of just above $5 million.

The husband's expert also performed a valuation that considered the tax effects related to a possible sale of the ownership interests. He said he used the current tax rates. He explained that, since the tax rates and the husband's current income were known, the valuation was not based on speculation. He did not believe the tax rates would change much in the near future. Under this calculation, the value of the husband's interest dropped by over $1 million.

In support of tax affecting, the husband cited the applicable code, ORC Ann. Section 3105.171(F)(6), which provides that "the Court ... consider the tax consequences of the property division upon the respective awards to be made to each spouse."

The husband claimed "there will be some tax consequences associated with the disposition of these assets ... at the time the asset is distributed." At this particular time, he said, the parties were dividing the assets, which meant a distribution, disbursement, or transfer of assets was occurring." There was "a known set of economic circumstances and a known and determinable tax calculation as a result."

The wife's expert did not tax affect because it was "speculative" and not done as "a general practice."

The wife acknowledged the cited statutory provision but argued against factoring in the tax consequences where the asset was distributed pursuant to divorce but was not liquidated at the same time.

The trial court favored the husband's position even though "the considerations and offsets made at this time may in fact not be actually what would occur at the disposal of the asset in the future due to the changing nature of the economic conditions of the parties individually or any changing tax code."

According to the trial court, the wife's argument would make it impossible to consider the tax consequences except in a case in which there was an immediate disposition of the property. "Under the statute the Court can determine the current tax consequences and consider the same in distributing the property," the court decided.

The trial court valued the interests in the four businesses at approximately $3.3 million. The court's calculation also factored in noncompete clauses at $100,000 for two businesses. Applying a 40% tax rate to them, the court added the remaining $60,000 to the value of the two businesses. Even though the wife questioned whether it was appropriate for the trial court to value the noncompetes, she did not raise this issue on appeal. In the final analysis, the trial court deducted more than $1 million for tax consequences from the valuation of the husband's business interests.

Test for 'too speculative.' The wife appealed. The gist of her argument to the state Court of Appeals was that the taxes in this case were too speculative based on prior appeals court decisions that dealt with similar circumstances. The trial court erred when it factored the tax consequences of a potential sale of the businesses into its valuation, the wife contended.

The Ohio Court of Appeals agreed with the wife's argument. At the start of its analysis, it noted that, notwithstanding the statute, the very court in an earlier decision said: "Tax consequences of property division … awards are proper considerations … as long as those consequences are not speculative." *See Day v. Day*, 40 Ohio App. 3d 155 (1988).

The appeals court noted that cases that have found taxes were "too speculative" involved the following situations:

1. It is uncertain whether, or at what point in the future, a business will be sold;
2. It is uncertain that the tax rates will be similar in the future; and
3. A sale is not made necessary by the trial court's division of the marital assets.

Under this "logic," the appeals court said, the tax consequences in the instant case were too speculative for the trial court to factor into its valuation. The husband indicated a desire to sell his businesses at the time of retirement, but the retirement date was uncertain. And retirement likely would occur in the distant future considering the husband was only in his 40s at the time of divorce.

The trial court used the current tax rates, but doing so required it to assume the tax rates would be the same or substantially the same in the future. But, said the appeals court, by the time the husband was ready to sell his business interests, "they could be worth far more, or far less. His percentage share could have grown larger or smaller, or the capital gains tax could rise or could be abolished." Consequently, a court would "necessarily" engage in speculation if it imposed "a present-day tax-affect upon the value of the businesses in this case."

Moreover, there was no indication that the distribution of the assets required the husband to sell his businesses, the Court of Appeals found.

The husband contended that the earlier appellate court decisions erroneously cited to the "speculative" language in *Day* even though in that case the appeals court allowed the trial court to deduct future tax consequences from a retirement plan. He also cited to other cases in which he claimed Ohio appellate courts gave trial courts discretion to consider speculative tax consequences.

The Court of Appeals dismissed the husband's claims. It noted that the line of cases the husband cited related to retirement plans; as such they were not as persuasive as the cases the wife cited. The latter decisions were "directly on point and related to business valuation in particular," the court said.

Under the facts, the taxes were too speculative, the Ohio Court of Appeals concluded, ordering the trial court to recalculate the value of the husband's business interests without factoring in tax consequences of a potential sale. The appeals court added that the redetermination would require the trial court to distribute additional assets.

Pattridge v. Starks

Citation: 2016 La. App. LEXIS 315
Date of decision: Feb. 24, 2016
Country: US
State/Jurisdiction: Louisiana
Court: Court of Appeals
Type of action: Contract
Experts: Benjamin Woods (plaintiffs); none (defendant)
Judge: Drew
SIC: 1389 Oil and Gas Field Services, NEC (except construction of field gathering lines, site preparation and related construction activities performed on a contract or fee basis)
NAICS code: 213112 Support Activities for Oil and Gas Operations

Breach of Noncompete Means Damages for 'Loss Sustained' *and* Lost Profits

An economic damages case stemming from the breach of a noncompete agreement features a noteworthy discussion on the difficulty of quantifying losses where the injured company is of a "volatile nature." The plaintiff's' expert used commonly accepted valuation methods for his calculation, but the defendants' attorney, who was not an expert, suggested there was a simpler way. The trial court credited the expert's approach but modified the amount based on the defendant's objections. Interestingly, the trial and appeals courts allowed for an expansive interpretation of the noncompete both in terms of the contract's geographical reach and expiration date.

Defendant enables competition. Four investors formed a company that manufactured and sold rod guides to the oil and gas industry. They all signed an agreement that prohibited a terminated shareholder from competing with the company within 24 months of termination. The company eventually fired one of the investors, the defendant. A dissolution fight ensued that resulted in two investors (the plaintiff) buying the company's stock at auction and terminating the defendant as a shareholder in July 2013.

Subsequently, the defendant worked for another energy-related company that marketed products to many of the subject company's customers. He used proceeds from the subject company's stock auction to assist his son with forming a new company. The son's company became a direct competitor of the subject company and began operations in March 2014. The son's company was in the same building in which the defendant worked. Three of the subject's sales reps switched from selling the subject's rod guides to selling the competitor's products. For the subject company, sales in the areas the deserters covered stopped. It lost about one-third of its customers and a sizable chunk of its domestic revenue.

The subject's two owners sued the defendant, claiming his conduct violated the noncompete and damaged the company's business. The trial court found the defendant liable. It noted that the defendant's funds, obtained from the sale of the subject company's stock, helped seed the son's company and his post-termination contacts with the subject company's salespeople and customers caused both to abandon long-standing relationships with the subject company in favor of the son's company. The sales reps and their customers committed to the competitor's products even before they had any experience with those products.

The court held a separate trial to determine the damages the premature competition caused the subject company.

Nonexpert's take on damages. Only the plaintiff offered expert testimony from a CPA and credentialed business valuator. The defendant chose not to present rebuttal expert testimony or an alternative calculation of damages.

The plaintiff's expert noted that he was not hired to determine causation but to calculate damages resulting from the loss of customers. (To protect proprietary business information, the trial court sealed large parts of the expert report as well as testimony from the subject's remaining owners.)

In a pretrial report, the expert used "two generally accepted methods for determining damages to a company as a result of impaired operations." The main method was a "before and after" analysis that compared the company's performance before the alleged misconduct with its performance after the event. At trial, the expert emphasized this was "a typical model used in damages cases." It considered the company's sales history, avoidable costs, and variable expenses. As a "sanity check," he also performed a discounted future earnings analysis to compare the company's fair market value before and after the event. Both methods produced a similar result: The loss to subject was a little over $1 million.

The expert based his calculation of damages on a list of lost customers the plaintiff provided after discussing the names with a company owner. The point was to err on the side of caution and not claim a customer that should not be on the list. The expert said he compared sales to lost customers to sales to customers the plaintiff did not lose to the competitor, and he prepared a graph that showed the subject company's performance over time. The graph indicated both a significant quarter-to-quarter volatility in sales as well as a "very loose" correlation between the sales the subject company made and the price of oil. A decline in the price of oil did not directly result in a decline in sales, the expert concluded.

At trial, he testified that he first estimated lost sales for quarters for which there were actual sales data and then extrapolated the information from the fourth quarter of 2014 to the fourth quarter of 2020. To go beyond 2020 "wouldn't be meaningful … because we're discounting it at such an aggressive 28% rate," he said. Also, "2020 is far enough to kind of recover … these lost sales become less and less meaningful over time."

He also said he increased the amount of avoidable costs after his deposition to account for greater sales commissions and shipping costs. As a result, he revised the loss through 2020 to $985,000 and allowed that it might actually be as low as $934,000.

When cross-examining the expert, defense counsel claimed the proper measure of damages was "gross sales minus expenses equals net income or net profit." The plaintiff's expert responded that he had "never seen a damage report that calculated damages that way from an event. It's never been a net income number." This method was "way too simplistic," the expert said. It was not an approach he was taught nor was it included in any valuation practice guide. He also claimed it did not follow the industry standard.

The expert noted that his calculation was based on several assumptions. For example, he assumed that the subject company would never regain the sales it lost within the first year of the defendant's exit from the company. He also assumed the quarterly loss would remain consistent from 2014 through 2020. He said he calculated costs based on the current cost of production, including labor costs, but agreed the cost could be reduced. He assumed the subject company would achieve an annual 14% increase in sales even though the company's historical performance did not support this number. He said to do so was necessary because "the expectation that they will grow it back is what gives it value—any value today."

In response to the defendant's contention that the number of sales the subject claimed to have lost did not match the number of sales the competitor actually made, the expert pointed to the volatile nature of the rod guide business, which, he said, led to variation. He explained the number of sales would be more equal when averaged over time.

Trial court adjusts for risk of speculation. The trial court recognized that the plaintiff's expert was the sole expert in the case. Even though defense counsel cross-examined him rigorously, the expert's method held up. "I think his numbers are acceptable," the court said.

However, it found that the longer damages were projected into the future, the greater the degree of speculation. And even though the parties did not raise the issue of technology, the court said it needed to be taken into consideration. "There may be a point in time where the rod guide is … not even necessary or useful anymore for whatever reason." In its own words, the court "somewhat arbitrarily" decided to grant damages only through 2016—not 2020. By its recalculation of the expert's figures, damages were about $632,000, which the court rounded down to $600,000.

Appeals court declines to reinterpret noncompete. The defendant challenged the award to the plaintiff on multiple grounds. For one, it claimed the trial court erred when it allowed for compensation of losses resulting from the defendant's business activities outside the narrow geographical reach of the noncompete.

The plaintiff countered that the genesis of all the wrongful activity that led to profits the subject company lost to companies inside and outside the state was within the noncompete zone. The competitor was located in the same building in which the defendant worked after his termination. The noncompete covered that location. The competitor did not have offices anywhere else, and all of its products were manufactured and shipped from that location. All of the marketing and promotional activities occurred on behalf of an entity active in the noncompete zone. Moreover, until the defendant was found in violation of the noncompete and ordered to vacate his office, he worked exclusively out of that one location. The close proximity of the defendant to the son's company, the competitor, meant easy access to the latter's operations.

The appeals court sided with the plaintiff. It noted all the competitive activity was "primarily concentrated" in the noncompete area. It also pointed out that the defendant had failed to raise this particular objection at trial, which made it difficult to separate the harm the defendant's actions caused within the covered area from the harm caused outside the covered area at this late stage in the litigation. Therefore, the appeals court declined to limit damages based on a strict reading of the noncompete.

Another objection was that damages were too speculative and uncertain. For one, the plaintiff's expert used the wrong measure of damages. Damages should be gross profits minus expenses, the defendant contended.

The appeals court was not convinced. Although this might be an accurate statement in cases where the only issue was lost profits and where those could be established with greater certainty, here the damage to the subject company was harder to quantify, the court observed. It also emphasized that under the applicable statute an injured party may recover damage for "the loss sustained *and* the profit of which he has been deprived." In other words, the party is entitled to damages for "the loss sustained" in addition to lost profits, the court clarified.

It pointed out that the subject's quarterly sales figures were highly inconsistent, reflecting "irregularly large and small orders from customers whose needs differed depending upon their own circumstances." The expert vouched that his methodology for calculating damages was standard industry practice, it said. Also, the figures he obtained by way of two different methods "were in fairly close agreement." Here, knowing the competitor's sales did not make damages more "susceptible of mathematical precision," the court found. It noted the expert's explanation that there were many reasons for the competitor's sales numbers to be lower than expected over the short term. However, the expert also explained that, when traced over time and averaged, they would eventually align with the numbers he used in his model.

What's more, the trial court recognized the "significant and generous assumptions" the expert used to develop his damages model and substantially discounted damages by awarding only 60% of what the plaintiff asked for, the appeals court said.

The defendant further claimed it was error for the trial court to award damages for time beyond the expiration of the noncompete.

At trial, one of the owners and the plaintiff's expert claimed the date specified in the agreement became almost meaningless once the defendant's improper actions enabled the competitor's early entry into the market. The expert extended damages past the end of the noncompete because the premature competition did not give the subject company sufficient time to prepare for the competition. Had there been no early competition, the expiration date would be "a big date," the expert said. But since there was a violation of the noncompete, the agreement's expiration date was no longer important; "the damage had already been done."

Approving of this argument, the appeals court found it was not legal error for the trial court to award damages for lost sales beyond the agreement's expiration date. The evidence showed that customers lost to the competitor were not likely to return to the subject company. The court noted again that damages in this case were not easy to measure precisely, and the trial court already "gave the defendant a substantial break" by denying damages for all of the years the plaintiff claimed. The appeals court upheld the award.

Pearson v. Westervelt Co.

Citation: 2016 Ala. Civ. App. LEXIS 17
Date of decision: Jan. 8, 2016
Country: US
State/Jurisdiction: Alabama
Court: Court of Civil Appeals
Type of action: Dissenting Shareholder
Experts: None (plaintiff); Dr. B. Perry Woodside (defendant)
Judge: Thompson
SIC: 2611 Pulp Mills (pulp mills producing paper except newsprint)
NAICS code: 322121 Paper (except Newsprint) Mills

Demand for Executive Compensation Data Lacks 'Proper Purpose'

A recent Alabama dispute over the right to inspect corporate records turned on the question of what information the plaintiff needed to value her minority interest in a closely held corporation. Besides the company's financial statements, she demanded to see the compensation records of certain officers of the company, purportedly to determine whether there was waste and mismanagement. The company resisted. After hearing expert testimony from a business valuator on behalf of the company, the trial court rebuffed the plaintiff's demand, finding it was not based on a "proper purpose." The plaintiff appealed.

Bad blood. The company (defendant) was a 132-year old papermaking business that has since become active in land resource management. It is incorporated in Delaware but has its principal place of business in Alabama. The plaintiff was an attorney and the great-granddaughter of the company's founder. The company's current chairman of the board was the plaintiff's cousin. The plaintiff held a minority interest in the company in her own name and by way of two trusts that held some company stock. Earlier, she served for about 20 years as an active member of the company's board of directors.

Sometime in 2011, shortly before the records dispute unfolded, she was one of several plaintiffs who unsuccessfully sued the company, including her cousin in his capacity as chairman of the board, over the company's approval of a reorganization plan. Also in 2011, she advertised in *The Wall Street Journal* that she was interested in selling a 33% interest in the company. It appears nothing came of her plan.

After the resolution of the litigation, the plaintiff sent a letter to the company demanding to see its most recent financial information and compensation data for four officers, including information pertaining to her cousin. The company provided certain financial data but not the compensation information. In response, the plaintiff sued to compel access to the information, citing Alabama law and the Delaware statute on books and records, 8 Del. C. § 220(b). While litigation was pending, the company was willing to provide her with the total compensation figure but not the individual compensation records.

Allegations of excessive compensation. Almost four years later, the trial court conducted a hearing on the matter. The plaintiff did not present expert testimony on valuation, but the company did. In her testimony, the plaintiff essentially gave two reasons for why she needed the compensation information. One reason was to value her stake in the company; a related reason was that the officers she targeted were overpaid, which deprived shareholders such as her of additional distributions and by extension an increase in the value of her shares.

In her testimony, the plaintiff seemed particularly preoccupied with the compensation her cousin received as chairman of the board. At the same time, she never explained why her demand letter also targeted the other three officers. The latter were not the highest paid executives in the company. She said that the reason why she had not tried to sell her interest since 2011 was because she had not been allowed to review the records she had demanded.

She said she knew the company had hired Mercer—nationally recognized compensation consultants—to determine the appropriate salary ranges. She claimed that in 2007 her cousin's compensation exceeded the proposed range by 100%. She said as a shareholder she also knew the company had hired Duff & Phelps—a global valuation firm and corporate financial advisor—to value the company. She said the shareholder information advised that the Duff & Phelps valuation was for the purpose of "planning and for estate tax purposes" only.

Finally, she claimed that, if she were to obtain access to the compensation records, she would find information on the Internet on compensation for similarly situated executives to determine whether the subject company overpaid officers.

The company retained an expert in business valuation to refute the plaintiff's claim that the contested records were necessary to value her minority interest in the company. He said he had reviewed the financial records the company had made available to the plaintiff and had discussed corporate governance issues with an officer.

He said that the plaintiff's claim about possible excessive compensation and its effect on dividends might be an issue in terms of valuing the company under the income approach. But he thought it would assist only in valuing a controlling interest. A minority interest, the expert said, "is not valued using a 'normalization' adjustment"; rather, he said, a minority shareholder's interest would be valued based "only" on the financial information from the company's operation. The financial data the company provided to the plaintiff contained the information necessary to value her interest.

On cross-examination, the expert said the Duff & Phelps valuation of the company did not adjust for excessive compensation to officers; therefore, the expert surmised the valuation firm considered the amounts paid to executives reasonable. However, he admitted that he had not personally reviewed the Duff & Phelps report but had relied on representations from the subject company's chief financial officer.

Moreover, the expert noted that Duff & Phelps valued the company under the fair market value standard of value. Under that standard, a minority interest "is often discounted to reflect the absence of a controlling interest in the company and the lack of marketability of the shares," the expert explained.

In contrast, he said, in a valuation under the fair value standard of value, the discounts are removed. But, he added, "minority interests are not commonly offered for sale according to their 'fair value,' i.e., without minority discounts." Paying excessive compensation to some officers "may or may not be" relevant to the fair value determination of the plaintiff's stock.

He said the company had internal structures in place to prevent excess compensation to officers, and it used well-regarded outside consultants to determine compensation and to value the company.

Valuation not the 'true purpose.' The trial court sided with the defendant. It said it was not convinced that the plaintiff's "true purpose" for demanding the compensation records was to value her shares and investigate possible waste and mismanagement at the company. The plaintiff did not limit her demand for inspection of the corporate books to her cousin's compensation records, the trial court noted. Instead, she included documents related to the compensation of three other individuals without having reason to suspect these officers were overpaid and without actually determining who were the company's most highly paid executives.

Although the valuation of a person's shares qualifies as a legitimate reason for a records inspection request, the court found in this case "the request was made merely to harass the company" and the individuals whose compensations were the subject of the request.

It observed that the plaintiff, who was not a financial expert, failed to explain how she could use the compensation information to determine the value of her shares. She also failed to offer expert testimony about the effect of unreasonable executive compensation on the value of her minority interest.

In contrast, the court credited the defense expert testimony that said the information was not necessary. This "highly qualified" expert based his opinion "on the non-controlling nature of [the plaintiff's] minority interest" as well as the adoption of principles of corporate governance that would ensure management acted in the best interests of the shareholders, the court said. Accordingly, the company obtained annual valuations from an independent, internationally renowned valuation firm that did not adjust for unreasonable compensation and received assessments of executive compensation by nationally known and respected compensation consultants.

After the trial court refused the plaintiff's request to compel disclosure of the compensation information, she appealed.

The state Court of Civil Appeals affirmed without further discussion. It simply noted that there was no evidence that the trial court had erred when it decided the plaintiff did not have a proper purpose to seek the requested documents.

PECO Logistics, LLC v. Walnut Inv. Partners, L.P.

Citation: 2015 Del. Ch. LEXIS 311
Date of decision: Dec. 30, 2015
Country: US
State/Jurisdiction: Delaware
Court: Court of Chancery of Delaware
Type of action: Contract
Experts: Duff & Phelps (plaintiff); N/A (defendants)
Judge: Bouchard
SIC: 2448 Wood Pallets and Skids
NAICS code: 321920 Wood Container and Pallet Manufacturing

Value Determination Accords With Parties' Contract, Chancery Says

Investors in a company committed themselves to having a nationally recognized valuation firm determine the value of their units in accordance with a specified formula. Displeased with the valuation, they subsequently claimed the appraiser made problematic judgment calls and the company's board made bad-faith business decisions that decreased the valuation. The Delaware Court of Chancery (Chancellor Bouchard) saw no reason to "second-guess" the valuator's work product.

Valuation-related agreement. The plaintiff, PECO Logistics LLC, owned an equity interest in PECO Pallet Holdings, a company that rented pallets to manufacturers for the shipping of groceries and consumer goods. The defendants were related companies that owned preferred units of PECO Logistics.

In the context of a merger involving the PECO companies, in March 2011, the plaintiff and the defendants agreed that the plaintiff would purchase all of the defendants' preferred units within three years of the agreement, following notice that the defendants wanted to sell. The agreement required the plaintiff to retain a valuation firm to determine the fair market value of the defendants' put units.

In terms of the valuation methodology, the agreement provided that "there shall be no minority or non-marketability discount applied." Also, "fair market value" meant an arm's-length sale to an unrelated third party. And, for purposes of calculating the "total equity value," the value of the assets would be subject to an EBITDA collar to ensure that the value of the assets was at least 6.5x but no more than 7.5 times the company's "EBITDA less Maintenance Capex" for year-end 2013. Further, the resulting number was to be reduced by the company's obligations and liabilities. Finally, the resulting amount would be run through a waterfall calculation to determine the amount allocable to each preferred unit.

Most importantly, both parties agreed to be bound by the determination of the valuation firm as to the price of the put units. The agreement did not provide for judicial or any other form of review of the valuator's determination.

After the company furnished the defendants with a calculation of the value of their units based on its understanding of the valuation methodology, the defendants rejected the result. At the same time, the defendants gave notice that they wanted to exercise their put right. The defendants' notice included language that the defendants reserved the right to participate in the fair market value determination, to confer with the valuation firm on the value determination, and to object to the firm's valuation.

Judgment calls. Upon receipt of the notice, the plaintiff considered three valuation firms before settling on one, a highly reputed national firm. Two months later, the valuation firm submitted a report that explained the key assumptions underlying the valuation and stated the final value.

Specifically, the valuation firm decided to use June 1, 2014, as the valuation date because the most recent financial information available when it started its work was from May 2014.

The firm based the fair market value of the plaintiff's assets on the value of the company's sole asset, PECO Pallet. Because the plaintiff was a holding company with no operations or income, the valuator applied the EBITDA collar "as a limitation of the enterprise value of PECO Pallet (the operating company), before deducting debt to conclude on a value of the equity which is owned by the company [PECO Logistics]."

The firm pointed out that it used the term "fair market value" as defined by the U.S. Tax Code, that is, "the price at which property would change hands between a willing buyer and a willing seller, neither being under any compulsion to buy or sell, and both having reasonable knowledge of relevant facts."

And the firm explained that it used a combination of an income approach—discounted cash flow method—and a market approach—comparable companies and precedent transactions analyses—to determine the value of the operating company, PECO Pallet.

The valuation firm determined that the operating company's total enterprise value was about $275 million. Since that value was higher than the cap under the EBITDA collar, it reduced the value to approximately $209 million—7.5 times the "2013 EBITDA less Maintenance Capex" of $27.95 million. It then subtracted about $114.4 million of debt and made some other minor adjustments to arrive at a total equity value available for distribution to the unit holders of about $93.12 million.

The defendants rejected the valuation report and refused to transfer their units to the plaintiff.

Consequently, the plaintiff asked the Delaware Court of Chancery for a declaration that it had complied with the agreement's valuation provisions and that the defendants were bound by the valuation firm's determination. The defendants, in turn, claimed the plaintiff violated the obligation of good faith and fair dealing.

The defendants also raised several arguments in defense of their refusal to honor the valuation agreement. For example, they said that, by accepting the defendants' put notice, the plaintiff in fact agreed to honor the defendants' reserved right to weigh in on the valuation and to object to the valuation firm's determination. According to the defendants, the put notice in effect modified the valuation agreement, which provided no right and no mechanism to contest the valuator's calculation.

The court disagreed with the defendants. As a matter of law, there was no modification of the valuation agreement, it said. The parties were bound by it. The court observed that all the defendants did was "reserve" pre-existing rights they claimed to have but did not actually have and for which they gave up nothing in return.

Moreover, the defendants attacked three decisions—judgment calls—the valuation firm made in applying the valuation formula. One concerned the valuator's choice of the valuation date, a second concerned the deduction of long-term debt, and a third concerned the application of the EBITDA collar to the EDITDA of the operating company, PECO Pallet. As the defendants saw it, whenever there was ambiguity in the agreement as to what to do, the valuation firm took a position that benefited the plaintiff rather than the defendants.

The court found all of these objections were baseless. In terms of the valuation date, the defendants averred the correct date was Dec. 31, 2013, which was the date used for applying the EBITDA collar. They claimed the valuator's decision to use June 1, 2014, added an additional $14 million in debt to the liabilities and, therefore, decreased the valuation.

But the court noted the defendants failed to point to any provision in the agreement that mandated the use of Dec. 31, 2013, as the valuation date. The agreement merely required that the "fair market value" of put units be calculated "as of the date of valuation." Since the defendants exercised their put right by way of their notice, dated May 2014, the valuator made a reasonable decision to use a June 2014 valuation date to include the latest financial information available to it. That information was prepared as of May 2014. The court pointed out that the defendants admitted that the valuator's choice of date was reasonable but tried to argue it was "the lesser of the two reasonable explanations." The court further said that, even though the agreement specified that for purposes of the EBITDA collar certain multiple calculations had to be as of December 2013, the parties were free to select a different date to value the preferred units, the court concluded.

The court also concluded the valuator's treatment of long-term debt was entirely consistent with the agreement. The contract expressly required that the units' fair market value be derived from the company's total equity value, which meant accounting for all of the company's obligations and liabilities to arrive at the amount "hypothetically available to distribute to the unitholders for purposes of determining the value of the Put Units."

Lastly, the court rejected the defendants' EBITDA collar argument. It noted that in their briefing the defendants acknowledged that applying the valuation collar to the plaintiff, the holding company, "would have reduced the Company's valuation to zero, which would have produced a meaningless valuation." The reason, the court said, was that the plaintiff's only asset was its equity interest in the operating subsidiary, PECO Pallet. To avoid "the absurd result of a zero valuation," the valuator made the rational decision to apply the collar to the operating subsidiary's EBITDA.

No review process. The court pointed out that, to the extent there were judgment calls, the valuation firm, which was a third party chosen in accordance with the parties' agreement, made them. "Critically in that regard, both the Company and [the defendants] expressly agreed that they 'shall be bound by the determination of the Valuation Firm ... with respect to the Put Price as established by the Valuation Firm,'" the court observed. "When parties to a contract agree to be bound by a contractually established valuation methodology, this Court will respect their right to order their affairs as they wish and refrain from second-guessing the substantive determination of value." Had the agreement provided for judicial review, the court might have entertained questions as to the reasonableness of the valuator's assumptions, the court said. But, since no such provision existed, "the Court will not take mere allegations of ambiguity about the valuation methodology as an invitation to circumvent the structure of the deal to substitute its own judgment for that of the valuation firm."

The defendants' claim that the plaintiff somehow breached the implied covenant of good faith and fair dealing also had no traction with the court. The Chancery observed that the defendants failed to allege any facts that raised doubts about the propriety of the valuation. The valuation firm was a nationally recognized firm that the plaintiff's board vetted in accordance with the agreement. There was no question as to the valuator's independence, and there was no evidence that the plaintiff engaged in conduct that tainted the valuation process, the court said.

It dismissed the defendants' allegation that the company acted in bad faith when it incurred a $50 million long-term debt in the second half of 2013 and an additional $14 million in the first five months of 2014. The company was in a business that required significant capital investment when carried out on a large scale, the court noted. Both parties agreed that the company had to buy a lot of pallets and store them so they were available to customers anytime, anywhere. Also, when the defendants exercised their put rights, they were aware of the company's 2013 debt. In terms of the 2014 debt, the valuation firm, not the company, decided to consider this debt by using a June 2014 valuation date. The defendants admitted that the valuation date decision was reasonable.

No trial ensued. Based on the parties' motions alone, the Chancery decided in favor of the plaintiff. It declared that, in valuing the defendants' put units, the plaintiff fully complied with the parties' agreement. Therefore, the defendants were bound by the valuation firm's determination of value.

Perez v. Bruister (Bruister II)

Citation: 2016 U.S. App. LEXIS 8046
Date of decision: May 3, 2016
Country: US
State/Jurisdiction: Federal/5th Circuit
Court: United States Court of Appeals
Type of action: ESOP
Experts: Z. Christopher Mercer (plaintiffs); Dana Messina (DOL/plaintiffs); Gregory Range (defendants)
Judge: Jones
SIC: 4899 Communications Services, NEC (satellite communications)
NAICS code: 517410

In Unusual ESOP Case, 5th Circuit Validates FMV Computation

In a gnarled ESOP case, the 5th Circuit Court of Appeals largely upheld the trial court's findings that the plan's trustees violated their fiduciary duties and engaged in a prohibited transaction. An appraiser's discreditable conduct enabled the wrongdoing, which resulted in the ESOP's overpaying for the company stock. In its decision, the trial court said the remedy questions were harder to resolve than the liability questions, and it suggested its valuation-related findings might be "vulnerable" on appeal. The findings gave rise to the parties' appeals, but the decision withstood appellate scrutiny. In fact, the appeals court commended the trial court on employing a "thoughtful" approach that "was founded in established valuation methodology."

Backstory. The owner of a closely held company that installed and serviced satellite television equipment for its sole client, Direct TV, was looking for a way to divest himself of the company. In a series of transactions that took place between 2002 and 2005, he sold 100% of the company's shares to its employees by way of an employee stock ownership plan (ESOP). The company stopped operating in 2008, after negotiating a deal with Direct TV under which the latter assumed the company's debt and acquired its assets in a foreclosure sale.

In 2010, the DOL and two plan participants filed separate lawsuits in federal district court raising essentially the same claims related to three of the ESOP transactions. In each transaction, the plan bought company stock through an employee stock ownership trust (ESOT) for which the owner-seller and two persons who had a close working relationship with the owner served as trustees. Two of the three transactions involved a combination of cash payments and transaction loans.

The trustees based the share price on valuations an appraiser, who also was closely aligned with the owner-seller-cum-trustee, had performed. Both lawsuits alleged the trustees paid too much for the stock because the appraiser's valuations did not reflect the fair market value (FMV) of the stock.

After consolidating the suits, the district court conducted a 19-day bench trial to determine liability and the applicable remedies, if any. The crux of the matter was whether the appraiser and the trustees were truly independent and looking out for the interests of the ESOP and whether it was reasonable for the trustees to rely on the appraiser's valuations. The trial court answered no to both questions.

The district court awarded over $4.5 million in "equitable restitution" (damages) based on its determination of overpayment related to each of the three transactions. Overpayment, the court decided, was a function of the contract price and the stock's fair market value on each transaction date. For its FMV determination, the court considered the testimony of three noted valuation experts retained by the plaintiffs, the DOL, and the defendants. The court considered all experts equally credible. Different experts used different methods, different assumptions, and different estimates, and they reached different conclusions. But they all used multiple approaches to produce several FMV estimates on the transaction dates, the court pointed out. To arrive at a final value determination, or range of values, they all averaged or weighted the results. "This method tempered the outliers that some methods produced," the court observed with approval.

Accordingly, the district court took a number of valuations resulting from different methods and assumptions and averaged them. It weighted the results the defendants' expert achieved at 50% and the much lower valuations the DOL's expert and the individual plaintiffs' expert proposed at 25% each. It entirely disregarded the appraiser's valuations made at the time of the transactions. (An expanded discussion of *Perez v. Bruister*, 2014 U.S. Dist. LEXIS 148314 (Oct. 16, 2014), is available at *BVLaw*.)

Liability review. The defendants appealed the liability and remedy findings of the district court, and the DOL cross-appealed on the remedy. The 5th Circuit Court of Appeals performed an extensive review. Its dense decision includes the following key findings.

Breach of fiduciary duties. One of the claims was breach of the duty of loyalty. A threshold issue at trial was whether the owner-seller met the definition of "fiduciary" under ERISA. The defendants argued that, even though he was a named fiduciary of the ESOP, he abstained from all votes related to the transactions and, therefore, was not a fiduciary.

The district court found that under the "two hats" legal doctrine he was. He "exercised fiduciary authority," the court said, providing the following examples:

- He fired the first appraiser for being too thorough;
- He hired a replacement appraiser who was beholden to him;
- He influenced the valuations;
- He made his preferences known to the two other trustees;
- He actively participated in all meetings concerning the subject transactions; and
- His personal lawyer was deeply involved in ESOP decision making and impressed on the appraiser the need to "tweak" proposed valuations to ensure a higher price for the owner-seller.

The appeals court said the district court "applied the law correctly." In a footnote, the 5th Circuit pointed out the owner-seller's personal lawyer "plays multiple roles in the story of this litigation."

His involvement in the ESOP led to his being a material witness in the case. At the same time, he was the lawyer of record on appeal. "The reader may judge the prudence of [the lawyer's] 'multiple hats' service, and whether different counsel may have helped [the owner-seller] avoid the trouble he is now in."

The duty of loyalty requires the fiduciaries "to keep the interests of the beneficiaries foremost in their minds." The district court found, and the appeals court affirmed, that the trustees breached it "from start to finish." In addition to the misconduct listed earlier, the owner-seller caused the appraiser to show valuation drafts to him *before* sending them to the buyers, i.e., the ESOP trustees, the court stressed. He also cut counsel for the ESOP out of all valuation-related communications and changed assumptions and figures for the appraiser to reach a higher valuation.

The other two trustees acknowledged a concern for the owner-seller's interest, and one of them testified she based her decisions on what "was best for everyone, including [the owner-seller]."

The defendants argued on appeal that the appraiser's valuations, and by extension the price the ESOP paid, proved not to be inflated when compared to the FMV the defendants' expert at trial proposed—which the district court at least in part accepted in setting damages. Therefore, the defendants did not breach their duty of loyalty by relying on the appraiser's valuations.

The appeals court rejected this "all's well that ends well" argument, noting that, as concerns ERISA liability, the key question is whether there was a conflict of interest and the trustees avoided it by making decisions with "an eye single to the interests of the participants and beneficiaries." Here, the trustees did not separate the owner-seller's personal interests from the valuation process to avoid a conflict of interest," the 5th Circuit decided.

Engaging in a prohibited transaction. Under ERISA, a fiduciary must not cause the plan to engage in the "sale or exchange ... of any property between the plan and a party in interest." But, even if this type of violation occurs, the prohibited transaction rule does not apply if the defendant can show that the sale "is for adequate consideration," i.e., "for the FMV of the asset," as determined in good faith by the fiduciary. Fiduciaries may point to expert guidance to show there was a good faith investigation.

How justifiable reliance on an expert advisor is depends on a host of factors, including the expert's reputation and experience, the thoroughness of the expert's work, the appropriateness of the expert's methods and assumptions, and whether there is support for his or her opinion.

The appeals court pointed out that an independent appraisal is not a guarantee that the fiduciaries satisfied their duty of care. Whether the fiduciaries acted with care, is, in turn, an open-ended inquiry because the fiduciary's responsibility is open-ended.

Here, the district court found the trustees failed to meet the duty of care standard when it came to reliance on the appraiser. The trustees did not sufficiently examine the appraiser's checkered professional past, and they overlooked communications that showed the appraiser was working in concert with the owner-seller's lawyer to set the stock value. The trustees themselves failed to relay important information regarding the company to the appraiser, and they did not properly review the appraiser's ultimate conclusions.

The appeals court essentially affirmed the district court's finding. It observed that the defendants "made no effort at trial to validate [the appraiser's] work," which the district court found to be "not credible." According to the appeals court, "[t]he flawed valuation process, in other words, led to an insupportable fair market value calculation, notwithstanding that it coincidentally fell within a range later estimated by reliable methodology during the *damages* portion of this case." The defendants failed to show they paid adequate consideration. Consequently, ERISA prohibited the subject transactions, the appeals court concluded.

Remedy review. On appeal, the defendants and the DOL gave different reasons why the district court's remedy determination in their view was defective.

Rescission. According to the DOL, the district court should have rescinded the transactions because it was impossible to determine the stock's FMV at the times of the sales. This drastic action would require the return of the entire purchase price paid by the ESOP.

The 5th Circuit disagreed. "There may be some cases in which rescission is the proper recovery or FMV cannot easily be determined, but this is not one," the appeals court said. In denying rescission, the district court did not abuse its discretion.

'Hypothetical' expenses. The parties objected to different aspects of the district court's computation of FMV. For example, the DOL's expert decided the company's financial statements were unreliable because they failed to adhere to generally accepted accounting principles (GAAP). Therefore, he used the actual revenue numbers appearing on the company's financial statements but used industry average numbers for comparable companies to estimate expenses and profits.

The defendants claimed the district court erred when it relied on the DOL expert's "hypothetical" expense figures.

The appeals court saw it differently. It noted that the defendants' expert himself used a guideline public company approach for one of his valuations. Therefore, just as the DOL's expert used "hypothetical" expense figures, the defendants' expert used *comparable* expense figures based on other companies, the court emphasized.

In an aside, the court noted "*all* valuation methods use projections of future income in some form, which would necessarily be 'hypothetical' and not actual information. It is not wrong to rely on these sorts of projections if they are done correctly and have a sound basis."

Most importantly, the 5th Circuit said, the district court's averaging the different valuation results "blunted" the effect of any problem resulting from the methodology the DOL's expert employed.

Company debt. The defendants faulted the district court for not making a finding about the company's outstanding debt on the date of each transaction.

The three experts used "dramatically" different debt figures in their FMV determinations.

The DOL and the plaintiffs' experts looked to the company's financial statements to determine debt. On appeal, the defendants equated this to looking only at the discredited appraiser's valuations, whereas their expert relied on the company's debt amortization schedule. Since the district court rejected the appraiser's valuations, it erred in accepting the opposing experts' "inherently flawed valuations," the defendants said.

The appeals court was not persuaded. "None of the approaches was necessarily incorrect, much less superior," the court said. It noted that the district court's "averaging process" took into account differences in valuation methodology.

Averaging expert valuations. The defendants and the DOL objected to the district court's "averaging process," whereas the plaintiffs defended it.

The defendants contended the result of the averaging was a valuation that was "not presented in evidence." In other words, the court should have accepted only one expert's valuation: the defense expert's.

The appeals court disagreed. Prior decisions "frequently accepted an average of expert valuations or estimates falling within a range of evidence offered," the court said.

The DOL objected because the averaging meant the district court had to "reconcile greatly divergent estimates." Specifically, it meant taking into account the defense expert's valuation, which the DOL thought was based on the wrong assumption that at the relevant time the company was a growth company. The DOL's and the plaintiffs' experts treated it as a "no growth company."

The appeals court said the district court knew how the defendants' expert arrived at his assumption and was free to accept or dismiss his testimony. Ultimately, it decided that the pessimistic projections the opposing experts offered would offset the defense expert's overly optimistic, "though not completely incredible" assumption. Overall, the district court took a "thoughtful approach to a complex question," rooted in accepted valuation methods, the appeals court said.

Sales price. One of the defendants' major objections to the sales price computation had to do with the transactions that involved cash and loans. Essentially, the company stock was placed in a suspense account and released as the ESOP paid off the loans. The defendants argued the damages calculation should have been based not on the contract price but on the price the ESOP actually paid.

For example, the contract price based on 100% debt financed was over $10.5 million, but the ESOP's cash payments of principal and interest were only about $762,000. The court arrived at an FMV of nearly $7.2 million. As the defendants saw it, until the ESOP paid at least $7.2 million, the plaintiffs had no damages claim. To base damages on the unpaid debt would result in a windfall for the plaintiffs, the defendants maintained.

The appeals court disagreed. "Every court to consider this question has rejected the Defendants' contention that the proper measure of recovery excludes the debt that remains unpaid or is later forgiven," it said, citing to a string of district and appeals court decisions from various jurisdictions. Even if the debt was not all paid off, there were damages to the plan participants, the court observed. If the ESOP had not assumed debt for overpriced company stock, "it could have made other, more fruitful investments."

The court clarified that damages could only include interest on the debt "to the extent that it was wrongly paid due to an inflated purchase price." Here, the district court's methodology followed this principle, the appeals court said, affirming the lower court's damages findings.

Post-Confirmation Comm. for Small Loans, Inc. v. Martin

Citation: 2016 U.S. Dist. LEXIS 44270
Date of decision: March 31, 2016
Country: US
State/Jurisdiction: Federal/Georgia
Court: United States District Court
Type of action: Bankruptcy
Experts: James Hart (plaintiff); Christopher S. Edwards (defendants)
Judge: Sands Sr.
SIC: 6141 Personal Credit Institutions (except installment sales finance, industrial nondeposit banks, and credit card issuing)
NAICS code: 522291 Consumer Lending

Daubert Flexible as to Solvency Determination for Multiple Debtor Entities

Pretrial motions in a bankruptcy case raised many substantive valuation issues, but, perhaps more important, begged the question of what it is the court decides when ruling on the admissibility of expert opinions. Both parties' experts provided solvency analyses in a case that involved a debtor parent and its debtor subsidiaries. The experts had fundamental disagreements on methodology, including whether or not to determine solvency on a consolidated basis, whether GAAP-based financials were an appropriate basis for the determination, and whether upward balance sheet adjustments were defensible under the facts of the case.

Fraudulent transfer claims. The case revolved around a group of corporate entities that provided small loans to individuals with limited access to credit. The decedent had formed the parent company, The Money Tree (TMT), in 1987, and eventually organized numerous corporate affiliates of TMT in other states.

By 2000, the entities had run out of money. To keep operating, they raised funds by selling various debt instruments to investors. The debtors filed for Chapter 11 bankruptcy in December 2011. Their reorganization plan was confirmed in May 2013.

Prior to his death, the decedent, aware of exposure to legal claims against him and his heirs related to the way the businesses were run, also set up several trusts. The decedent's estate, family members, and other insiders, who were officers and directors in the various businesses, were the defendants. The plaintiff, the Post-Confirmation Committee for Small Loans, represented the debtor enterprises, including in matters of litigation. The Committee sued, claiming certain transactions involving the debtor entities and other entities the defendants controlled or owned were avoidable fraudulent transfers.

For recovery purposes, the issue was whether the debtors were insolvent at the time of the transfers. Both parties relied on well-qualified experts to support their positions, and both parties filed dueling *Daubert* motions in which they asked the court to exclude the opposing expert's testimony.

Strong position against GAAP. The defendants' expert was a CPA and certified valuation analyst. For 27 years, he had practiced in the areas of audit, tax, forensic examination, valuation, and litigation.

In his initial report, he analyzed the solvency of TMT on a consolidated basis. He considered SEC filings, including TMT's original and restated annual and quarterly financials, as well as the plaintiff's complaint and TMT's prospectuses and consolidated financial statements from 2000-2002. He ignored subsidiary-level financial statements and the sworn testimony of the debtors' former CFO.

He objected to using generally accepted accounting principles (GAAP), declaring them to be "unsuitable for use in determining the 'value' of a company and is not indicative of the actual value of the company's assets." Instead of considering the actual values of an entity's assets, liabilities, and equities, GAAP "requires the presentation of capital assets at historical costs," he explained. Also, because of GAAP's conservative approach, the value of other components such as a business's investments, accounts receivables, loan portfolio, and goodwill tended to be lower. He contrasted GAAP with the International Financial Reporting Standards (IFRS), which he said allowed for valuation of assets based on a fair value standard. (The defendants subsequently clarified that their expert did not rely on IFRS to value TMT's assets and liabilities.)

The defendants' expert decided a valuation based on the fair value standard of value required upward balance sheet adjustments in this case. The assets "undoubtedly" would have had greater than book value, he said, because of TMT's "proven ability to produce positive cash flows and its name recognition." He decided to add almost $3 million in goodwill for the years 2008, 2009, and 2010, after acknowledging the debtors had removed nearly $1 million in goodwill from their books in 2008. He did not give a reason as to the other two years. He added nearly $8 million to TMT's actual bad debt recoveries, finding the credit loss reserves numbers in the company's prior financial statements were "overly conservative" and did not reflect the true value of the company's assets.

In a hypothetical, he considered how the company might fare if its management considered selling the business despite its reported net deficit in stockholder equity. For this comparative transactions analysis, he considered a U.K. lending company, a Canadian lender, and a smaller U.S. lender. He noted that, in each case, the company sold for more than the book value of its total assets. Based on the analysis, he found TNT would have sold for 0.99 to 2.06 times its total assets, which would suggest solvency from 2003 to 2010. The multipliers were reasonable, he said, particularly when one considered TMT's established infrastructure and customer base.

He also said any acquiring entity would pay at least a 10% premium on the company's loan portfolio "merely for the opportunity to continue the relationship with the existing customers." Without further explanation, he decided to apply a 15% premium. Ultimately, he added over $71 million to the company's assets between 2003 and 2010.

He found that the company was balance sheet solvent until the fall of 2007. It ultimately became insolvent as of the fiscal year ending September 2008. The company was "balance sheet" insolvent as of the year ending September 2009 and during all of the following years and remained a "going concern" through 2010, he stated.

No to any upward adjustments. The plaintiff's expert was equally accomplished. A CPA and credentialed business valuator, he also was certified in the areas of insolvency and restructuring, financial forensics, and fraud examination. He had practiced for over 30 years and written and taught about subjects in his areas of expertise.

He discussed the solvency of each of the debtor entities and their nondebtor affiliates. He reviewed TMT's initial and amended SEC filings, consolidating financial statements, restated trial balances, and audited work papers and schedules. The debtors' SEC filings were prepared in accordance with GAAP.

The expert's report took the reader through each fiscal year, from 2001 to 2012, of TMT's and its subsidiaries' consolidated financial statements. The expert compared the company's SEC filings and pointed out where balances matched and did not match as to total assets, income, interest expenses, shareholders' equities or deficits.

After sifting through the parent company's consolidated financial statements, he was able to compile the company's rising shareholder deficits. He found that in the year ending September 2001, TMT's shareholders' deficit was about $1.6 million. By the time, the company filed for bankruptcy, in late 2011, the deficit had increased to about $62.4 million. He determined shareholders' equities and deficits for the individual subsidiaries and showed that over the years all subsidiaries became entirely dependent on the parent company for their funding. He said the result was that TMT, the parent, provided large intercompany lines of credit to its subsidiaries. This drain, along with "incurred increasing annual net losses, interest expense ..., and shareholders' deficit," impeded TMT's ability to make a profit on a consolidated basis, he said.

Moreover, he stated that the parent company's mode of operation, which was to attract new investors and rely on new debt issuances to repay existing debt holders and fund operations, "together with its large and growing losses and deficits, mirrored certain ... characteristics of [a] Ponzi scheme."

The plaintiff's expert determined "with a reasonable degree of professional certainty" when each of the debtors became continuously insolvent. The parent company became insolvent in the fiscal year ending in September 2001, and the last debtor entity became insolvent by the fiscal year ending in June 2008, he concluded.

Rebuttal testimony. In a rebuttal opinion, the defense expert criticized the plaintiff expert's decision to rely on subsidiary information and determine solvency on an individual subsidiary basis.

There were numerous reasons for why solvency in this case should be considered on a consolidated basis, he claimed. The consolidated statements were "inherently more reliable" than the subsidiary financial information because they were statements filed with the SEC and were uniformly available. He said TMT's audits were done on a consolidated level, investors invested in the parent company rather than the subsidiaries, there was significant intercompany debt among subsidiaries and between subsidiaries and the parent company, and the subsidiaries expected that debt owed to the parent company would be forgiven.

He also objected to the opposing expert's reliance on GAAP to determine the fair value of assets for the reasons he had stated in his initial report.

For its part, the plaintiff intended to use its expert's initial report also as a rebuttal to the defense expert's reports.

A matter of reliability not persuasiveness. The primary reason for excluding the defense expert's testimony, the plaintiff said, was that he did not examine solvency on a subsidiary level. Focusing exclusively on the solvency of the parent company, the defense expert opinions were unhelpful to the trier of fact.

Further, the plaintiff contended the opposing expert considered irrelevant and misleading evidence (presumably the IFRS) and made arbitrary and speculative adjustments to TMT's financial statements.

In discussing Federal Rule of Evidence 702 and *Daubert* and related cases, the court noted "the Court's focus will strictly be on the reliability of the expert's testimony and not persuasiveness of arguments or 'whether it fits within the narrow confines of lawyer-urged litmus tests.'" (citation omitted)

The court also pointed out that a ruling on a *Daubert* motion "is merely considering the admissibility of expert opinion." The decision does not represent a ruling on the substantive issue: whether a debtor entity was solvent or insolvent.

In terms of the defense expert opinion, the court noted there were "legitimate concerns" about providing an expert opinion on the solvency of the debtors on a consolidated basis. In fact, the court found that "solvency should be determined on an individual subsidiary basis where the claim requires a solvency determination as to an individual Debtor or Debtors," which was the case here. But, rather than excluding the defense expert opinion completely, the court allowed the expert to speak to the solvency of TMT on a consolidated basis but said he could not discuss the solvency of the individual debtors on a subsidiary level.

As for the plaintiff's other objections, the court said it sufficed that the defendants had stated their expert had not relied on IFRS to reach his conclusions. The court agreed that some of the defense expert's goodwill adjustment lacked support or a rationale. At the same time, it found the bad debt recovery adjustment was more reliable. The court said concerns over the expert's comparable transactions analysis went to the weight of the testimony rather than its admissibility. Similarly, the expert's unexplained use of a 15% premium was a proper question for trial.

In sum, the court decided the adversary system was the way to "properly vet[]" the expert opinion.

Expert's work 'careful' and 'well-reasoned.' The defendants' arguments for exclusion of the plaintiff's expert focused on the expert's use of GAAP and the decision to determine solvency on a subsidiary level. Further, they asked the court to strike the plaintiff expert's Ponzi scheme comments and not to allow the plaintiff to use the plaintiff expert's initial expert report to rebut the defense expert reports.

The court said the law on GAAP in the bankruptcy context is that "courts in making their determinations are simply not bound by GAAP." At the same time, case law "strongly suggests that GAAP is relevant to the solvency inquiry." Consequently, the court declined to exclude the opinion on this ground.

The court observed that the plaintiff expert's testimony indicated that he not only based the opinion on the fair value standard of value, but he also made a "conscious decision" not to perform any upward adjustments. The court commended the expert for his "careful review of over a decade of the Debtors' voluminous financial records," which "led to a well-reasoned and supported decision to not increase or adjust the Debtors' assets upward."

The court declined to adopt a bright-line rule on how to determine solvency as to a parent and its subsidiaries. In this case, the record showed that each of the individual debtors operated distinctly from the parent company during the relevant periods, it found. Consequently, an individualized determination, as the plaintiff's expert had performed, was appropriate.

But the court agreed to strike the plaintiff expert's Ponzi scheme comment, finding it was irrelevant to the issue of solvency and other issues in the case. Also, since the purpose of the plaintiff expert's original report was to bolster the plaintiff's main case against the defendants, rather than to rebut the opposing experts' opinions, the testimony could not also serve as a rebuttal report.

Based on the legal principles the court highlighted, it admitted most of the testimony the parties' solvency experts proposed.

Redstone v. Commissioner

Citation: 2015 Tax Ct. Memo LEXIS 242
Date of decision: Dec. 9, 2015
Country: US
State/Jurisdiction: Federal
Court: United States Tax Court
Type of action: Federal Taxation
Experts: Gordon Klein (petitioner); Steven C. Hastings (IRS/respondent)
Judge: Lauber
SIC: 7812 Motion Picture and Video Tape Production
NAICS code: 512110 Motion Picture and Video Industries

Subsequent Transaction Too Remote to Allow for Reliable Valuation

In this tax dispute featuring media mogul Sumner Redstone and a 43-year-old transfer of shares in his company to trusts benefitting his children, the U.S. Tax Court found the very late IRS examination was proper, the transfers were gifts, and the IRS expert's "mergers and acquisitions" method best captured the then fair market value of the shares.

Voluntary and involuntary stock transfers. Redstone Sr. established the family business by building drive-in movie theaters in the Northeast. Eventually, he and his two sons, Edward and Sumner, incorporated National Amusements Inc. (NAI) as a closely held company. The three decided that each of them would own a third of the company's stock (100 shares each of common voting stock) but would make different amounts of contributions, with Redstone Sr. contributing nearly 48% of the company's capital. In 1968, Redstone Sr. transferred 50 shares of his common stock to a trust benefitting his grandchildren (Grandchildren's Trust).

In 1971, when Edward decided to leave the company, he demanded his 100 shares, but Redstone Sr. in particular refused to give the stock certificates. He argued his greater capital contribution to the company meant he had gratuitously given more stock than Edward was entitled to. To honor Redstone Sr.'s intent, the "extra" shares should be held in trust for Edward's children. Edward threatened to sell his interest to an outside party—a plan that contravened the other stakeholders' determination to keep the business in the family. Negotiations between the parties went nowhere. Ultimately, litigation resulted in a settlement that specified Edward was the owner of only 66 2/3 shares of NAI stock; the remaining 33 1/3 shares that had been in Edward's name would be held in trust for the benefit of his two children.

Under a June 1972 settlement, the company would repurchase the two-thirds of stock Edward was said to own. In a redemption agreement, the parties specified the 66 2/3 shares of stock were worth $5 million—an amount Edward would receive in quarterly installments. Edward then executed irrevocable declarations of trust for the benefit of his children. Under the parties' agreement, Sumner would be the sole trustee of each of the two trusts.

Three weeks after this settlement agreement, Sumner on his own volition decided to make the same arrangement for his two children. In July 1972, he transferred 16 2/3 of NAI shares to a trust benefitting his son and the same amount of shares to a trust benefitting his daughter. The remaining 66 2/3 shares were reissued to Sumner. He did not file a gift tax return for that calendar year.

In 1975, Sumner was the subject of a review from the Internal Revenue Service based on his contributions to political committees from 1970 to 1972. The IRS concluded "there was no necessity to solicit a gift tax return for 1972."

In 1984, NAI redeemed 83 1/3 shares held by the Grandchildren's Trust (50 shares) and the shares in the trusts benefitting Edward's children (33 1/3 shares). The aggregate redemption price was over $21.4 million—approximately $257,000 per share.

In a subsequent litigation involving family members, Sumner explained his motivation for transferring 33 1/3 of his NAI shares to the trusts benefitting his children. "Nobody sued me. I gave my kids a third of the stock voluntarily, not as the result of a lawsuit. In [s]o doing I did what I wanted and appeased my father too." And "Eddie had to find a justification for what he was doing in transferring. I wasn't sued. I just made an outright gift."

As a result of that litigation, in 2010, the IRS began to focus on the transfer of these shares and in 2011 initiated a gift tax examination covering the 1972 calendar year. The examination lasted for over a year. The agent working on it was not aware of the earlier 1972 review. The IRS determined the two transfers to Sumner's children were gifts and calculated a deficiency of over $737,600. It added nearly $369,000 for fraud and, in the alternative, $37,000 for negligence and $184,400 for failure to file a timely tax return.

Expert valuation testimony. Sumner petitioned the United States Tax Court for review. At trial both parties presented expert valuation testimony. The crux of the matter was to determine the value of the NAI shares in 1972.

IRS expert. The agency retained an expert in valuing closely held companies and stock interests in closely held companies. He explained he mainly relied on a "mergers and acquisitions" approach, basing his valuation of the NAI stock as of July 1972 on the price the company paid three weeks earlier to redeem Edward's stock in accordance with the parties' settlement agreement. The expert considered that agreement the result of an arm's-length transaction that took place at essentially the same time as the transfers Sumner made. The $5 million price for Edward's 66 2/3 shares yielded a value of $75,000 per NAI common share.

According to the expert, the redemption of Edward's 66 2/3 shares of NAI stock was "a private transaction for a minority interest." Accordingly, the redemption price valued the shares "on a minority, non-marketable interest basis." He concluded that the 33 1/3 shares Sumner transferred to his children's trusts at about the same time had a value of $2.5 million.

The IRS's expert also performed "direct capitalization" and "guideline public company" analyses. He concluded that these methods required the application of a 34% discount for lack of marketability. The resulting values for the 33 1/3 shares were $2.4 million and nearly $3 million.

Petitioner's expert. Sumner's expert was an attorney and CPA with extensive experience in accounting, finance, and valuation. He used what he called "the engrafting method." When the IRS's expert objected that this was not a recognized method for valuing corporate stock, Sumner's expert said it resembled the direct capitalization method. Under this approach, he calculated ratios between the per-share price NAI paid to redeem the trust's shares in 1984—$257,000 per share—and NAI's net income for 1981 to 1983 and the book value of NAI's common shareholder equity in 1984. He explained that he then "applied these same ratios to comparable NAI data existing at or about the time" of Sumner's transfers. He concluded that the shares Sumner transferred into his children's trusts in 1972 were worth about $736,000—$22,079 per share.

Petitioner's objections. Besides contesting the valuation determinations, Sumner made various arguments as to why the court should set aside the deficiency determination.

For one, the 2011 examination amounted to an impermissible second examination in light of the 1975 review the IRS had undertaken in connection with political campaign contributions. The court dismissed that contention. The IRS's position has been that "compliance checks" and "compliance initiative projects" do not amount to "examinations," the court observed. Also, the focus of the 1975 review concerned taxpayers' political contributions that did not comply with the rules applying to the annual gift tax exclusion.

But even if the 2011 examination were a second inspection, the remedy would not be to set aside the gift tax deficiency the IRS calculated during the examination, the court said. Further, Sumner failed to object to the deficiency ruling on that ground during the examination, which lasted more than a year. He first broached the argument in 2014, nearly a year after the IRS had issued its deficiency notice. In other words, Sumner waived this argument.

Sumner also contended that the transfer was not a gift but a transaction that occurred "in the ordinary course of business," just as Edward's transfer had. He sought to portray the transfer as an overall reconfiguration of stock ownership, which helped to bring an end to Edward's litigation.

The court found that argument very unconvincing considering there was no evidence of a dispute surrounding Sumner's shares and or evidence of an arm's-length negotiation surrounding the ownership of the transferred shares. Even if the settlement agreement with Edward provided an impetus for Sumner to transfer stock to his children and to please his father, the transaction was not "in the ordinary course of business." Sumner was motivated by kinship for his father and his children, the court decided. Most importantly, when testifying in the earlier family litigation, Sumner himself called the transaction "an outright gift."

Court's ruling centers on valuation date. In determining the amount of gift tax deficiency, the court adopted the IRS expert's approach. It noted that valuing the 33 1/3 shares of NAI stock Sumner transferred to his children based on the price the company paid only weeks earlier for Edward's stock made sense. These transactions occurred within a reasonable time of each other and the price the parties decided to put on Edward's stock was the result of hard bargaining between Redstone Sr. and Sumner on one side and Edward on the other side.

All parties had thorough knowledge of the company's financial condition. Their interests diverged: Edward tried to obtain as much as possible for his shares, whereas Redstone Sr. tried to pay him as little as possible. According to the court, the outcome of this negotiation—a per-share price of $75,000—represented the fair market value of the company's common stock as of the valuation date, that is, Sumner's transfer of stock into the trusts benefitting his children. The total value of the 33 1/3 shares was $2.5 million.

Finding the 1972 redemption price NAI paid to Edward was the most reliable indicator of value of the stock at issue, the court declined to examine the results the IRS's expert achieved under the direct capitalization and guideline public company methods. It noted, however, that the parties disagreed over inputs informing these other analyses. The disagreements were hardly surprising considering the valuation date was 43 years ago, the court said. To find data on NAI's then cost of equity, the appropriate "beta," NAI's growth rate, and a set of comparable companies presented a special challenge. At the same time, the $2.5 million valuation the court adopted fit within the range of values resulting from "various permutations of these other formulas."

The court objected to the valuation methodology Sumner's expert used principally because it relied on a stock sale that occurred much later than the valuation date.

The court acknowledged that under Tax Court law later occurring events, including sales of stock, "may be taken into account as evidence of fair market value of the valuation date," but it noted that those subsequent events must have occurred within a reasonable time in relation to the valuation date. Sumner failed to cite a case "in which a court employed, as its principal valuation metric, a stock sale that occurred as many as 12 years after the valuation date," the Tax Court observed.

It added that, even if it were possible to rely on the 1984 redemption price for determining the value of the NAI stock in July 1972, there would have to be adjustments to mark the passage of time. Specifically, the value calculation would require modifications for macroeconomic factors (inflation, interest rates, and stock market values) as well as factors specific to the industry (movies) and specific to the company (changes in NAI assets and lines of business). Sumner's expert made no such adjustments, nor did he provide reasons for failing to make the adjustments. The failure to do so or show why he did not do so rendered his valuation "altogether unreliable," the court decided.

No additions to gift tax. At the same time, the court found the IRS failed to prove that Sumner engaged in fraud to avoid paying a gift tax or even was negligent. In contrast, the evidence showed that he had relied on the advice of competent tax professionals who had advised him on his gift tax filing requirements on 34 occasions, beginning in 1970. When Sumner consulted with them regarding the tax consequences of transferring shares into the trusts benefitting his children, he was told a gift tax return was not necessary. Therefore, there was no justification for penalties. Sumner was liable for the $737,600 gift tax deficiency only, the Tax Court held.

RMS of Wisconsin, Inc. v. S-K JV

Citation: 2016 U.S. Dist. LEXIS 64224
Date of decision: May 16, 2016
Country: US
State/Jurisdiction: Federal/Wisconsin
Court: United States District Court
Type of action: Contract
Experts: Michael Betters (plaintiff); Terence Rodgers (defendants)
SIC: 1629 Heavy Construction, NEC (except industrial nonbuilding structures, irrigation systems, sewage and water treatment plants, petrochemical plants and refineries, power generation plants [except hydroelectric dams] transmission and distribution stations
NAICS code: 237990 Other Heavy and Civil Engineering Construction

Flawed Lost Profits Analysis Leaves Plaintiff Bereft of Damages Evidence

In a recent *Daubert* case involving a major construction contract, a relatively inexperienced damages expert faced exclusion because his lost profits calculation was based on insufficient facts and an "ad hoc" methodology. But, as the court's analysis made clear, in the end, the shortcomings in the work product stemmed from the expert's lack of experience. He had never done a damages analysis in a construction industry case before and failed to appreciate how industry- and fact-specific lost profit calculations are. His exclusion left the client scrambling for other means with which to show damages. This case serves as a reminder that it may be best to decline an engagement that is outside or beyond the expertise of the expert.

Backstory. The plaintiff was certified as a minority- and/or women-owned business (MBE/WBE) by the City of Indianapolis. It entered into a subcontractor agreement with the defendants to perform work on a major construction project, the "Indianapolis Project." The price of the lump-sum contract was nearly $6.8 million. The parties' relationship deteriorated. The plaintiff ended up alleging the defendants never intended to honor the contract but used the plaintiff to fulfill a city requirement to use an MBE/WBE on the job.

The plaintiff sued on theories of breach of contract and fraud in the inducement. The defendants counterclaimed for breach of the subcontractor agreement.

Both sides offered damages expert testimony. The plaintiff performed a lost profits calculation and a calculation of other damages to the plaintiff in connection with the aborted project. (It is not clear from the opinion whether the defendants' expert did his own lost profits analysis or simply provided rebuttal evidence.)

Many 'shortcomings.' The defendants filed a *Daubert* motion to exclude the plaintiff expert's testimony. Their main arguments were that his lost profits determination was based on insufficient data and that his methodology was unreliable.

Qualifications. Although the defendants did not challenge the plaintiff expert's qualifications, the court itself found the expert's experience wanting and spent time discussing the expert's professional background. He was a CMA who for about 10 years served as the plaintiff's tax preparer and provided outside accounting services. Both he and the opposing damages expert acknowledged that a lost profits calculation depended on the industry.

The plaintiff's expert admitted his experience of determining lost profits was limited. He stated that, in a few cases, he was asked to compute lost revenue to businesses that had to close after a fire or flooding. He also had done a business valuation in a marital dispute case. He said he had never developed a report as involved as the one he prepared for the plaintiff. The court noted that he "has not previously offered expert lost profit opinion in a construction industry case." It further observed that, given the liberal interpretation of expert qualifications and the defendants' decision not to challenge the expert's qualifications, the testimony might be admissible if there were no other shortcomings.

Reliability and fit. However, the court found numerous other reasons to exclude the opinion having to do with reliability and fit.

1. *Data.* The defendants argued that a principal flaw in the expert's analysis was that he used insufficient and inappropriate data for his analysis. The court agreed.

Specifically, the expert relied on data concerning another construction project, the "Milwaukee Deep Tunnel Project," on which the plaintiff worked with the defendants. However, unlike the contested project, the Milwaukee Project did not involve a lump-sum contract but was based on time and materials spent.

The plaintiff claimed it had performed nine lump-sum contracts in the past, but it conceded that none of them had been on the scale of the Indianapolis Project.

The plaintiff's expert admitted that, unlike a time and materials contract, a lump-sum contract carried with it a degree of risk of not making any profit. On the other hand, he said, it had the potential to be more profitable.

The court stated that using historical data was a proper tool for ascertaining lost profits with reasonable certainty. However, the expert must provide some kind of analysis as to why and how the data can reliably project the future loss to the project at issue. Here, the expert failed to do so. He gave no explanation why and how the conditions in the Milwaukee Project were comparable to those in the Indianapolis Project both in terms of the type of contract and the scope of work. Without the analysis, the court rejected the proposition that the data relating to the Milwaukee Project were credible comparable evidence.

2. *Labor costs.* Next, the defendants attacked the plaintiff expert's calculation of labor costs.

In essence, the expert used actual hourly rates as they appeared on payroll records for the two months the plaintiff worked on the Indianapolis Project, averaged them, added payroll tax, and came up with an average hourly rate for labor.

To determine revenue, the expert averaged the cost of operated equipment for 10 machines. He relied on an equipment rate sheet the plaintiff had developed and assumed that all machines would be used equally. He admitted he did not try to find out how the different machines actually were used during the two months the project was moving along.

He then divided the average labor cost by the average equipment cost to determine the average cost of labor by hour of revenue. Next, he multiplied the resulting rate by the contract sum of $6.8 million to arrive at the total labor cost. After certain adjustments, he found that the plaintiff's labor costs were close to $2 million. He assumed it would take the plaintiff five years to complete the contract because that's how long it took to complete the Milwaukee Project. The expert stated he did not have a projection of how many hours it would take to complete the work, of the scope of the job, or a timeline. He also said he never reviewed any estimates the plaintiff had created.

He admitted that his calculation lacked critical components and was "not the best scenario." But when comparing the costs he determined to the plaintiff's historical data, he "believed he was in the ballpark" of the plaintiff's historical labor costs.

The expert's testimony did not align with statements from the plaintiff's field and job site supervisor, who had done much of the preliminary research into the project and who was part of the team that decided to enter into the subcontract. The supervisor said he had prepared an analysis of the total labor costs related to the project as part of the bidding process. He also said it was impossible ahead of time to determine how many man-hours it would take for each piece of equipment. He intended to use all 10 vehicles, but often they were used on an "as-needed" basis.

The court said it was "not convinced of the propriety of using an average of all employees' hourly rates." It observed there were different types of employees—union and management—who performed different work. The plaintiff's payroll records showed "greatly differing" hours of work performed. "[H]ow does lumping these categories of employees together create an accurate hourly rate for all employees?" the court asked.

The expert's cost of equipment analysis also lacked nuance, the court found. It noted the field supervisor's cautionary statements as well as the expert's failure to justify averaging where there was a distinct possibility that the plaintiff might not use all of the equipment on the list.

Finally, the court found it problematic to assume the job would be completed in five years based on the Milwaukee Project. The expert failed to show that the two projects were sufficiently similarly in terms of scope and type of work to justify the assumption. Considering the project at issue was a lump-sum contract, it was critical to establish the scope of work and the number of hours needed for completion, the court pointed out.

It noted the expert acknowledged these components were missing in his lost profits calculation. All flaws considered, there was "simply too great" an analytical gap between the data the expert used and his opinion, the court found.

3. *Methodology.* The defendants also contended the methodology the expert used was unreliable. The court agreed again.

The plaintiff's expert said that his approach to calculating lost profits or valuing a business was to "use whatever tools I have in front of me to try to make the most accurate educated estimate of loss I possibly can." He went on to say that, "if he does not have the requisite tools, he goes to the next best thing he has."

The court called this an unreliable "ad hoc method" with which to calculate lost profits. Because the approach was specific to the situation at hand, it did not lend itself to independent testing. "The uniqueness of the case cannot justify using a method that cannot be tested or replicated," the court noted. It excluded the lost profits testimony.

Expert analysis not necessary. Finally, the defendants were able to exclude the expert's testimony regarding other damages the plaintiff sought, arguing those damages required no expert testimony at all. They concerned losses the plaintiff incurred when it sold assets to deal with a cash flow squeeze resulting from the loss of the contract, money spent to upgrade equipment the plaintiff intended to use on the project, and administrative fees.

On cross-examination, the expert admitted in calculating those damages he simply added up the numbers the plaintiff provided to him.

Performing basic arithmetic with numbers the plaintiff provided does nothing to assist the trier of fact, the court said. Therefore, it also barred the expert from testifying as to these additional damages.

Fact witness route foreclosed. After the court excluded the damages expert testimony, the plaintiff tried to introduce lost profits testimony by having the expert testify as a fact witness in accordance with Federal Rule of Evidence 701.

The court was alert to the backdoor maneuver. "Surely [the expert] cannot offer expert testimony through the cloak of a lay witness," the court said.

And, even though the expert had served as the plaintiff's accountant for years, the court noted that, since the plaintiff did not attempt to qualify the expert as an accounting expert, he could not give expert testimony as an accountant.

The court did allow the president of the company as well as the field and job site supervisor to testify as lay witnesses as to "the facts of the business underlying [their] profit expectations." But it warned them "not to cross the line into expert testimony by giving economic analysis."

Rubin v. Bedford

Citation: 2015 Ill. App. Unpub. LEXIS 2919
Date of decision: Dec. 24, 2015
Country: US
State/Jurisdiction: Illinois
Court: Appellate Court of Illinois
Type of action: Dissenting Shareholder
Experts: Raphael Puga (plaintiffs); Gilbert Matthews, Dr. Elizabeth Eccher (defendants)
Judge: McBride
SIC: 2092 Prepared Fresh or Frozen Fish and Seafoods
NAICS code: 3117 Seafood Product Preparation and Packaging

Expert's Poor Grasp of Valuation Issues Undercuts Shareholder Suit

A dissenting shareholder suit in state court challenged a going private transaction. But the plaintiffs' attack on the sales process and sales price fizzled in trial court based in part on questionable valuation testimony from an "expert" witness who admitted to having no formal training in accounting or valuing a company and compelling countertestimony from the defendants' experts. The appeals court affirmed, pointing to the plaintiffs' expert lack of awareness and understanding of issues affecting the company's value.

'More than fair' offer to buy. Vita Foods was a two-headed company: One division processed and sold high-quality fish (smoked salmon, herring) and seafood; the other sold sauces, including marinades and salad dressings. The divisions were legally and financially intertwined.

One of the plaintiffs was the company's former CEO who, prior to 2006, was the company's largest shareholder. When the company required a $3 million cash infusion to keep operations afloat in early 2006, the named defendant contributed $1 million in exchange for stock in the company. He also became a member of the company's board of directors. A year later, the defendant investor was able to consolidate his position when the company required additional equity. He contributed $3 million in exchange for stock. At that time, the plaintiff CEO and the defendant investor executed a voting proxy agreement that gave the defendant investor a controlling vote.

In late 2007, the board decided to delist the company from the American Stock Exchange and trade on the over-the-counter market to save on regulatory costs applicable to public companies.

In late 2008, the company stock traded between $0.23 and $0.30 on the over-the-counter market. Around that time, the board received notice that the controlling stockholder would make an offer to buy the outstanding shares and take the company private. The board immediately created a special committee to assess the offer. The committee then hired a known investment bank "in anticipation of possibly rendering a fairness opinion." But when the committee learned the majority shareholder's offer was for $0.30 per share, it told the offeror that the company was not interested unless there was a higher bid. About two weeks later, the controlling shareholder came back with a $1.00-per-share offer. The committee's financial advisor determined the price was "more than fair." Regardless, the committee went back to the offeror asking for $1.20 per share. The parties ultimately settled on $1.05 per share. The deal also included nonmonetary requirements.

One of them was obtaining the approval of a majority of the minority shareholders. Another was a 30-day "go shop" period during which the company could pursue alternative transactions with other interested parties. The committee issued a press release in a trade publication aimed at the fish industry to announce the deal to competitors to avoid contacting them directly. Also, the committee contacted about six companies, and it hired another investment bank to solicit offers from a list of 10 companies. The initiatives generated little interest. At trial, a member of the special committee explained the reason was the "two-business nature" of the company. A third party interested in buying only the fish business was unable to do so because the divisions were inextricably linked. At the same time, a fish purveyor might not be interested in the sauce business. One direct competitor wanted more information and an extension of time during the "go shop" period and received both. But it declined to move forward.

The company announced the merger to the public on February 2009. At that time, the plaintiff CEO "made a voluntary decision *** to sell [his] stock to [the controlling shareholder] at a dollar-five." In April 2009, a majority of the minority shareholders voted in favor of the merger.

Subsequently, the former CEO and a number of other shareholders sued the controlling shareholder, the former chairman of the board, and members of the special committee. The plaintiffs alleged in essence that the sales price undervalued the company and claimed the defendants breached their fiduciary duty by allowing the deal to go forward. At the same time, the defendants contended the former CEO had breached his fiduciary duty by not informing other board members of a purported 2007 offer to buy the company at $3.50 per share.

'One of the easiest fairness opinions' ever. A bench trial ensued, featuring expert valuation testimony from both sides.

The plaintiffs' expert had worked for years in the seafood industry and most recently for a big Norwegian seafood company that operated in countries around the world. He described his current employer as "the largest salmon farmer in the world." He said he originally sold raw salmon to Vita Foods, the subject company, for smoking. Eventually, this expert's company made products for Vita Foods that the latter sold under a private label. The expert said he realized how successful Vita Foods was when his own company was unable to fulfill all the orders it received from Vita Foods.

He said his company would have paid "[a]nywhere between 20 and $30 million" for the subject company between 2006 and the end of 2008, including assuming any debt Vita Foods had at the time. He said this figure related only to Vita Foods' fish division because his company was not interested in the sauce division of Vita Foods. He believed the valuation was appropriate because of Vita Foods' sales volume, its well-known brand name, and its commanding shelf space in supermarkets. He stated that Vita Foods' sales were "approximately 25 to $30 million in seafood and something similar in other products, sauces and something else." He valued the company using "one time [sales], plus assumption of debt." He said it did not matter to him that Vita Foods was not profitable in 2007 and 2008 because his company would have been able to make Vita Foods profitable by closing one of the subject's plants and using the buyer's own smoking facility. "[I]n our industry where we are producers and we owned also smoked salmon operations, *** we do know what our costs would be to produce. So basically, once you know the sales numbers, you can extrapolate those numbers and say, 'Okay. This is the value for us.'"

He admitted that he was not aware of the legal and financial interconnectedness of Vita Foods' two divisions. And he acknowledged that he had no information as to the extent of Vita Food's shelf space after 2006. He said his statement on shelf space was based on what he had observed walking through his local supermarket. He was unaware that Vita Foods had lost shelf space to major retailers from 2003 to 2007. He said he did not know the company's fair market value as of the valuation date, April 2009. Moreover, he was not a trained and certified accountant, nor an economist. Nor did he have training in how to value a company. He said he knew Vita Foods was "going private" in 2009, and he acknowledged that, between 2004 and 2009, his own company never made an offer to buy Vita Foods even though nothing prevented it from doing so.

The defendants offered testimony from the reputed investment banker and business valuator who had provided the company with fairness opinions in 2006, 2007, and 2008. He explained that a fairness opinion was "an opinion given to a fiduciary as to the fairness of a particular transaction to a specific group of investors." He explained in 2006 he had found Vita Foods was "highly leveraged" and had "negative tangible net worth." By then it had operated at a loss for two years. Similarly, in 2007, the company again risked becoming insolvent if it was unable to raise capital.

In terms of the 2008 fairness opinion that related to the contested merger, he said that by then the company had "gone from losses to a *** small profit." However, the company faced debt maturity in April 2010 that it might not have been able to meet; "its inability to reach that would have caused the company to become bankrupt." The company was "troubled," the expert said. At the same time, given the economic conditions in 2008, it seemed unlikely that investors that were unwilling to put money into good companies would invest in troubled companies.

The expert explained that for the 2008 fairness opinion he performed a comparable companies analysis, considering eight companies "in the food products industry, *** smaller companies engaged in selling products through the same distribution channels that Vita was using." He found Vita Foods had "very little cash flow"; it "was not generating enough cash to come close to meeting its debt maturities"; and "it had very low profit margins." In terms of evaluating the $1.05-per-share price, he said, "[F]rankly, [this] was one of the easiest fairness opinions I ever worked on. I would say it was a very generous price." As he saw it, an offer to buy out the minority shareholders for $0.60 to $0.70 per share would have been a fair offer.

He disputed the suggestion that one could value the company by looking only at revenue or sales, as the plaintiffs' expert had done. "Revenues are not very relevant at all because the important thing is how much profit you're able to get from those revenues," the defendants' expert said. Also, the company's EBITDA margins were less than 5%, which was below the median of all the comparable companies, he observed. Therefore, valuing the company based on sales "is not meaningful" where the sales were not profitable.

The defendants offered other expert testimony from a principal with an economic, financial, and strategy consulting firm. This expert echoed the first expert's value conclusion when she found that the shares were worth "between 66 and 69 cents." Moreover, she considered it inappropriate to value the company by "taking its revenues, adding the debt, and using that to compute a total value." Revenue, she explained, was only one input in valuing a company and specifically in determining its ability to generate cash flow. She focused on "EBIT or EBITDA," which she called a "lower-down-the-line number on an income statement," which sought to capture the value of all of a company's assets, including brand and shelf space.

Yet another financial expert affirmed that the sales process under the direction of the special committee was proper. He said he had "represented special committees as an investment banker," including in situations similar to the contested merger, "where an insider at a company was either purchasing some or all of the company." He explained the lack of interest among third parties to buy Vita Foods by noting that buyers typically are willing to pay a 30% premium over the price at which a stock is trading. Here, the controlling shareholder offered to pay "significantly more than that." The offer, therefore, might have had a "chilling effect" on potential third-party bidders.

The trial court found for the defendants. The board of directors had pursued a "sound" sales process and the directors' conduct related to the contested transaction complied with their fiduciary duty to the minority shareholders, the trial court decided. Also, the plaintiffs had failed to provide evidence of offers that the special committee had not considered. Therefore, the plaintiffs failed to establish damages. At the same time, the court dismissed the defendants' counterclaim regarding the plaintiff CEO's alleged failure to apprise the company of more lucrative offers prior to the buyout.

No better offers, no evidence of damages. Both sides appealed the trial court's findings at the state appellate court. Besides attacking the special committee and its decision making surrounding the sales process, the plaintiffs claimed they showed damages by way of their expert's statement that his company "would have paid $30 million plus the assumption of debt" for Vita Foods.

The appellate court found this argument unconvincing. It pointed out that the expert's statement specified the offer was for the period of 2006 through the end of 2008. The expert's company "notably" did not make an offer during the go shop period, when Vita Foods solicited competing bids, or subsequently, when the contested merger closed. Yet nothing prevented it from doing so. The record failed to show that there were better offers "that were realistically available to the company," the appeals court observed.

The court further found the testimony of the plaintiffs' expert itself was problematic. By his own admission, the expert had no valuation experience; what's more the defendants' experienced valuation witnesses both discredited his proposition to calculate value based on one times revenues plus debt. The plaintiffs' expert "also appeared to be either unaware or mistaken as to several other significant issues affecting the company's value," the appellate court added. In light of these weaknesses, the trial court did not err in finding the plaintiffs had failed to establish damages. The appeals court upheld the trial court's judgment, which approved the contested merger.

Showers v. Pfizer, Inc. (In re Pfizer Inc. Sec. Litig.)

Citation: 2016 U.S. App. LEXIS 6622
Date of decision: April 12, 2016
Country: US
State/Jurisdiction: Federal/2nd Circuit
Court: United States Court of Appeals
Type of action: Securities
Experts: Daniel R. Fischel (plaintiffs); Dr. Paul A. Gompers (defendants)
Judge: Livingston
SIC: 2834 Pharmaceutical Preparations
NAICS code: 325412 Pharmaceutical Preparation Manufacturing

2nd Circuit Chafes at Wholesale Exclusion of Loss Causation Testimony

It's not over until the appeals court has had its say. The 2nd Circuit Court of Appeals recently resuscitated a securities fraud lawsuit involving the drug giant Pfizer after the class action had died following the district court's exclusion of the plaintiffs' loss causation and damages expert. The appeals court objected to the district court's drastic move, which left the plaintiffs unable to prove critical elements of their claim. According to the 2nd Circuit, "parsing" expert testimony and excising the unreliable part(s) from the reliable testimony accords with the "liberal admissibility standards" of *Daubert* and the Federal Rule of Evidence 702.

Backstory. Shareholders in Pfizer sued the pharmaceutical company and several of its directors and officers, alleging the defendants made fraudulent misrepresentations, and fraudulently omitted to disclose information, about the safety of the company's Celebrex and Bextra drugs during the class period—October 2000 to October 2005. Celebrex and Bextra were part of a class of nonsteroidal anti-inflammatory drugs to treat chronic pain and inflammation. Vioxx, a similar drug that belonged to the pharmaceutical giant Merck, achieved particular notoriety and was withdrawn from the market in 2004.

Celebrex and Bextra originally belonged to two different companies with which Pfizer maintained co-promotion agreements going back to 1998. Pfizer obtained the exclusive rights to manufacture, promote, and sell the two drugs when it acquired the company holding the rights to them in 2003.

The gist of the plaintiffs' claim was that Pfizer and the earlier owners of the drugs knew about the drugs' dangerous side effects as early as 1998. But, because the drugs were commercially successful, the financial stakeholders in the drugs issued press releases and other public statements denying the risks and touting the drugs' safety to keep the public's misperception going.

In 2012, more than eight years after the suit began, the district court (S.D. N.Y.) certified the class.

Star expert calculates artificial stock inflation. The involvement of various players in the misrepresentations raised an issue for the plaintiffs as to how to show whether Pfizer's fraud, as opposed to the fraud by the prior owners of the drugs, caused Pfizer's stock price to fall.

The plaintiffs solved this problem by presenting an "inflation-maintenance" theory of liability. It said that, even though during part of the class period Pfizer did not yet own the drugs, it was responsible for all of the misrepresentations because it had control over the statements the then-owners made. Further, Pfizer made its own misrepresentations and engaged in fraudulent omissions, the plaintiffs said. By its actions, Pfizer *maintained* the public's misperception about the drugs. As a result, during the five-year class period, investors continued to value the Pfizer (and the other owners') stock as if the Pfizer drugs were free of the risks the market came to associate with Merck's Vioxx. But when the public learned about studies linking Pfizer's drugs to cardiovascular risks soon afterward, the company's share prices fell. Had Pfizer not continued to conceal the risks, the market would have adjusted its valuation of Pfizer's stock. Pfizer was responsible for the full amount by which its stock fell, the plaintiffs claimed.

To prove liability and to determine the amount of money shareholders lost because of the fraud, the plaintiffs retained one of the highest-ranked experts in this area of the law. In his initial report, the expert performed an event study to determine whether and to what extent Pfizer's stock price changed when investors discovered the risks associated with the two drugs.

From the start, the expert made it clear that he was asked to assume liability in step with the plaintiffs' theory. He was hired to identify the "artificial inflation" in the company's stock as a result of the alleged fraud. The centerpiece of the expert's theory was that there were seven days during which there were disclosures about the risks. On the days the "corrective disclosures" occurred, the stock price showed negative residual returns. But, the expert explained, around the same time as the corrective disclosures, on five days, the stock price actually rose more than expected. In other words, on five days of "positive disclosures," the stock price showed positive residual returns. To account for the positive residual returns, he offset the stock price movement on the corrective disclosure days by the movements on the positive disclosure days. He found that, at the beginning of the class period, Pfizer's stock was inflated by $1.46 per share and that the inflation went as high as $3.95 per share before it dropped to $0 by the end of the class period, October 2005.

The expert stressed that offsetting the positive disclosures against the corrective disclosures resulted in a more accurate measurement of the effects of the alleged fraud. Ignoring the price increases, he said, would overstate the artificial inflation. He observed that, on two of the five positive disclosure days, as the market became aware of the risks associated with Merck's Vioxx, Pfizer's stock price rose, presumably because investors anticipated greater sales for Celebrex and Bextra after Merck's withdrawal of Vioxx. He said the subsequent corrective disclosures revealed both concealed information about the two drugs and showed the market was mistaken in predicting greater sales. He said he needed to offset the price increases on the two positive disclosure dates against those of the corrective disclosure dates to isolate the artificial inflation associated with the concealed information.

The defendants offered rebuttal expert testimony only. The defendants' expert did not object to the use of the event study as a methodology and had "no major criticism" of how the opposing expert arrived at the residual return, that is, the difference between the actual return of the company's stock and the predicted return. But the defendants' expert objected to the opposing expert's assumptions that certain corrective disclosures revealed information about the drugs that had been concealed fraudulently.

District court identifies two weaknesses. After discovery began, Pfizer filed a motion for summary judgment, which the district court granted in part. It found two problems with the expert testimony.

The court first said that the losses on two corrective days were not attributable to disclosures that exposed Pfizer's alleged misrepresentations. Further, the court took issue with the plaintiffs' theory that Pfizer was liable for all misrepresentations during the class action period, even those made by the previous owners of the drugs on account of Pfizer's co-promotion agreements with them. The district court ruled that only one out of 10 contested misrepresentations was attributable to Pfizer.

Based on the court's decision, the plaintiffs' expert submitted a supplemental report. The report did not adjust for the court's ruling on the number of misrepresentations essentially because the expert believed that, under the plaintiffs' inflation maintenance theory, it did not matter which of the companies made the misrepresentation. The expert explained that he proceeded from the assumption that Pfizer's claimed misrepresentations maintained the market's "false expectations" about the drugs. These expectations were put in place before the class period and kept there based on Pfizer's misconduct. Each of Pfizer's misrepresentations was responsible for maintaining the same amount of artificial inflation.

As for the district court's ruling about the two corrective disclosures, the expert first removed them from his event study. The elimination of the two days reduced the total stock price declines by about 9.7%, he found. He then decided he had to "proportionally reduce the residual stock price increases measured" by 9.7%. At the same time, he did not identify a one-for-one relationship between a particular positive disclosure and a particular corrective disclosure. The only rationale he articulated to support his assumption that there was such a relationship was that "inflation cannot come out of a stock unless it goes into the stock."

In another rebuttal, Pfizer's expert criticized the opposing expert for ignoring the district court's decision on the number of misstatements for which Pfizer was responsible. The plaintiffs' expert failed to "disaggregate" the price inflation attributable to misstatements by the prior owners of the two drugs, Pfizer's expert contended.

Moreover, Pfizer's expert contended the proportional reduction the plaintiffs' expert performed was an unreliable methodology. The plaintiffs' expert should have just removed the rejected corrective disclosures from his calculations, without proportionally reducing the amount of inflation attributable to the positive disclosures.

Based on its expert's critique, Pfizer filed a *Daubert* motion to exclude the plaintiffs' expert testimony on loss causation and damages, which the district court granted.

In so doing, the district court noted the plaintiff expert's failure "to account in any way for the impact" of the statements attributable to the prior owners of the drugs, which made the expert testimony unhelpful to the jury in terms of calculating damages attributable only to Pfizer's alleged misrepresentations and omissions. Also, the plaintiffs' expert "proffered no explanation of the analytical basis" for his proportional reduction and no "explanation of the relationships among the events triggering the respective price decreases and increases" nor "reference or peer review information … in support of [his proportional] adjustment method."

The district court excluded the entire expert testimony. This sweeping ruling meant the end of the plaintiffs' case because they no longer were able to establish loss causation and damages. Accordingly, the district court granted judgment in favor of Pfizer.

District court 'misapprehends' expert's role. The plaintiffs appealed the district court's rulings with the 2nd Circuit Court of Appeals. Their overriding argument was that, in excluding the expert testimony, the district court improperly applied Rule 702 and the *Daubert* standard.

Disaggregation issue. The appeals court first discussed the district court's finding that the plaintiffs' expert failed to disaggregate the stock price inflation attributable to Pfizer's own statements from the inflation based on the misrepresentations of the drugs' previous owners.

According to the Court of Appeals, the district court's reasoning was based on a "misapprehension" of the plaintiffs' theory of liability and the expert's role in the plaintiffs' claim. Specifically, the district court mistakenly believed that, if the case eventually were to go to the jury, members of the jury would be left to calculate "damages proximately caused by [Pfizer's] alleged misrepresentations and omissions." But, said the Court of Appeals with emphasis, this idea "is directly contrary" to the plaintiff's theory of liability, which is that Pfizer is liable for *all* of the artificial inflation related to the drugs because Pfizer's own fraudulent conduct concealed the same information as its predecessors.

The appeals court observed that the plaintiffs' expert "did not assign damages on a statement-by-statement basis." Rather, his loss causation model was based on the assumption that Pfizer's misrepresentations repeated the same false messages and served to maintain Pfizer's stock price at a constant, inflated level. In the context of this theory of liability, the expert's testimony could be helpful to the jury, the Court of Appeals noted. The testimony showed that the discovery of the concealed information caused shareholders to lose money and the amount of money they lost.

The district court's decision to prevent the expert from testifying based on the failure to disaggregate the effects of Pfizer's specific misrepresentation was an abuse of discretion, the 2nd Circuit found.

The Court of Appeals pointed out that its ruling on this point did not mean that the plaintiffs' theory was legally or factually successful. It meant that, under *Daubert* and Rule 702, there was no justification for the district court to conclude the testimony was unreliable or unhelpful to the jury.

Proportional reduction issue. Excluding the expert testimony based on the expert's failure to provide an adequate explanation for the proportional reduction was a "more complicated matter," the 2nd Circuit found.

After the district court ruled Pfizer was not responsible for the stock-price changes related to two of the corrective disclosures, the plaintiffs' expert "clearly needed to remove the price changes associated with those disclosures from his calculation of artificial inflation," the appeals court said. The problem was the expert's decision to also adjust the positive disclosures even though the district court's ruling left this part of the expert's initial report untouched. The adjustment seemed based on an "implicit conclusion regarding the relationship between the Corrective and Positive Disclosures," the appeals court noted. But the expert never "offered" an explanation of whether and how the information in the positive disclosures related to the information in the excluded corrective disclosures. He merely "asserted" that the exclusion of the corrective disclosures "*must have*" had an effect, the appeals court emphasized.

The district court, therefore, did not abuse its discretion when it found the proportional reduction was an unreliable application of the general methodology the expert had outlined, the Court of Appeals said. By his own account, the expert was to evaluate the "relationship between" the excluded disclosures and positive disclosures to determine how to "allocate the" price changes on the positive disclosure days "between what is fraud related and what [] is not fraud related."

District court goes 'astray.' But, said the Court of Appeals, the district court "went astray" when it decided to exclude the entire expert testimony based on one flaw in the testimony. The proportional reduction issue "was but one small part of an extensive economic analysis," the appeals court observed. The expert had performed an event study to identify whether and how the market responded to new information about the drugs' cardiovascular risks. Although Pfizer's expert objected to the proportional reduction, "overall" he did not have "any major criticism" of the event study, the 2nd Circuit noted.

"When faced with expert testimony that contains both reliable and unreliable opinions, district courts often exclude only the unreliable testimony," the 2nd Circuit observed. This is what the district court should have done in this case. The expert's error regarding the proportional reduction did not invalidate his opinion that the stock price fell during the class period, when the market learned about the risks associated with the drugs. Nor did it put into question his methodology for identifying and calculating the residual returns related to the positive and remaining corrective disclosures. And eliminating the proportional reduction from the expert's testimony did not make the remainder of the expert's analysis useless, the Court of Appeals noted.

The district court simply should have prevented the expert from making the proportional reduction, the court said. The remainder of the testimony met the *Daubert* standard.

Excluding the expert's entire opinion was an abuse of discretion, the 2nd Circuit concluded. Accordingly, it set aside the district court's judgment and remanded "for further proceedings consistent with this opinion."

Spencer Franchise Servs. of Ga. v. WOW Café & Wingery Franchising Account, LLC

Citation: 2016 U.S. Dist. LEXIS 50919
Date of decision: April 15, 2016
Country: US
State/Jurisdiction: Federal/Louisiana
Court: United States District Court
Type of action: Contract
Experts: Mark A. Dayman (plaintiff); Ralph A. Litolff (defendant)
Judge: Barbier
SIC: 5812 Eating Places (limited-service restaurants)
NAICS code: 722513 Limited-Service Restaurants

Rebuttal Opinion Helpful to Jury Because Valuation 'Not a Common-Sense Subject'

Even a veteran appraiser is not immune to an attack on his qualifications, as a contract case involving a franchise agreement gone wrong illustrates. Attorneys and experts working in the litigation arena also know that most attempts to exclude an expert under the *Daubert* qualification prong fail. But lawyers keep making the argument. It typically says that the expert lacks specialization in the underlying field. In the instant case, the plaintiff contended the expert damages opinion was inadmissible because the expert had a background in accounting and not in the franchise industry. The court disagreed. The plaintiff's attacks under the other *Daubert* prongs also failed.

Contract or no contract? In 2007, the parties entered into an area development agreement (ADA) giving the plaintiff the exclusive right and option to "establish, operate, and/or provide guidance to multiple WOW Café Franchise businesses" in all but two counties in Georgia. The plaintiff promised to pay $175,000 upfront and open two franchises; in return, the defendant agreed not to grant a franchise in Georgia to any other entity. The plaintiff was to receive weekly operating fees and royalty payments from Georgia franchises, as well as broker fees for newly opened franchises, and advertising fees.

Critically, the ADA designated the plaintiff as the "Developer" and the defendant as the "Franchisor."

Eventually, the parties fell out. The plaintiff sued for breach of contract in federal court (E.D. La.). The defendant countersued, also alleging breach of contract. The dispute centered on a single word in one of the ADA's provisions, which said: "In addition to Developer's obligation to open its own Franchise Units as described above, *Franchisor* shall, at a minimum, sell or cause some third party to sell the number of Franchise Units set forth on the Minimum Development Requirements, which is attached hereto as Schedule 2." (emphasis added)

The defendant claimed "Franchisor" should have said "Developer," meaning the plaintiff, not the defendant, had the obligation to sell a minimum number of franchise agreements. In other words, this was a terrible drafting error. The court agreed, saying the current language made the contract "absurd." It rescinded the agreement based on "clear mutual error." Without an enforceable contract, the plaintiff's claims failed. The court entered summary judgment in favor of the defendant.

The plaintiff appealed to the 5th Circuit Court of Appeals and won. The appeals court said there was a legitimate question as to whether the parties entered into a contract containing an error. It sent the case back for a fact finder to decide whether the contract was enforceable.

The plaintiff retained a damages expert to evaluate the terms and conditions of the ADA and determine the number of WOW franchises that could have been sold and the stores that could have been opened pursuant to the ADA but for the defendant's alleged breach. The defendant hired a rebuttal expert who did not prepare his own damages analysis but critiqued the opposing expert's calculation.

Report complete enough. Both experts had similar credentials and titles, but in a pretrial motion the plaintiff sought to exclude the rebuttal testimony, saying it failed all the *Daubert* requirements as well as a requirement under Federal Rule of Civil Procedure 26(a)(2)(B), which concerns expert reports.

1. Daubert. The defendant's rebuttal expert had undergraduate and graduate degrees in accounting, was a CPA, and had credentials in business valuation and financial forensics. He also had over 20 years of experience working on valuations and performing economic damages, financial, and forensic accounting analyses.

In preparation of his report, he reviewed the ADA, the opposing expert's report, the defendant's website, and data specific to casual dining brands in the U.S.

The plaintiff maintained the defendant's expert was not qualified to testify as an expert on franchise development. He lacked credentials in franchising, publications in franchising journals, and the knowledge or expertise of how the industry operated.

The court rejected the argument. An expert witness is not strictly confined to his or her area of expertise but may testify about "related applications," the court noted. According to case law, "specialization in the underlying field is unnecessary for an expert on business valuation," the court pointed out (referencing *Willis v. TRC Companies, Inc.*, 2008 U.S. Dist. LEXIS 64870) (available at *BVLaw*). In *Willis*, the court allowed a CPA with 30 years of experience, including as the CEO of a tech company, to testify about the valuation of an engineering firm, even though he had not taught business valuation, was not published, and had no business valuation certificates.

A lack of specialization goes toward the weight not the admissibility of the testimony, the court noted. It concluded that in the instant case the expert's qualifications "speak for themselves."

Next, the plaintiff questioned the reliability of the rebuttal testimony. It suggested the rebuttal report was unreliable because it dealt solely with subjects the defendant could use in its cross-examination of the plaintiff's expert. Further, it said the rebuttal expert did not identify what methods or principles he used to support his opinion.

The defendant countered the expert used a methodology that met the standards of the American Institute of Certified Public Accountants (AICPA).

The court pointed out that this was a rebuttal report that questioned aspects of the plaintiff expert's opinion. Since the plaintiff's expert used a market approach, the defendant's expert "can be said to use the same methodology," the court observed. The market approach was one of three recognized business valuation methods. Therefore, the defense expert's opinion was based on reliable principles and methods.

Finally, the plaintiff contended that since the defense expert's report "merely criticizes" the plaintiff expert's report it was irrelevant. It would not assist the trier of fact because the jury could decide on its own whether or not to accept the opinion of the plaintiff's expert based on his performance on direct examination and under cross-examination.

The defendant claimed the rebuttal expert was a business valuator and CPA whose opinion would help the fact finder determine whether or not to rely on the damages the plaintiff's expert calculated.

The court sided with the defendant. It said business valuation was "not a common-sense subject" that jury members could evaluate based on common experience or knowledge. Accordingly, the rebuttal testimony was helpful to the jury and relevant.

2. *Rule 26(a)(2)(B).* Rule 26 requires that witnesses who are "retained or specially employed to provide expert testimony in the case" provide expert reports to the other party in the case.

Among other things, the expert report must contain "a complete statement of all opinions the witness will express and the basis and reasons for them." The plaintiff claimed the defense rebuttal report failed this requirement.

The court again disagreed. The rebuttal expert report included a section, "Summary of Conclusions and Opinions," which described each of the expert's opinions, the court noted. The body of the report sufficiently explained the basis and reasons for the individual opinions. The gist was that the defendant's expert took issue with the opposing expert's conclusions about the number of franchises the relevant market could support. The statement of opinions was not incomplete just because the rebuttal expert did not provide his own opinion on the subject, the court said.

The rebuttal testimony met the *Daubert* requirements, and the report met the Rule 26 requirements, the court concluded. It admitted the testimony, leaving it up to the adversarial process to test the strength of the testimony by way of cross-examination, countervailing testimony, and jury instructions on the burden of proof.

St. Jude Med. S.C., Inc. v. Biosense Webster, Inc.

Citation: 2016 U.S. App. LEXIS 6658
Date of decision: April 12, 2016
Country: US
State/Jurisdiction: Federal/8th Circuit
Court: United States Court of Appeals
Type of action: Contract
Judge: Smith
SIC: 3829 Measuring and Controlling Devices, NEC (medical thermometers)
NAICS code: 339112 Medical Equipment and Supplies

8th Circuit Validates Employment Contract and Damages Related to Breach

An employment contract is different from a restrictive covenant because it is enforceable by damages rather than an injunction. And goading an employee into breaching his employment agreement may expose the poacher to lost profits damages. These were the takeaways from an economic damages case in which a salesperson breached his agreement with the employer to join a competitor that had courted him aggressively. Both the employee and the competitor were liable for replacement costs. In addition, the competitor was liable for lost profits under a theory of tortious interference. The case highlights the critical role causation plays in establishing lost profits. The plaintiff prevailed because it offered sufficient evidence that tied the loss claimed directly to the defendants' wrongful conduct.

Double exposure. The plaintiff and the defendant company were manufacturers of medical equipment. The defendant employee initially worked as a sales representative for the plaintiff. In January 2011, he and the plaintiff signed a three-year agreement that limited the plaintiff's ability to terminate the employee and prevented the employee from working for someone else during that period. However, a year into the contract, the defendant employee left to join the defendant company, which had pursued him based on his business relationship with a hospital that the defendant company wanted to gain as a client. Shortly after the employee began to work for the competitor, he introduced the client hospital to the competitor's cardiac mapping system for a free trial period.

After the employee left to join the competitor, the latter unsuccessfully asked the court to declare the employee's agreement with the plaintiff invalid. The plaintiff, in turn, sued the employee for breach of contract and the competitor for tortious interference with the employee's employment agreement. A federal district court (D. Minn.) ruled for the plaintiff on summary judgment on the issue of liability.

A trial on the issue of damages followed. The plaintiff apparently engaged an expert, who produced a report but did not testify in a deposition or at trial.

The jury found the employee's breach cost the plaintiff nearly $47,700 to replace him. Further, the competitor caused the plaintiff to incur another $47,700 in replacement costs. In addition, the jury awarded the plaintiff nearly $551,000 in lost profits based on the competitor's wrongful interference with the employment contract.

'Ample' evidence to support lost profits. Post-trial, the defendants first challenged the damages verdict in a motion for judgment as a matter of law or for a new trial, which the district court denied.

In terms of lost profits, the defendants made a two-prong argument. First, they said the plaintiff had no right to lost profits because the applicable Minnesota law limited damages for a claim of tortious interference with a contract to breach of contract damages, which means replacement costs only.

Second, the defendants claimed there was insufficient evidence for the jury to consider the defendants' conduct the direct cause of the plaintiff's lost profits. The plaintiff failed to take into account other factors causing a decline in its profits, including the superiority of the competitor's product and changing market trends.

Also, the defendants dismissed the importance of the correlation between the plaintiff's decline in profits and the almost identical rise in the defendant's profits, arguing by itself the correlation did not prove causation.

The district court found both arguments unconvincing. It noted that under Minnesota law lost profits were available as a remedy for tortious conduct "where the evidence sufficiently establishes such losses." Here, the plaintiff furnished "ample evidence" to support the jury's conclusion that the employee's leaving the plaintiff to work for the competitor caused the plaintiff's lost profits. The plaintiff not only showed a direct correlation between its financial performance and the employee's departure and work for the competitor, but it also showed the competitor had induced the employee to breach his contract and go to work for it as part of a strategy to convert a coveted client account from the plaintiff to the competitor.

Further, the plaintiff offered testimony from a physician at the hospital that neither party's cardiac mapping system was superior and that the cardiology group's founding physician continued to use only the plaintiff's system even after having access to the competitor's product.

The plaintiff established direct causation and proved the loss stemming from the alleged misconduct with reasonable certainty, the district court concluded.

In their motion for a new trial, the defendants also challenged a number of evidentiary rulings. For example, they claimed the district court erred in admitting evidence about the defendant's strategy to hire the employee in order to secure his business, saying this evidence was only related to the issue of liability. The court disagreed, finding the evidence was relevant to prove causation and lost profit damages; at the same time, the court said evidence as to the employee's subjective reasons for breaching the agreement with the plaintiff had no relevance to the issue of damages and, therefore, was excludable.

The court also affirmed its decision to admit evidence of the defendant company's sales, finding this information, too, was relevant to the elements of causation and damages.

Damages rulings stand. The defendants appealed the district court's rulings with the 8th Circuit Court of Appeals. First they argued the district court erred when it declined to consider the employment contract an unenforceable restrictive covenant. Although the contract was enforceable by damages and not an injunction, damages in this case had the same effect as an unlawful restrictive covenant, the defendants claimed.

The appeals court rejected this argument. The contract did not amount to a "perpetual prohibition of competition" because it limited to a fixed number of years the employees' "lock-up." Moreover, the employer bargained for the lock-up period with employees by providing them with valuable compensation and giving a promise not to terminate them. Also, the penalty for the breach of contract was related to the damages the employer actually incurred as a result of the breach. Therefore, the Court of Appeals concluded, the district court correctly found the contract was enforceable and the defendant company was liable for tortious interference with the agreement.

Next, the Court of Appeals dismissed the defendants' argument that lost profit damages were not available here because they were not contract damages. This claim was based on a misreading of the applicable case law, the court said, and it affirmed the district court's decision to allow for the recovery of lost profits.

Finally, the Court of Appeals rejected the defendants' attack on the evidence the plaintiff introduced to show lost profits. According to the defendants, there was counterevidence that suggested a salesperson such as the employee had no role to play in a hospital's decision as to which technology to use. Also, testimony from a physician suggested the hospital began looking at the competitor's product before the employee left the plaintiff.

According to the Court of Appeals, the jury as the fact finder was free to decide whose testimony to credit and what parts of a witness's testimony to believe or disbelieve. And, although a corresponding shift in profits by itself may not be sufficient to show causation, here the plaintiff offered specific information about the purchasing decision of the client and the comparability of the two systems in addition to the correlation in the companies' financial performance. The district court correctly found a jury could conclude the defendant company's conduct caused the plaintiff's lost profits, the Court of Appeals concluded. It upheld all of the damages.

Sternat v. Sternat

Citation: 2015 Wisc. App. LEXIS 776
Date of decision: Oct. 28, 2015
Country: US
State/Jurisdiction: Wisconsin
Court: Court of Appeals
Type of action: Marital Dissolution
Experts: Marcia Teal (husband); Kris Disbrow (wife)
Judge: Per Curiam
SIC: 7299 Miscellaneous Personal Services, NEC (except diet and weight reducing services, personal care services, valet parking services, babysitting bureaus, debt and credit counseling, consumer bartering services, and formal wear and costume rental)
NAICS code: 561311 Employment Placement Agencies

Business Debt Renders Expert's Lack of BV Credentials Inconsequential

A recent divorce case featured a noteworthy challenge to the prevailing testimony of the wife's expert. The husband claimed the opinion of the wife's expert was unreliable because the expert had fewer credentials as a business valuator than did the husband's expert. The court found under the circumstances business valuation experience did not matter very much.

Business awash in tax problems. The company was a healthcare staffing agency that the wife set up in 2005. The wife was its president, and the husband was responsible for payroll processing and invoicing. Throughout the company's history, the wife ran into problems with the Internal Revenue Service for failing to pay payroll taxes. She defaulted repeatedly on a formal repayment plan the agency put in place, but she made "good faith" payments. To keep the business operating and deal with its debt, she secured several loans. At the time of divorce, the business had accumulated approximately $200,000 in debt.

At trial, both parties presented expert testimony. The husband's expert was a CPA and credentialed business valuator, who also was certified in financial forensics. She was experienced in testifying in a litigation setting in business valuation matters. She determined that the company's fair market value was $230,000, notwithstanding its debt. She acknowledged that, for the company to have any marketable value, it would need to be a going concern.

The wife's expert was an experienced CPA with no business valuation credentials. His practice specialized in working with "problem tax clients," he stated. He also said he had performed business valuations for buyers and sellers. Further, he had represented the company in its dealings with the IRS and was "intimately familiar" with its income, expenses, and the nature of its tax debt. The source of the company's financial problems was "mismanagement," he acknowledged. He concluded the company was no longer a going concern and assigned zero ($0) value to it.

The trial court adopted the zero value the wife's expert proposed.

A related issue was how to treat the business's $200,000 in debt stemming from the wife's failure to pay payroll taxes. The husband argued, under controlling case law, the debt represented marital waste. By her conduct, the wife had squandered marital assets.

The trial court disagreed. It allowed that the wife's decision not to pay payroll taxes "wasn't a very smart business decision, in fact, it was probably very bad." It likely could "cause the collapse of this company," the court added. But the court decided to treat this liability as marital debt subject to equal division. Both spouses worked for the business, and the husband, almost from the beginning, was aware that the taxes remained unpaid. The husband, in fact, testified the debt did "not really" create a problem between him and the wife, the court noted. And it pointed out that the wife made continuous, albeit unsuccessful, efforts to pay down the debt.

Post-trial, the husband filed a motion for reconsideration, arguing that the opinion of the wife's expert was inadmissible under the state's statute on expert testimony. That statutory provision essentially adopted the *Daubert* standard on reliability. The wife's expert lacked the necessary business valuation expertise and was unqualified to testify, the husband contended.

The trial court allowed that the husband's own expert was "eminently qualified" and "did a very good job." She "might have come out ahead," had it been a question of who was "the better expert on business valuation." But, given the company's ever-increasing liabilities, it was not a going concern, the trial court decided. Accordingly, the court denied the husband's motion.

Valuation a 'non-issue.' The husband appealed the judgment with the state Court of Appeals. He argued the trial court committed two errors. One, it admitted the opinion of the wife's expert even though that expert had less business valuation experience and fewer credentials and professional affiliations than the husband's expert. In that regard, the husband also noted the wife's expert based his opinion only on the expert's experience working with the company and on the company's financials. This narrow approach made the expert's opinion unreliable. In contrast, the husband's expert used a "broader array of data and valuation methods," the husband contended.

The appeals court was not persuaded. The key issue for the trial court was whether the business was a going concern and would still be in business in 12 months, the appeals court said. There was ample evidence to support the trial court's conclusion that it was not a going concern. "Valuation thus was a non-issue," the appeals court said. Even if allowing the wife's expert to testify were error, the error would be harmless. The testimony did not interfere with the husband's substantial rights, the appeals court added.

According to the husband, the trial court also erred when it declined to consider the business's debt marital waste. The appeals court again disagreed. The trial court's decision to assign the debt to both parties was based on the involvement of both spouses in the business and the husband's awareness of the unpaid taxes, the court observed. It was not error for the trial court to find that both parties benefited from the business when it was doing better and "that the debts were incurred in the interest of the marriage," the appeals court said. It added that the trial court's "reasoned refusal" not to divide the debt equally was a proper exercise of its discretion. The appeals court affirmed the trial court's valuation of the business.

In re Sunedison, Inc.

Citation: 2016 Bankr. LEXIS 2959
Date of decision: Aug. 11, 2016
Country: US
State/Jurisdiction: Federal/New York
Court: United States Bankruptcy Court
Type of action: Bankruptcy
Experts: Homer Parkhill (Rothschild, Inc.) (debtors); unknown (equity holders)
Judge: Bernstein
SIC: 4911 Electric Services (other electric power generation)
NAICS code: 221114 Solar Electric Power Generation

Debtors' Balance Sheet Not Reliable Indicator of Assets' Market Value

It is not uncommon for shareholders in a bankruptcy to resist the idea that the company they invested is insolvent and to question the accuracy of post-petition valuations offered by other stakeholders. But, as a recent bankruptcy court ruling involving a renewable energy business confirms, it is common for bankruptcy courts to reject the demands of equity holders for an equity committee. Cost concerns related to the formation of an equity committee tend to outweigh concerns that equity holders are not adequately represented in the reorganization discussions.

Questionable prepetition financials. The debtors group included Sunedison, a holding company, and many affiliate entities. The companies were in the business of developing renewable energy projects. The debtors filed for Chapter 11 bankruptcy on April 21, 2016 (petition date). The day before the petition date, there were approximately 436 million shares of Sunedison common stock outstanding and approximately 214 holders of record. At the time, the stock was trading at $0.34 per share.

Sunedison had two principal assets ("Yieldcos") that were not debtors and also were publicly traded.

Sunedison issued financial information that suggested its group of businesses was solvent on a consolidated basis as of the petition date. According to the last published unaudited balance sheet as of Sept. 30, 2015, shareholder equity was about $4.5 billion and total assets were $20.7 billion.

However, a March 2016 Form 8-K suggested that this information was not reliable. It mentioned the company's internal controls over financial reporting showed "material weaknesses" and said the company's audit committee was unable to complete its audit for the year ended Dec. 31, 2015. A subsequent Form 8-K said that the Department of Justice was investigating Sunedison regarding a problematic acquisition and that it had received an "informal nonpublic inquiry" from the Securities and Exchange Commission into similar issues.

A third Form 8-K that came out just before the petition date said the audit committee did not identify material misstatements in the company's historical financial statements but did identify problems related to cash flow forecasting. The projections were overly optimistic, and the company lacked adequate internal controls to manage cash flows.

In statements in support of the petition, Sunedison's vice president cast more doubt on the previously published financial data. The executive said that the Sunedison group owed secured and unsecured funded debt of about $3.8 billion and trade debt of at least $357 million. Moreover, he noted that stock prices for Sunedison and the Yieldcos had fallen.

A number of shareholders clung to the financial information the company had published, which indicated equity in excess of $4 billion, and asked the Bankruptcy Court to appoint an equity committee to protect their interests. The shareholders contended there was no valuation evidence that specifically discredited or contradicted the $4 billion equity value that appeared in the prepetition financials.

Several parties objected to the formation of an equity committee. They claimed that Sunedison's new management team and the creditors committee would adequately represent the interests of equity holders. They contended the debtors were hopelessly insolvent. Forcing creditors to shoulder the financial burden of paying for the professionals working on behalf of the equity committee when there was a substantial likelihood that the creditors would not get paid in full was improper.

Asset valuation revised. At an evidentiary hearing on the equity committee issue, the court received additional information regarding the company's solvency from the debtors' financial advisor and investment banker.

In a prehearing submission to the court, the advisor had made a conservative determination that, excluding debtor in possession financing, the debtors would be able to liquidate assets during the bankruptcy proceedings for about $850 million. This amount included $650 million from the sale of Yieldcos. He said his estimate was based on the average public trading price of shares in Yieldcos over a month-long period. The remaining $200 million resulted from liquidating other assets.

At the hearing, he revised the valuation of the debtors' assets upwards. He said share prices for the Yieldcos had risen, and as a result Sunedison's interest had increased by about $150 million. He also said his earlier estimate did not include a control premium for the Yieldco shares, which they might command and which might enhance share value by another 20% to 30%. Sunedison's Yieldco stock might be worth about $1.1 billion, the debtors' financial advisor concluded.

In addition, he noted there was more interest than anticipated from potential buyers of other assets. There currently was an expectation of significant realizable value in those assets. He determined that the debtors might be able to gain as much as $1.5 billion from the sale of the various assets.

At the same time, the debtors' secured and unsecured debt was about $4.2 billion, and contingent liabilities could amount to another $1.2 billion, or more. He said that Sunedison's debt was trading at around $0.06 as of late May 2016.

Connection between solvency and equity's representation. The court noted that Bankruptcy Code Section 1102(a)(2) authorizes the formation of an equity committee "if necessary to assure adequate representation of creditors or of equity security holders." Courts look to "the number of shareholders, the complexity of the case, and whether the cost of the additional committee significantly outweighs the concern for adequate representation."

The court explained that the issue of solvency was "intertwined with the concept of adequate representation because it defines the extent of the interests that require adequate representation." If a debtor is solvent, there is concern that creditors will propose a reorganization plan "based on a conservative estimate of the debtor's worth that captures all of the value of the reorganized entity, including value possibly in excess of the unsecured claims, through the issuance of new stock to the creditors at the expense of old equity whose shares will be cancelled." In a nutshell, creditors may take control of the company by paying less than adequate consideration for it.

On the other hand, the court explained, if the bankruptcy estate is hopelessly insolvent, the equity holders have no economic interest in the case and no right to any distribution under a reorganization plan. In that situation, the estate should not have to finance an equity committee.

The court also pointed out that, for purposes of deciding whether or not to appoint an equity committee, it was not required to hold an "exhaustive valuation" hearing on the issue of solvency. The main question, the court emphasized, is whether the debtor "*appears to be* hopelessly insolvent."

Equity holders have the burden of showing an equity committee is "necessary." Here, the Bankruptcy Court concluded, they did not meet their burden.

The court agreed the case was complex and the number of outstanding common shares and shareholders was significant. At the same time, based on the financial evidence to date, the company appeared to be hopelessly insolvent, the court decided. It declared the prepetition financial statements showing shareholders' equity of roughly $4 billion unreliable. It noted, with emphasis, the last published *unaudited* data spoke as of September 2015. Subsequent Forms 8-K reported on problems related to financial reporting. Many of the financial statements also were consolidated statements that failed to differentiate between assets and income attributable to the debtors and assets and income attributable to the Yieldcos.

Insolvency, the court said, "turns on a comparison between the debtor's debts and the 'fair valuation' of its property." In terms of a going concern, fair value means the fair market price the debtor's assets could command "if sold in a prudent manner within a reasonable period of time to pay the debtor's debt." The court emphasized that fair value is not the value appearing on a company's balance sheet, even if many shareholders have relied on that balance sheet when deciding to invest in the company.

Here, there was some evidence of market value, the court noted, pointing to the revised valuation of the debtors' financial advisor. But, even assuming the fair market value of the debtors' assets reached $1.5 billion, "[t]his is $2.5 billion less than the undisputed funded debt and trade debt totaling over $4 billion," the court said. Also, the trading price of Sunedison's debt was about $0.06. Although this steep discount was not conclusive, it was an indication that the company was insolvent. According to the court: "Trading on six cents on the dollar does not imply solvency."

Early evidence points toward insolvency. The court noted that proponents of the equity committee relied on case law that was not on point. The court gave attention to a recent bench decision in *In re Horsehead Holding Corp.* (Bankr. D. Del.). There, the judge ruled in favor of an equity committee notwithstanding evidence that the debtors were insolvent. The court in *Horsehead* said it had significant doubts about the valuation information the debtors presented and that it was unable to decide whether there was a reasonable or substantial likelihood that equity would receive any value in the case.

The court in the instant case said the *Horsehead* bench decision put into relief the dilemma a court faces when ruling on a request for an equity committee early in the case. It has to decide based on evidence in front of it whether or not the debtor is or appears solvent. Where that evidence is unreliable or ambiguous and other factors point toward the formation of an equity committee, a court has discretion to appoint a committee.

In contrast, here the evidence suggested that an equity committee was not necessary, the court said. The debtors were hopelessly insolvent. "The appointment of an Equity Committee … will not create value where it does not exist." The court said the shareholders would be able to renew their request if the facts changed—a possibility it considered "substantially unlikely."

In re Trulia Stockholder Litig.

Citation: 2016 Del. Ch. LEXIS 8
Date of decision: Jan. 22, 2016
Country: US
State/Jurisdiction: Delaware
Court: Court of Chancery of Delaware
Type of action: Dissenting Shareholder
Experts: J.P. Morgan (defendant); N/A (plaintiffs)
Judge: Bouchard (Chancellor)
SIC: 6531 Real Estate Agents and Managers (except property managers, condominium associations, cemetery management, agents and brokers, operating housing authorities, and appraisers)
NAICS code: 531 Real Estate

More Valuation Data Do Not Ensure Fair Class Action Settlement

Class action shareholder suits contesting a merger have become commonplace and so have "disclosure settlements." The latter require plaintiffs to drop their legal claims against the defendant(s) in exchange for additional information that in theory may help stockholders in deciding on the proposed transaction. Courts are increasingly skeptical about the fairness of this bargain. Recently, the Delaware Court of Chancery's chief judge gave full expression to his misgivings about disclosure settlements when he evaluated the benefit to shareholders of additional valuation-related information.

Too much information. The case centered on the real estate site Zillow and its acquisition of Trulia, an online provider of information on homes for purchase or rent. Four Trulia stockholders objected to the merger and filed a class action in the Delaware Court of Chancery, claiming in essence that

Trulia's board of directors breached its fiduciary duty when it approved the transaction. The merger took place, and, less than four months later, the parties had worked out an agreement-in-principle to settle. In exchange for a very broad release of claims, the class of plaintiffs would receive information that was not in the proxy statements the Trulia stockholders had available prior to voting on the transaction.

Once the parties agree to settle the dispute, the dynamics of the litigation typically change. Both sides work to obtain the court's approval of the settlement. Usually, the only party gaining a monetary benefit from the settlement is the plaintiffs' counsel.

In the instant case, prior to voting on the proposed merger, the Trulia and Zillow stockholders received a 224-page proxy statement that discussed the board's reasons for supporting the transaction and explained the opinions of the financial experts advising the boards. It included a 10-page, single-spaced summary of the opinion of Trulia's financial advisor, J.P. Morgan.

In advocating in favor of the settlement agreement, the Trulia plaintiffs claimed that four additional disclosures related to the various financial analyses J.P. Morgan had performed in regard to the transaction were of sufficient benefit to warrant the release of existing and future claims. The disclosures included: (1) synergy numbers in J.P. Morgan's value creation analyses; (2) selected transaction multiples; (3) selected public trading multiples; and (4) implied terminal EBITDA multiples for a relative discounted cash flow analysis.

In assessing the value of the extra disclosures, and by extension the fairness of the settlement, to the absent class members, the chancellor noted the Chancery's historical practice of approving such settlements, even though they frequently were of marginal value to the plaintiffs. The chancellor considered this past attitude of the court one of the causes for the explosion of deal litigation "beyond the realm of reason."

He said the lack of an adversarial process required the court to assume the role of forensic examiner of proxy materials to determine what stockholders would "get" from the additional disclosures in relation to what they would "give" when agreeing to drop claims against the defendants and their affiliates. "It is all too common for a plaintiff to identify and obtain supplemental disclosure of a laundry list of minutiae in a financial advisor's board presentation that does not appear in the summary of the advisor's analysis in the proxy materials," he observed. According to the chancellor, "the optimal means by which disclosure claims in deal litigation should be adjudicated is outside the context of a proposed settlement."

He cautioned that, barring that, "practitioners should expect that the Court will continue to be increasingly vigilant in applying its independent judgment" when assessing the reasonableness of the settlements in the individual case. To be of genuine benefit, the supplemental disclosures have to be "plainly material," the chancellor stated. For information to be material to a reasonable stockholder means it "significantly alter[s] the 'total mix' of information made available."

Immaterial and not helpful data. None of the four supplemental disclosures in the instant case met that standard, the chancellor decided.

1. *Synergy numbers.* In advising Trulia, the target of the merger, J.P. Morgan prepared two value creation analyses, one using an intrinsic value approach and another based on a market approach. In the former analysis, J.P. Morgan compared the implied equity value resulting from a discounted cash flow analysis of Trulia on a stand-alone basis to the Trulia stockholders' pro forma ownership of the implied equity value of the combined company. Under the market approach, J.P. Morgan compared the public market equity value of Trulia on a stand-alone basis to the stockholders' pro forma ownership of the implied equity value of the combined company.

Based on the parties' proposed settlement, the additional disclosure would show that, under the intrinsic value approach, J.P. Morgan assumed after-tax synergies of $175 million. In contrast, the proxy already showed that, under the market approach, J.P. Morgan used synergies of $100 million.

The plaintiffs claimed that having both numbers available was of significance to stockholders: "Had [stockholders] initially known that the market-based approach analysis was skewed downward by using lower synergies numbers, their view of the resulting implied value and reliability of [J.P. Morgan's] analysis may have changed appreciably."

The chancellor dismissed this argument. It seemed logical that the two different approaches would call for different synergies, the court said. An intrinsic value approach would use synergies based on long-term management projections, whereas a market-based approach would use synergies based on what would be publicly announced to investors. The proxy materials accurately explained which synergy assumptions the financial advisor used for which analysis, the court added.

It also observed that the $175 million synergy figure in fact appeared in a table that explained management's synergy expectations and that was included in the proxy materials. Inserting that figure a few pages later, without an explanatory context, was not only of no benefit to the stockholders, but also could have created confusion more than anything else, the chancellor said.

Finally, the court noted that the plaintiffs exaggerated the importance of being able to juxtapose the synergy figures considering the proxy materials made it clear that the market-based value creation analysis was secondary to the intrinsic value analysis.

The proxy gave a fair summary of the methods and assumptions J.P. Morgan used for its two value creation analyses, the court said. Additional minutiae underlying some of the assumptions would not alter the total mix of information, and, therefore, the supplemental disclosure was not material. It was "not even helpful to stockholders," the chancellor concluded.

2. *Individual company multiples in transaction analysis.* The proxy showed that J.P. Morgan also performed a precedent transactions analysis for which it considered 32 transactions featuring companies it considered similar to Trulia. The proxy further indicated the low and high forward EBITDA multiples for the transactions. Based on this analysis and considering other factors, J.P. Morgan created a narrower range of multiples to arrive at an estimated range of equity values per share for Trulia's common stock.

In advocating for the settlement, the plaintiffs claimed that it was significant that stockholders would receive the multiples for each of the 32 transactions for which there was publicly available information. This information was not in the proxy. The plaintiffs contended that the additional information showed that there was no publicly available information for 15 of the 32 transactions. Knowing this, they said, might make stockholders realize that J.P. Morgan's precedent transactions analysis was less "robust" than the proxy suggested.

The chancellor disagreed. No one argued that having 16 similar transactions was an insufficient number for J.P. Morgan's analysis, he noted. The revelation that some of the individual multiples were not publicly available "could not reasonably have been expected to significantly alter the total mix of information," the court added. Most important, under the law, the stockholders are entitled to a "fair summary" of the financial advisor's methodology and assumptions. But there is no requirement to provide stockholders with sufficient data to allow them to conduct their own valuation, the court observed.

3. Individual company multiples in selected public trading analysis. The proxy gave the names of the 16 publicly traded companies J.P. Morgan used as comparables to develop ranges of forward EBITDA and revenue multiples for Trulia and Zillow. The multiples for Trulia and Zillow were based on the last unaffected trading day before the announcement of the merger. The proxy showed the median multiples for the three categories into which the financial advisor grouped the comparable companies, but it did not include the individual multiples for the companies.

In contrast, the supplemental disclosure would show the revenue and EBITDA multiples for each of the 16 companies.

Citing case law, the plaintiffs claimed that the individual company multiples were material per se. And they claimed that providing the individual multiples allowed stockholders to compare the EBITDA growth rates and multiples of the comparable companies to those of Trulia's.

The chancellor disagreed that the multiples were material. In the case the plaintiffs cited, the original disclosures listed the comparable companies without providing any summary multiple data at all, the court noted. Here, the financial advisor provided data for the three categories of companies but not the individual company multiples. Also, in the instant case, the individual company multiples were already publicly available. The Trulia proxy essentially started where the prior case on which the plaintiffs relied ended, the court said.

In terms of the ability to compare growth rates and multiples, the chancellor said that basic valuation principles suggest to stockholders that higher growth rates should correspond to higher multiples. And he pointed out that the supplemental disclosures did not contain EBITDA growth rates, "so the figures necessary to make that comparison are not present in any event."

4. Implied terminal EBITDA multiples in DCF analysis. J.P. Morgan conducted a DCF analysis to determine the per-share equity value of Trulia and Zillow, respectively, based on management projections showing cash flows from 2014 through 2028 and using the perpetuity growth method to calculate the companies' terminal values.

The proxy indicated unlevered free cash flows, discount rates in the range of 11% to 15%, and perpetuity growth rates in the range of 2.5% to 3.5%.

The supplemental disclosures would show the EBITDA exit multiple ranges that the range of terminal values for the two companies implied. According to the plaintiffs, the implied multiples were important to stockholders that were concerned that the exit multiples for the companies were nearly identical, even though the companies' EBITDA growth rates showed differences, and that were concerned because the exit multiples were much lower than the current EBITDA multiples of Trulia and its peers.

"The logic of the plaintiffs' argument is flawed," the chancellor said. For one, it should not be surprising that the implied exit EBITDA multiples would be similar for both companies where the financial advisor used the same range of perpetuity growth rates to calculate the terminal values for both companies. Also, the exit EBITDA multiples were based on growth assumptions *as of 2028, not 2015,* the court said with emphasis. Trulia's then current EBITDA growth rate was high, but basic valuation principles suggested that it would eventually fall to a market-based rate.

The supplemental disclosure was not only immaterial, but it also "serves none of the purposes that plaintiffs allege," the court found.

In sum, the proxy provided a "more-than-fair" summary of J.P. Morgan's financial analysis in all four respects, the court concluded. Therefore, from the Trulia stockholders' perspective, giving up a host of claims to the defendants and their affiliates in return for the supplemental disclosures did not result in a fair or reasonable settlement, the chancellor concluded. He declined to approve the proposed agreement.

Verghetta v. Lawlor

Citation: 2016 N.Y. Misc. LEXIS 845
Date of decision: March 9, 2016
Country: US
State/Jurisdiction: New York
Court: Supreme Court of New York (Trial Court)
Type of action: Judicial Dissolution (incl. Withdrawal, Buy Out)
Experts: Bruce S. Schaeffer (plaintiff); Gary R. Trugman (defendants)
Judge: Scheinkman
SIC: 7991 Physical Fitness Facilities
NAICS code: 713940 Fitness and Recreational Sports Centers

No Place for DLOM and Tax Affecting in N.Y. Fair Value Determination

The most recent New York statutory fair value proceeding has oodles of drama—all of it valuation related. It featured unevenly matched valuation experts and a gaping difference in values. The court, in trying to make sense of the conflicting testimony and the financial evidence, ruled on contentious issues such as the appropriateness of the marketability discount and tax affecting. Coursing through the court's decision is the concern for achieving a plausible and fair result.

Backstory. The case involved three (roughly equal) partners who owned Planet Fitness franchises and the two limited liability companies they had formed to manage the existing fitness clubs and establish new ones. One company was JGJ Holding (JGJ), which the partners set up in 2012 to hold 29 existing franchises in New York City and develop new facilities pursuant to a development agreement with the franchisor. The second company was JGJg Holding Co. LLC (JGJg), which they set up in December 2013. Three months later, in March 2014, JGJg paid the franchisor $180,000 for the right to develop and operate fitness clubs in Southern California. The funding came from the New York entity, JGJ. The three partners held equal interests in JGJg, and the named defendant, who served as in-house counsel, owned a 5% interest.

The fitness industry is extremely competitive, with health club models coming in all shapes and forms to accommodate the public's ever-changing tastes and needs. The court said for background information it relied mostly on the defendant expert's "thorough, researched, documented and credible analysis of the general economy, the regional economies, and the health fitness industry."

In terms of the competition, Planet Fitness is one of the largest health club chains in the country—in large part because of its low membership fees. For the franchisee, this distinction comes at a cost. Development agreements heavily favor the franchisor, requiring the franchisee to open a certain number of clubs per year and to buy the gym equipment from the franchisor. The franchisor has the right of first refusal regarding any sale the owner contemplates, it sets membership fees, and it must approve changes to the brand's fitness model. Franchisees also must contribute to a national advertising fund. Further, the clubs are not set up to provide services and amenities that might generate extra revenue.

Under the franchise agreement, JGJ had to open six clubs per year through 2028. The JGJg development agreement required the company to open 18 new clubs in California with 18 leases to be signed by the end of 2017. The California agreement included a provision prohibiting JGJg from reselling development rights at a profit.

After the partners fell out, the plaintiff sued the other two partners (brothers) and the lawyer, alleging breach of contract and tort claims and asking for judicial dissolution. Ultimately, the parties asked the court for a fair value determination of the two companies to enable a buyout of the plaintiff's interest. The valuation date was June 2014.

No totally reliable valuation. Both sides presented expert testimony to support their positions. The plaintiff's expert was a tax lawyer with no formal valuation training or certification. In contrast, the defendants' expert was one of the intellectual leaders of the valuation profession.

The plaintiff's expert valued the two corporations at over $162 million and the plaintiff's interest at over $53 million. The defendants' expert valued one company at $6.2 million and the other at $208,000. Assuming a total value of $6.4 million, he found the plaintiff's interest was worth about $2.2 million.

Since this was a bench trial, the court allowed the plaintiff's expert to testify on valuation. But it said it considered "his expertise in the area of valuations to be lacking" and found his analysis "seriously flawed." Even if his valuation approach were valid, his "execution of it is fraught with misjudgments and errors," the court said. At the same time, it declined to adopt the defense valuation as presented. Instead, it decided to adjust two components of the defendant expert's valuation to raise the value of the one-third interest to $8.8 million.

California entity's value. A preliminary issue was how to value the California entity, JGJg. The plaintiff's expert argued the two companies essentially represented a single entity in that they were centrally administered and supported by a single credit facility. Each company added synergistic value to the other. Based on historic data from the New York operation, he created projections as to the net present value of each newly opened club. He used that number for the eight clubs he projected would open in New York and the three clubs he projected would open in California in 2015. Based on this analysis, he arrived at a total enterprise value of over $150.6 million, $23.2 million of it attributable to JGJg, the California operation.

The defendants' expert used an asset approach. He found that, at the valuation date, JGJg had about $28,200 in cash and another $169,200, which represented the capitalized value of the $180,000 development, less amortization. Because the funding came from JGJ, JGJg owed the New York entity over $235,400. Consequently, members' equity was nearly -$39,000.

The court discredited the plaintiff expert's "construct" with which he tried to calculate positive cash flow from as yet nonexisting California clubs. It agreed with the defendants' expert that extrapolating the net present value of a nonexisting California club from the net present value of a future New York club was "highly speculative." It pointed out that, on the valuation date, the California operation had no facilities, no employees, no leases, and no budgets or forecasts. The plaintiff's expert failed to consider how the environment in California differed from the operating reality in New York. He prepared no revenue forecasts or an analysis accounting for startup costs related to equipment and other capital items.

The court said the plaintiff's $23 million valuation of the California operation "defie[d] economic reality." It observed that, just three months before the valuation date, JGJg had paid $180,000 for the right to develop facilities in California. It was "highly improbable, if not inconceivable" that the franchisor, which by all accounts made agreements that were highly in its favor, would agree to sell development rights that were worth $23 million for only $180,000, the court said.

The court dismissed the proposition that there was "synergistic" value in operating the New York and California entities together. It decided to value JGJg as a stand-alone entity, adopting the defendant expert's view that this entity represented an early-stage development company that should be valued under the asset approach. The assets, the court said, were the $28,200 in cash and the $180,000 paid to the franchisor (the court chose to ignore the impact of capitalization). It found that, since the funding came from JGJ, a total of $208,200 should be added to the value of JGJ. It assigned zero value to the California entity.

New York entity's value. In terms of the New York operation, JGJ, the court said, "Both valuations are fraught with issues."

Plaintiff's expert. The plaintiff's expert basically valued each of the existing 32 clubs individually and determined what the plaintiff's one-third interest was worth. This approach in itself was flawed, the court said. In this case, a hypothetical buyer would want to buy and, therefore, know the value of the integrated enterprise. It would not want to buy "club-by-individual club."

Although the expert stated he performed a discounted cash flow analysis, "he did not actually do so," the court said. He performed a future earnings analysis that did not account for depreciation or capital expenditures or working capital.

Unjustifiable adjustments. The court observed that, in valuing the existing clubs, the expert made adjustments that had no support in the financial evidence. For example, for 2014, management predicted an 8.86% rate for "returns and allowances"—nonpaid monthly membership fees. At the valuation date, in June 2014, the actual rate was 8.7%. However, the plaintiff's expert capped the rate at 7.5% without "basis for doubting management's figures and without understanding the actual facts," the court said. Moreover, because he found it "unfair and abhorrent" that JGJ was obligated to pay the franchisor royalties for uncollected membership fees, the expert declined to treat the royalties as a real expense. He reduced depreciation for existing clubs ostensibly "to conform to New York's tax code," without considering actual depreciation stemming from the need to replace worn-out exercise equipment. Cross-examination showed the adjustment the plaintiff's expert made was unnecessary since the company did not take accelerated depreciation, the court noted.

A propensity to inflate revenues and diminish expenses was in evidence throughout the expert's analysis of the existing clubs, the court observed. The valuation of "future clubs" was similarly problematic. The court was skeptical of the expert's sampling of prevaluation date clubs to determine a net present value of cash flows for hypothetical future clubs. It found the analysis failed to consider costs related to building and equipping each new club and did not account for the operating costs the company incurred prior to opening a new club.

This was "not a genuine effort to place a fair value on JGJ," the court summed up its assessment of the valuation testimony. It was an attempt to maximize recovery for the plaintiff, as evident from the plaintiff expert's assigning a $139 million enterprise value to JGJ, which excluded $29 million in debt outstanding as of the valuation date. The court dismissed this approach as "not professional"—adding that the valuation also included $6.8 million in uncorrected math errors.

Defendants' expert. The defendants' expert was "a true valuation professional," the court said. But it found his value determination came with its own set of problems.

Flawed DCF analysis. The expert relied on the income approach—discounted cash flow (DCF) analysis—but performed a market-based analysis as a sanity check. In normalizing historic statements, he adjusted officer compensation by doubling it. The new levels aligned with compensation in other companies, he said.

The court was troubled by the degree of adjustment, noting that the principals of the company were the three officers. It thought it immaterial that their compensation was low, considering they would receive the benefit in the form of profit distribution. It also noted that the expert failed to show that the companies he used as guidance to achieve reasonable compensation also were pass-through entities, similar to JGJ; further, the court said the expert failed to address the question of whether JGJ would need three officers—a CEO, COO, and CFO—as his calculation assumed.

As for the cash flow projections underlying the DCF analysis, since the company had no five-year forecast, the expert created a model analyzing the performance of 24 of the 32 existing clubs (he excluded eight that were too recent) from the clubs' inception to Year 5. He adjusted for depreciation, capital expenditures, and changes in working capital needs. He noted that membership fees were set by the franchisor, which had not increased them in 10 years. Therefore, the expert's model showed rising expenses but not rising fees.

Specifically, his analysis showed that, in Years 2 and 3, club membership was steadily increasing, but, in Year 4, growth slowed. By Year 5, there was a marked decline that continued. He acknowledged that, to avoid projecting the clubs' going out of business, he tweaked the model by cutting off the decline after five years and introducing a 2.5% terminal growth rate. "I cut it off intentionally because it wouldn't make sense to have negative growth until every one of these clubs went out of business at some point in time."

The court said the model suffered from an "analytical flaw." The court recognized that "it would be purely speculative" to assume the franchisor would eventually increase membership fees. But it also said it was "highly problematic and unfair" to assume there would be no increase in fees but an increase in expenses. It dismissed the expert's proposition that the franchisor might freeze fees on purpose "to swoop in and buy back the franchises at low prices." According to the court, it would be "suicidal" for the defendants to hold onto the companies "at any price" if the companies were on a perpetual downward descent. Yet, holding onto the business is exactly what they wanted to do.

Insufficiently explained DLOM. The defendants' expert applied a 35% marketability discount, which he admitted was "towards the high end" but found justifiable. One of the justifications was the franchise agreement, which, among other restrictions, gave the franchisor the right of first refusal on a sale of a franchise.

The defendants' expert also noted a significant deferred rent liability on the company's books. While paying lower rent, the company's owners were able to recognize a greater expense for accounting purposes, which reduced the profit passed through to them and lowered taxes. However, a hypothetical buyer would know that the favorable tax treatment inexorably would end. The expert suggested the unfavorable tax treatment might begin in October 2016 and accelerate and continue for another 30 years.

Finally, the expert assumed the company would be subject to a holding period given the restrictions on sale and transfer.

Of the three reasons, the only one that resonated with the court was the transfer restrictions the franchisor imposed. But since the defendants' expert had failed to provide a way with which to apportion to the effect of that reason ("discounting the discount"), the court found the defendants had not met their burden.

The court went on to say that, even if there were a way to determine the appropriate discount level, it would reject a DLOM under the circumstances. Referencing the 2014 *Zelouf* decision in which the court declined to apply a DLOM, the court in the instant case said no New York appellate court has mandated a marketability discount in a statutory fair value determination. See *Zelouf Int'l Corp. v. Zelouf*, 2014 N.Y. Misc. LEXIS 4341 (Oct. 6, 2014) (available at *BVLaw*).

Here, the defendants made it clear that they had no intention of selling the company and no amount of money would make them sell. Accordingly, the plaintiff "should not recover less due to possible illiquidity costs in the event of a sale that is not likely to occur," the court said. Applying a marketability discount in this situation would be the "economic equivalent of imposing an impermissible minority discount," the court added. The plaintiff, who was obligated to sell his interest based on the price the court determined, would get less for his interest while the defendants would "get to realize the full value by staying in control." This outcome would conflict with the court's effort to achieve a fair result.

<u>Problematic tax affecting.</u> Because JGJ was a pass-through entity, the defendants' expert thought it appropriate to apply an 18.5% tax rate at the entity level. Tax affecting was justified, he explained, because the buyer of the company would account for taxes when developing cash flow projections. A buyer only wants to pay for the true value on the investment. In developing the applicable tax rate, the expert followed the Delaware Court of Chancery's Kessler model. See *Delaware Open MRI Radiology Assocs., P.A. v. Kessler*, 898 A.2d 290 (Del. Ch. 2006) (available at *BVLaw*).

The 18.5% tax rate assumed a 10.85% rate to account for New York State and New York City taxes effective at the valuation date. But the expert conceded that "[p]ersonal tax rates may vary depending on many factors that have nothing to do with the investment. A valuation analyst cannot be expected to consider items such as personal exemptions and itemized deductions." Further, the amount of distributions an owner chose in a given year depended on factors specific to the owner's situation.

The court was not receptive to the arguments in favor of tax affecting. It said the expert's calculation ignored the tax effect on the seller and "unduly" focused on the buyer's side. The buyout of the seller's interest represented a taxable event to the seller with the proceeds from the sale taxed as ordinary income, not capital gain. The court noted that, if it were to allow tax affecting, the seller in effect would incur a double tax: once on the entity level and again on the personal level. It also credited the plaintiff expert's argument that the law allowed the buyers to step up the basis of the company's assets and reap significant tax savings. Finally, the court thought it inappropriate to account for New York City taxes when none of the parties resided there, and it even considered accounting for New York State taxes a matter of speculation.

There was no New York appellate law in favor of tax affecting, the court said. Moreover, there was disagreement in various jurisdictions over the appropriateness of the practice. It noted the U.S. Tax Court's consistent objection to tax affecting in decisions going all the way back to *Gross v. Commissioner*, T.C. Memo 1999-254, aff'd 272 F.3d (6th Cir. 2001) (available at *BVLaw*).

Pragmatic resolution. The court concluded that the value the defendants' expert proposed was unreasonably low. To require the plaintiff to accept a buyout based on that calculation was "fundamentally unfair." It decided that the most feasible way to increase the valuation was having the defendants' expert compute the value of JGJ without tax affecting and without applying a marketability discount. The resulting amount, about $26 million, plus the $208,200 related to the California operation, represented the fair value of the company, the court said. Since the plaintiff owned a one-third interest in the company, his share was worth about $8.8 million, plus interest starting from the valuation date, the court decided.

Wagner v. Wagner

Citation: 2016 Ida. LEXIS 128
Date of decision: April 27, 2016
Country: US
State/Jurisdiction: Idaho
Court: Supreme Court
Type of action: Judicial Dissolution (incl. Withdrawal, Buy Out)
Experts: Dennis Reinstein (plaintiffs/respondents/minority); Paul Hyde (defendants/appellants/majority)
Judge: Horton
SIC: 0191 General Farms, Primarily Crop
NAICS code: 111998 All Other Miscellaneous Crop Farming

High Court Pushes Back on Mandatory Discounts in Fair Value Determinations

When it comes to the use of discounts in fair value proceedings, most of the decisions that have galvanized the valuation profession have come out of New York. Think *Zelouf*, *AriZona Ice Tea*, and, most recently, *La Verghetta*. But, with its recent key ruling on discounts, the Idaho Supreme Court has become a key contributor to the conversation. The question the court answered—one of first impression in Idaho—was whether minority and marketability discounts should be mandatory when determining fair value.

Trial court rejects expert appraisals. The source of contention was a closely held family farming business whose assets included a mill, over 1,000 acres of land, lake property, and homes. The shareholders were the children of the founders of the business. Since 1998, they unsuccessfully had tried to affect a split under Section 355 of the Internal Revenue Code. A minority group of shareholders that owned 28% of the shares wanted the mill and adjoining land for employment and housing reasons. The idea was that the majority owners would receive the remaining assets.

At the end of June 2012, the shareholders obtained an appraisal that valued the corporation's net assets at $1.61 million under the cost approach. The company then hired an attorney to assist with crafting the split. At the beginning of July 2012, the attorney presented a spreadsheet that assigned a value of about $3.3 million to the corporation as an ongoing business—$3,344 for each of the company's 1,000 shares. He valued the mill at $1.7 million. His valuation was based on the June 2012 appraisal and a financial statement from the company's accountant. Some of the financial information turned out to be incorrect.

The majority was ready to sell the mill for this price, but the minority could not afford to pay this much. Ultimately, the majority gave up on the 355 split, shut down the mill, and liquidated its assets. In response, the minority sued for dissolution of the company. Subsequently, the parties stipulated to a buyout based on the court's determination of the fair value of the corporation's shares.

At a bench trial, both sides offered expert testimony. The minority's expert had extensive experience appraising closely held companies, many of them agricultural processing facilities. He considered many of the same sources the attorney had used, including the June 2012 appraisal and the financial information from the corporate accountant. But he caught and corrected the errors. He arrived at a value of $3,399 per share.

The majority's expert, who was not a CPA, used an August 2012 valuation date based on the applicable statute. He did not place a value on the mill as a going concern, arguing it was in poor condition and had substantial safety issues. He applied discounts for lack of control and marketability and valued the minority's voting shares at $1,540 per share and nonvoting shares at $1,490 per unit.

The trial court decided the attorney's valuation of $3,344 per share was the most credible appraisal, notwithstanding the problematic financial data underlying it. It noted that this value was "very close" to the value the minority's expert, who had corrected the errors, determined.

The court discredited the majority expert's opinion, noting his failure to include "numerous assets" in his calculation. The court particularly took issue with the expert's position on the mill, finding he lacked the expertise to assess the mill's safety issues. It also declined to apply any discounts.

Appeal homes in on discounts. The majority appealed the trial court's determination with the state Supreme Court. It made essentially three arguments: (1) the trial court's decision was not based on substantial and competent evidence; (2) the court used the wrong valuation date; and (3) the court erred in not using discounts.

Sufficiency of evidence. The majority shareholders contended the trial court credited an appraisal that was not done by a professional appraiser and that relied on flawed financial data.

The Supreme Court acknowledged that the attorney's spreadsheet "may contain inaccuracies and is not the sort of appraisal that would ordinarily be presented at trial." But it pointed out the appraisal was not prepared in anticipation of trial. Rather, at trial, the minority relied on an expert appraisal that was based on a more detailed analysis, used more or less the same data sources as the attorney's appraisal, and came in very close to the prevailing value determination. Therefore, even if "it is far from clear that [the attorney] possessed the requisite expertise to appraise the corporation, the valuation of the Minority's expert buttresses the district court's finding," the Supreme Court said.

Further, the high court found the record provided "substantial reasons" for the trial court's rejection of the majority expert opinion. A key flaw, according to the trial court, was the expert's refusal to consider the mill a viable operation when, in fact, he was not a CPA, nor an OSHA expert, and he could not identify specific code violations.

Appeals courts are not free to question the trial court's credibility determinations, the Supreme Court noted. Here, "the fact remains that the Majority failed to present the district court with an appraisal containing values it deemed to be credible." In a footnote, the court said: "The outcome of the trial brings to mind the acronym 'GIGO,' or 'garbage in, garbage out.'" Put differently: "The quality of a court's factual findings can be no better than the quality of the evidence the parties provide to it."

Valuation date. The majority argued that the applicable statute required the court to use a later valuation date—the day before the filing of the petition for dissolution. Using the later date was critical because between the valuation date in the prevailing appraisal and the majority expert's valuation date, the corporation allegedly lost nearly $840,000 after the majority shareholders closed down the mill. The trial court failed to take into account this loss, the majority contended.

The state Supreme Court noted the applicable statutory provision expressly gave the trial court discretion to use "such other date as the court deems appropriate under the circumstances." Here, the trial court considered the mill's economic feasibility and faulted the majority for closing it and liquidating its assets. For this reason, the court used its discretion and chose the earlier valuation date—before the mill closure—the high court observed.

Discount requirement. The crux of the appeal was the argument that there should be a bright-line requirement to apply minority and marketability discounts in fair value proceedings. For support, the majority shareholders looked to a comment in the American Bar Association's Model Business Corporation Act (MBCA), which is identical to the applicable Idaho statute, and which says: "In cases where there is dissension but no evidence of wrongful conduct, 'fair value' should be determined with reference to what the petitioner would likely receive in a voluntary sale of shares to a third party, taking into account his minority status."

In addition, the majority shareholders cited to a number of decisions from other jurisdictions, including New York (*Ferolito v. Arizona Beverages USA* (aka *AriZona Ice Tea*)), in which courts have sanctioned the use of discounts.

The Supreme Court found both arguments unpersuasive. It first noted that the comments to the MBCA were not controlling authority in Idaho, even though they were important to evaluating the meaning of "fair value." At the same time, the court pointed out that the comment on "taking into account his minority status" uses the word "should," in contrast to "must." This choice of words suggests that discounts for lack of control or lack of marketability are not mandatory.

The high court itself cited at length to treatises that have explained why courts have found that discounts should not be mandatory. As concerns the cases the appellant cited in support of discounts, they "simply demonstrate that minority and lack of marketability discounts may be applied in some cases," the state Supreme Court said. It emphasized that the majority "does not cite a case that supports its assertion that minority and lack of marketability discounts must be applied as a matter of law." In short, the discounts are "just another fact that a court may consider in determining fair value," the Idaho Supreme Court said. It "expressly" rejected the majority's proposition to require the use of discounts as a matter of law.

Court punishes majority. In rejecting the appeal, the court went further. It decided to grant the minority's request for attorney's fees. For one, the majority's insufficient evidence argument was but a "thinly disguised request for this Court to re-weigh the evidence," the court said. Therefore, this issue was frivolous.

Moreover, the majority raised the discount issue without identifying any jurisdiction that had a bright-line rule that "minority and majority discounts are always to be applied." The lack of support in case law made the majority's appeal on this issue "frivolous, unreasonable, and without foundation," the state Supreme Court concluded.

In short, the majority shareholders lost on the discount issue and had to pay the minority shareholders' attorney's fees for appealing the trial court's value determination.

Washington v. Kellwood Co. (Kellwood II), (Kellwood III)

Citation: 2016 U.S. Dist. LEXIS 92309
Date of decision: July 15, 2016
Country: US
State/Jurisdiction: Federal/New York
Court: United States District Court
Type of action: Damages (incl. Lost Profits)
Experts: Scott Barnes (plaintiffs); Gary Trugman (defendant)
Judge: Netburn
SIC: 5136 Men's and Boys' Clothing and Furnishings (merchant wholesalers of athletic uniforms)
NAICS code: 423910 Sporting and Recreational Goods and Supplies Merchant Wholesalers

Citation: 2016 U.S. Dist. LEXIS 136612
Date of decision: Sept. 30, 2016
Country: US
State/Jurisdiction: Federal/New York
Court: United States District Court
Type of action: Damages (incl. Lost Profits)
Experts: Scott Barnes (plaintiffs); Gary Trugman (defendant)
Judge: Netburn
SIC: 5136 Men's and Boys' Clothing and Furnishings (merchant wholesalers of athletic uniforms)
NAICS code: 423910 Sporting and Recreational Goods and Supplies Merchant Wholesalers

Court Sets Aside Big Lost Profits Award Based on Bad Yardstick Analysis

After more than a decade of litigation, a damages case featuring an upstart sportswear company that portrayed itself as a serious competitor to the market leader ended with a whimper. The court struck down the jury's lost profits award, finding it was based on expert testimony that was "sheer surmise and conjecture." Although the court was prepared to allow a retrial on lost value damages, it ultimately concluded the plaintiffs lacked admissible evidence to prove the loss. A new trial would be a waste of judicial resources. The court addressed its earlier *Daubert* ruling in which it allowed the expert to testify at trial even though the expert analysis might contain "seemingly improbable" damages conclusions.

Weathering *Daubert* challenge. The plaintiff and his company owned the "Sunday Players" brand and wanted to break into the compression sportswear apparel and accessories market. In late 2003, they reached an exclusive licensing deal with the defendant, a large "private label" clothing manufacturer that made clothes, including compression apparel, for retailers to sell under their own brand names. Under the agreement, the defendant could use the Sunday Players mark "in connection with the production, manufacture, advertising, merchandising, promotion, importation, distribution and sale" of apparel. During the parties' early negotiations, the defendant allegedly told the plaintiff that MTV was interested in partnering with Sunday Players. An MTV promotion would result in hundreds of millions of dollars in product sales.

Although the defendant and MTV got as far as a draft agreement and MTV, according to an MTV employee involved in the negotiations, was prepared to finalize the deal, the defendant called it off. In spring 2005, the defendant ended its arrangements with the plaintiff.

The defendant claimed it was unable to make a single sale even though it had pitched the brand to some 18 large retailers and spent about $220,000 in marketing. The defense expert calculated that total sales—made by the plaintiffs' sales team—during the license agreement period were less than $150,000.

The plaintiffs sued, alleging the defendant "fail[ed] to use its best, or even reasonable, efforts to generate profits under the agreement." Also, the defendant breached the license agreement and defrauded the plaintiffs by misrepresentations and omissions. The plaintiffs asked for damages exceeding $50 million.

Both parties retained experts and challenged the opposing testimony under *Daubert*. The plaintiffs' damages expert was a CPA and certified financial forensics expert with extensive experience in business valuation. His damages calculation was based on two approaches: a yardstick analysis and what he called a "Market Forecast Analysis." He then used the values from both analyses to calculate net sales, royalties, and lost value of the Sunday Players brand, both for the license agreement's initial three-year term as well as for a possible three-year renewal term.

Only the yardstick analysis survived the *Daubert* attack. The analysis used "Under Armour," the market leader in the compression sportswear industry, as a benchmark. The expert justified this choice by pointing out that both brands had similar products; therefore, it was reasonable to look to Under Armour's historical sales performance to value Sunday Players. He also made much of the fact that in 2003 Under Armour executed a promotion agreement with ESPN, which led to TV commercials and significant growth. He assumed that a successful sublicensing agreement between the defendant and MTV would have led to similar success for Sunday Players.

However, the plaintiffs' expert reduced the comparative figure he derived from Under Armour's sales history by 50%, ostensibly to account for the increased competition in the compression apparel market during the relevant period. He called this discount an "assumption" and allowed that, if there had been actual projections from the defendant and MTV, "we may not have used that methodology."

The defendant attacked the yardstick analysis on two grounds. First, it claimed "Under Armour and Sunday Players are so dissimilar as to render [the expert's] selection of Under Armour laughable." Moreover, the expert applied the analysis in an unreliable way in that he used the sales record of what was then a six-year-old company, Under Armour, for purposes of quantifying the loss to the startup Sunday Players. Moreover, the expert's 50% reduction was arbitrary.

The court found the expert's use of the yardstick method was not "so unrealistic and contradictory as to suggest bad faith." Therefore, testimony as to the yardstick analysis was admissible under *Daubert*. (A digest and the court's opinion in *Washington v. Kellwood Co.*, 2015 U.S. Dist. LEXIS 63457 (April 21, 2015) are available at *BVLaw*).

Pitching similarities. The issue at trial was whether the defendant was liable for failing to make reasonable marketing efforts before it terminated the agreement with the plaintiffs. The jury found liability and, based on expert testimony, awarded the plaintiffs $4.35 million in lost profits (exceeding by $567,000 the amount the plaintiffs' expert had calculated) or, alternatively, $500,000 in lost business value. The plaintiffs chose the lost profits award.

The defendants then filed a motion for judgment as a matter of law, asking the court to strike down the lost profits award and, in the alternative, order a new trial.

The court found liability but agreed with the defendants that there was no sound basis for the jury's lost profits award.

It noted the plaintiffs had failed to prove their "new and untested business" would have achieved the vast success their expert predicted but for the defendant's breaches. It said that the expert based his calculation on "superficial similarities" between Sunday Players and the market's dominating force, Under Armour. His proposition that a newcomer such as Sunday Players would be able to generate half the sales of Under Armour was little more than "speculation and conjecture," the court said.

The court was quick to say it earlier had admitted the very damages testimony it now rejected. It explained that testimony that was admissible under *Daubert* "need not be sufficient to sustain a verdict." "Admissibility" and "sufficiency of scientific evidence" required different inquiries and involved different stakes, the court clarified. "*Daubert* loosened the standard for *admissibility* of scientific evidence" but left the "traditional sufficiency standard intact," the court added with emphasis. The expert opinion here was admissible, but it was insufficient to prove lost profits.

The court took particular aim at certain expert claims, including that 2003 was a "breakout year" for both Under Armour and Sunday Players. The expert said the year Under Armour got its "channel of distribution into the major sports retailers" and entered into the marketing deal with ESPN also was the year Sunday Players made its agreement with the defendants. He said he believed the defendants actually had better relationships with retailers, superior manufacturing capability, and more efficient ways to get product to the market than Under Armour.

The court called those assertions "demonstrably false." In 2003, Under Armour launched its marketing offense whereas all year long Sunday Players negotiated a licensing deal with the defendant, which was not signed until November, the court pointed out. Sunday Players at that time had no relationships with major retailers, the court noted. It said the expert pitched the alleged similarities between the companies "at such high level of generality as to be totally meaningless."

Trial evidence showed, the court said, that the expert's claim regarding the defendant's superior marketing position was false. Under Armour had been in business since 1996 and had steadily built its position in the market. Even if one assumed Sunday Players could compete against Under Armour, which was a big if, it was unclear how Sunday Players would be different from other competitors such as Nike, Reebok, and Adidas. The court noted it took Nike from 2003 to 2005 and

$30 million in advertising to increase its 3.5% share of the compression market to 5% or 6%. The expert's 50% reduction of Under Armour's profit was "little more than an admission that Sunday Players was not like Under Armour," the court said.

According to the court: "The yardstick comparison can show the profits a company could have expected if it had maintained its market share; it cannot establish that a company without market share would have become an overnight success." Here, Sunday Players had no market share but used the market leader as a yardstick for its lost profits calculation. This proposition, the court said, was nothing more than "the entrepreneur's cheerful prognostications." It did not support the jury's lost profits verdict.

Case for lost value. On the other hand, the court said, the plaintiffs proved their business had value before the breach and the defendant's breaches "crippled" Sunday Players before the company had a chance to compete in the market.

The question was how to quantify the loss. Simply adopting the jury's $500,000 lost value verdict was inappropriate because it was based on the plaintiff expert's lost value estimate of $532,500, which in turn relied on the expert's speculative lost profits estimate, the court noted. Therefore, a new trial on this measure of damages was appropriate. (*See Washington v. Kellwood Co.*, 2016 U.S. Dist. LEXIS 92309 (July 15, 2016) (*Kellwood II*)).

Lack of nonspeculative evidence. In a subsequent opinion, the court decided there was no justification for a retrial on lost value damages. In pretrial proceedings, the plaintiffs "made clear that they had no intention of pursuing a realistic damages award." In fact, they increased the range of damages from the disallowed $4.35 million to $5 million to $140 million, the court said. After reviewing their evidence, it excluded virtually all of the lost business value evidence.

The plaintiffs made a last-ditch effort to salvage their lost value claim by trying to introduce two financial documents they claimed were new evidence. One concerned purported revenue projections from the defendant, which showed the plaintiffs were only making $1.35 million from 2004 through 2006. The court noted that this document was not previously unknown since the defendant produced it in 2010. The plaintiffs had various opportunities throughout the proceedings to introduce this document, but, seeking more in damages than $1.35 million, they instead decided to rely on the subsequently discredited testimony of their damages expert. Also, it was unclear who created the document and when, the court noted. Using this document was a "transparent effort to plug the evidentiary gap identified by the Court."

The second document was a business plan the plaintiffs made sometime between 2002 and 2003. It, too, was available to the plaintiffs at the time of the first trial and, therefore, was not new evidence, the court noted.

There were other reasons for rejecting this document. "The measure of lost value is what an informed, willing buyer would have paid for the business at the date of breach, in this case March 2005," the court explained. No willing buyer would rely on a document "this old" when determining the value of the company, said the court. Moreover, subsequent events made the document obsolete.

The document assumed over $500,000 in earned revenue during 2003, whereas the company's actual revenue was closer to $43,000. It also assumed the company would attract over $1.5 million in initial capital, when in reality it never received any significant investment.

The revenue projections were not based on fundamentals such as historic growth rate of sales or an appropriate point of comparison, the court said. They were based on speculation that the company would sextuple it revenue within a year and double it for two years thereafter. If the business plan was good marketing, it was irrelevant in terms of valuing the company from a bona fide buyer's perspective.

Finally, the plaintiffs tried to introduce the testimony of the company's founder, who was an experienced accountant, as lay testimony under Federal Rule of Evidence 701. The court rejected the request.

Rule 701 allows "the owner or officer of a business to testify to the value or projected profits of a business without the necessity of qualifying the witness as an accountant, appraiser, or similar expert." It requires that the witness is able to make a business valuation based on his or her personal experience running the company. It assumes knowledge of past sales, trends of historic growth, as well as knowledge of the company's capital structure and assets.

Here, the evidence showed the company had approximately $43,000 in revenue during 2003, yet the owner asserted the company "could achieve approximately a 20% share of the compression wear market" with the defendant's assistance. Owing to the defendant's breach, the plaintiffs lost about $3.3 million in income in 2004 and over $3.9 million in 2005, the plaintiff owner asserted.

The court noted it had already decided the defendant's breaches did not cause lost profits. Moreover, the plaintiff owner did not base those numbers on his own experience of selling compression wear. He did not explain how the company was going to increase revenue by a factor of 75 in the space of a year, the court noted.

Seeking permission to introduce this testimony under Rule 701 was an attempt to introduce revenue projections the court had found to be inadmissible, the court said.

"Accelerating the inevitable," the court decided to reconsider its prior order for a new trial on lost value damages and close the case. It awarded the plaintiffs one dollar in nominal damages. (*See Washington v. Kellwood Co., 2016 U.S. Dist. LEXIS 136612 (Sept. 30, 2016) (Kellwood III)).*

Wheelabrator Bridgeport, L.P. v. City of Bridgeport

Citation: 2016 Conn. LEXIS 16
Date of decision: Feb. 2, 2016
Country: US
State/Jurisdiction: Connecticut
Court: Supreme Court
Type of action: State Taxation (incl. Ad Valorem)
Experts: Alexander L. Hazen, Joseph Kettell (owner/plaintiff); Mark Pomykacz (city/defendant)
Judge: Zarella
SIC: 4911 Electric Services (electric power distribution)
NAICS code: 2211 Electric Power Generation, Transmission and Distribution

Highest Court Rebukes Trial Court Over Flat-Out Bar of DCF Approach

Special purpose facilities pose special valuation problems. Not too long ago, a Minnesota tax court stumbled when it ignored expert testimony and produced its own valuation of an ethanol plant in a tax assessment dispute. Now comes a Connecticut tax dispute in which the trial court got into trouble when it rejected expert testimony from both sides that said the best way to value a waste to energy plant was the discounted cash flow (DCF) method. In appealing the ruling with the state Supreme Court, the facility's owner argued the trial court's categorical rejection of the DCF approach for tax assessment purposes was improper. The state's highest court agreed.

Energy facility fuels controversy. The tax assessment of a waste to energy facility located in Bridgeport, Conn., touched off a tangled litigation between the facility's owner and the city. The facility burned municipal solid waste to generate electricity that it sold to a third party. The plant also earned income from tipping fees from municipalities for taking their solid waste.

The city initially listed the fair market value (FMV) of the property at over $365.6 million (excluding personal property). A year later, in October 2008, it conducted a citywide revaluation and assessed the property at about $401 million. The facility's owner unsuccessfully appealed the decision with the board of assessment appeals.

More appeals followed, which ultimately ended up in consolidated form in front of the trial court. The crux of the valuation dispute was the claim by the facility's owner (plaintiff) that the city (defendant) had overvalued the property.

Pretrial challenge to appraisal testimony. For trial, both sides offered expert testimony. The city filed two pretrial motions to exclude the facility owner's two appraisers. It argued that, in preparing their appraisal reports for the property, the experts violated a state statute that prohibited any person who did not have a real estate license to act as a real estate appraiser or "engage in the real estate appraisal business." The court did not immediately rule on the motions. But, when the city repeated its claim in a post-trial motion, the court found the testimony was admissible as long as the witnesses qualified as experts in real estate appraisal—which they did.

At trial, one of the owner's experts said that, of the three valuation approaches, "[t]he primary reliance would be on the income approach to value." He explained the reason was that the willingness of a potential buyer to pay for the facility depended on the asset's anticipated future income stream. The expert said he reviewed the facility's financial information and performed a DCF analysis to project future income from the sales of electricity and tipping fees. He concluded the property's FMV as of the valuation date (October 2008) was $199.3 million.

Both of the owner's experts also produced a valuation based on the replacement cost approach as a check "to make sure that you're not way off in left field someplace." Based on this approach, the facility was worth $211.3 million. After the experts reconciled the two results, they arrived at an FMV of $201.7 million, which dropped to about $190,900 based on an adjustment.

The city's expert also favored the income approach. He said he performed a direct capitalization analysis that showed a value of about $398.4 million and a DCF analysis that resulted in a value of about $376.2 million. The income approach, he explained, "is the method that the market participants put the most weight on." That approach provided "the strongest indication of market value for the [f]acility, as of the valuation date," he added.

Apropos appraising special purpose properties and highly engineered facilities, the city's expert did note that the cost approach was "especially informative." He explained that there were two variants: the reproduction cost approach and the replacement cost approach. He found sufficient data to analyze the subject facility "meaningfully and reliably" under either of these approaches. But he said he assigned less weight to the results of the cost-based analyses than the results stemming from the income-based analyses. In the end, he valued the property at $357.5 million.

Trial court opts for cost approach. The trial court acknowledged that both sides' experts relied "primarily" on the DCF analysis because "the subject facility is a special purpose type property in which there is no market from which to develop comparables." It also noted that the facility's being a special purpose plant made it "difficult to adapt the classic concept of market value" for income-producing property.

For its part, the court found the "process used in the [discounted cash flow] income approach lacks credibility." It gave a number of reasons why that was the case.

- The parties' "experienced and knowledgeable appraisers" used the same approach on the same basic facts and ended up being "over [$2 million] apart in valuing the same property";
- The plaintiff expert's value determination was not a "direct" valuation of "the real and personal property which are the subject of these [tax] appeals"; and
- The plaintiff's expert accounted for C corporation income taxes, which seemed "inapplicable to the appraisal of real estate generally" and to the property in particular since the latter was a limited partnership.

Finally, the trial court gave a nod to a New Jersey decision that dismissed the DCF analysis in the tax assessment context as an "amalgam of interdependent, attenuated assumptions of limited probative value." Worse, the DCF is an "exercise in financial haruspication," the New Jersey decision said. (Haruspication means "a form of divination from lightning and other natural phenomena, but especially from inspection of the entrails of animal sacrifices," the Connecticut Supreme Court explains in an helpful aside.)

In short, regardless of the experts' preference for the DCF analysis, the trial court in the instant case decided that the reproduction cost approach was "the only credible approach to use" for the valuation. Adjusting the historical cost figure the city's expert produced, the court arrived at a total taxable value of about $314 million for the waste to energy facility.

Highest court critiques analysis. After the facility's owner appealed the trial court's valuation with the state Supreme Court, the latter instructed the trial court to clarify whether it had objected to the use of the DCF approach for valuing a property that had no rental market as a matter of law or because it deemed the expert testimony regarding the DCF analysis not credible. The trial court said its problem was with the expert testimony.

However, the facility's owner argued the trial court unlawfully rejected the DCF approach as a matter of law. The state Supreme Court agreed with the owner.

As part of its analysis, the state high court repeatedly noted that the trial court was imprecise in its terminology. Specifically, the trial court used "going concern" and "discounted cash flow" more or less interchangeably when, in fact, the DCF approach is one form of the income approach, and the income approach is one way to value a going concern, the Supreme Court explained.

According to the state Supreme Court, the following were indications that the trial court in fact had no problems with the expert testimony but with the DCF approach as such:

- The trial court called the experts "experienced and knowledgeable appraisers."
- The trial court said the experts used a "going concern approach [which the trial court considered to be the same as the DCF approach] rather than directly valuing the real and personal property."
- According to the Supreme Court, this comment suggested the trial court considered the DCF approach "inherently improper and fundamentally incompatible with a property valuation for tax assessment purposes."
- The trial court cited with approval another state court's "disparagement" of the DCF method.
- The record showed that, throughout trial, the court "expressed doubts about the general propriety" of using the DCF approach for valuations used for tax assessment purposes.

The state Supreme Court, on the other hand, decided there was no reason to categorically bar "the general income approach" or the "specific discounted cash flow approach" in the tax assessment context. Further, it emphasized that in this case both parties' "experienced and knowledgeable" experts testified an income approach was the *best* method for valuing the subject facility. Therefore, the trial court's rejection was improper, the Supreme Court concluded.

But stops short of prescribing methodology. The facility's owner proposed one of two remedies to correct the trial court's ruling. It asked the Supreme Court either to order the trial court to adopt the value the owner's experts determined or to remand the case to the trial court with instructions to use the DCF approach in valuing the property. The state's highest court rejected both suggestions. Instead, it remanded for a new trial on valuation, granting the trial court discretion to assess the testimony of the parties' experts as concerns the appropriate valuation method and the credibility of their specific calculations.

Court affirms admissibility of experts. In its review, the state Supreme Court also rejected the city's counterclaim that it was error for the trial court to admit the testimony of the owner's experts considering they were not state-licensed real estate appraisers.

The high court pointed out that prior case law has established that witnesses who have the education, training, and experience to qualify as experts are not precluded from testifying just because they are prohibited by statute from engaging in real estate appraisal. Also, testifying as to the value of a property does not mean "engaging in the real estate appraisal business" for purposes of the applicable statute, the court observed.

The purpose of the rules of evidence governing the admissibility of expert testimony is to ensure a person qualifies as an expert who can "shed light on an issue that is beyond the ken of the ordinary juror or trial juror," the court noted. In contrast, the purpose of the statutory framework governing the licensing of real estate appraisers is to assist the public in assessing whether a person who wants to be in the business of real estate has the competence and honesty to do so. Nothing would be gained by barring a witness who has the qualifications to assist the fact finder in valuing a property from doing so merely because he or she does not have a real estate license, the court found.

In conclusion, the Connecticut Supreme Court sent the case back to the trial court for a new trial on valuation featuring the same experts.

Editor's note: Readers interested in the Minnesota Supreme Court case, Guardian Energy, LLC v. County of Waseca, *2015 Minn. LEXIS 437 (Aug. 12, 2015), can find a case digest and the court's opinion at* BVLaw.

Wisniewski v. Walsh (Wisniewski II)

Citation: 2015 N.J. Super. Unpub. LEXIS 3001
Date of decision: Dec. 24, 2015
Country: US
State/Jurisdiction: New Jersey
Court: Superior Court, Appellate Division
Type of action: Dissenting Shareholder
Experts: Gary Trugman (selling shareholder/plaintiff-appellant, cross-respondent); Roger J. Grabowski (buyers/defendants-respondents/cross-appellants)
Judge: Per curiam
SIC: 4213 Trucking, Except Local (general freight, truckload)
NAICS code: 484121 General Freight Trucking, Long-Distance, Truckload

Affirmation of DLOM Rulings Augurs End to Shareholder Fight

After two decades of fierce fighting among the parties in this shareholder dispute involving a closely held trucking company, the parties renewed their attacks on the trial court's findings regarding the applicable discount for lack of marketability. The selling shareholder reasserted his earlier claim that his expert's prevailing discounted cash flow analysis sufficiently accounted for factors related to marketability. The buyers, in turn, contended the trial court erred in failing to adopt their expert's considered DLOM analysis.

Circumstances justify DLOM use. Three siblings—a sister and two brothers—owned equal shares in a family trucking business that provided private fleets to customers across the country, with a particular focus on the retail industry. The sister's suit against the younger brother set off an avalanche of other suits. Most critically for this case, in 1996, the younger brother filed an oppressed shareholder action claiming his two siblings tried to oust him from the company. Subsequently, the trial court found that the plaintiff younger brother in fact was the oppressing shareholder and ordered him to sell his interest either to the company or to the two siblings at fair value.

Both parties retained illustrious valuators. Ultimately, the first trial court set a value without conducting an evidentiary hearing—a move that triggered the parties' first appeal. On remand, a different trial court heard expert testimony and largely adopted the discounted cash flow (DCF) approach the selling shareholder's expert proposed. However, the court agreed with the buyers' expert, who used a market approach to value the company, that a 15% key person discount was appropriate to account for the unique contributions the late board chairman (the older brother) had made to the company's success.

Neither party approved of the resulting value determination, and both appealed the valuation a second time on various grounds. The appeals court affirmed nearly all aspects of the trial court's findings, but it concluded that the valuation should have included a marketability discount.

It noted that a marketability discount was only applicable under "extraordinary circumstances" in forced buyout situations. Here it was justifiable. Under prevailing case law, "where the oppressing shareholder instigates the problems, ... fairness dictates that the oppressing shareholder should not benefit at the expense of the oppressed." The trial court specifically had found that the younger brother, i.e., the selling shareholder and minority owner, had engaged in conduct that harmed the other shareholders—the siblings defending against his suit—and that necessitated the forced buyout.

Accordingly, the appeals court remanded for a second time, ordering yet another trial court (two trial court judges had retired over the course of the litigation) to determine whether the prevailing DCF analysis embedded a DLOM and to set the applicable DLOM rate. (A further discussion of *Wisniewski v. Walsh*, 2013 N.J. Super. Unpub. LEXIS 724 (2013), as well as the court's opinion, is available at *BVLaw.)*

Trial court reviews DLOM testimony anew. To answer the DLOM-related issues, a third trial judge reviewed the existing record. He found that, for his DCF analysis, the seller's expert had built up a 12% discount rate from a number of components including a 7% equity risk premium, a 3.5% size premium, and a 4% company-specific risk premium. The latter accounted for the company's closely held nature, its dependence on the older brother (since deceased) as a key manager, relative undercapitalization, and concentration of its customer base on the retail industry.

At the valuation trial, the seller's expert explained that there was no reason to apply an independent DLOM because the company was successful and would likely take no longer to sell than other closely held companies of similar size and nature—typically about six to nine months—with assistance from "the right business intermediary." He foresaw no danger to the other shareholders of losing liquidity during the marketing period. They likely would continue to benefit from the company's generous cash flow. He noted that, in the years surrounding the valuation date, the business had distributed tens of millions of dollars to the shareholders.

He also explained that a marketability discount was more appropriate to valuing a minority share of restricted stock in a publicly traded company because owners have a difficult time selling their interests when the fluctuating market declines, making their interests relatively more illiquid. He pointed out that since he had accounted for certain risk factors in developing his discount rate he did not want to count those factors again by applying an independent discount for illiquidity.

Using a market approach to value the company, the buyers' expert considered factors specific to liquidity such as the company's size and closely held nature, its profitability, customer concentration in the retail sector, anticipated holding period, and dependence on the older brother's stewardship of the company to determine the DLOM. He said that studies on the subject and legal precedent supported a 35% rate.

The new trial court started its analysis by answering the appeals court's first question: Did the prevailing DCF analysis include a marketability discount? He found it did not. Even though the seller's expert, in building his discount rate, considered many of the same factors the buyers' expert considered for formulating his marketability discount, the seller's expert did not adjust for marketability specifically. He "utilized [the factors] in a different way" than adjusting for a lack of liquidity, the trial court noted.

In contrast, in analyzing those same factors, the buyers' expert "focused on the inherent illiquidity of closely-held companies and the anticipated holding period for a rational investor in his company," the court found. There was no danger that applying a separate marketability discount resulted in double counting since it did not appear the experts accounted for the same risks relative to marketability, the court observed.

In answering the follow-up question—what the applicable DLOM rate should be—the trial court rejected both expert opinions: the 0% the seller's expert proposed and the 35% the buyers' expert used. The prior appeals court decision specifically required the use of a DLOM, the court noted. At the same time, it said that applying a 30% to 40% rate, in accordance with the leading decision in *Balsamides v. Protameen Chems.*, 160 N.J. 352 (1999) (available at *BVLaw*), would unduly punish the seller and give a windfall to the buying shareholders. Other studies suggested a broader range, starting as low as 20%, the court said, depending on the equities in a given case. A relevant prior appeals court decision applied a 25% rate.

Just as the buyers' expert did, the trial court on second remand also considered Judge Laro's decision in *Mandelbaum v. Commissioner*, 69 T.C.M. (C.C.H.) 2852 (available at *BVLaw*) setting forth nine factors appraisers should weigh in determining a marketability discount. The court took particular issue with the buyers' expert's argument that the anticipated holding period in this case would be lengthy. It agreed with the seller's expert who noted that given the company's historical financial performance and growth it would not take long to sell the company and the shareholders would receive sufficient earnings while trying to sell. There were strong indicators of liquidity that the buyers' expert failed to weigh appropriately, the court decided. It concluded that the equities in the case suggested a DLOM at the low spectrum of normal, that is, 25%.

End of the valuation game? Both parties challenged the trial court's DLOM-related findings in a third appeal. The seller in essence claimed that since his expert considered all the factors related to marketability in calculating a discount rate for his DCF analysis, applying a separate DLOM based on the same factors amounted to double counting and improperly devalued the seller's interest in the company. Also, considering none of the shareholders planned to sell their interest to a third party, a DLOM should not apply.

The buyers argued the trial court should have used the rate their expert determined based on relevant statements in *Balsamides* and his analysis along the lines of the Tax Court's *Mandelbaum* decision.

The appeals court rejected both sides' arguments. It first cleared up what it considered to be a misunderstanding on the seller's part: that consideration of the same factors to build a discount rate for a DCF analysis and to apply a separate marketability discount inherently double counts the same risks. Not so, the appeals court said. The same factors affect the value of the company in two distinct ways. First, they account for uncertainty in receiving the expected income stream from the asset. Second, they affect liquidity by limiting the pool of interested buyers in a sale.

There was no dispute that the seller's expert considered the relevant factors to assess uncertainty in building his discount rate. He also considered several factors related to liquidity, but not exclusively so, the appeals court observed. On the contrary, the expert was firm that the company had no liquidity problems that required special consideration. Therefore, the trial court's finding that the expert's discount rate did not embed a discount for lack of marketability was sound, the appeals court said. It dismissed the seller's alternative argument that no DLOM was appropriate where no one contemplated a sale, noting that this issue had been decided in the earlier appeal against the seller.

The appeals court also upheld the trial court's 25% marketability discount rate. The judge had a right to find a figure other than the figures the experts proposed, "so long as it was plausible, based on evidence in the record, and—in the final analysis—fair and equitable." The appeals court added that neither side made a convincing argument for second-guessing the trial court's "thoughtful and well-reasoned determination in this most difficult case."

There is reason to think that, in upholding the trial court's DLOM-related findings, the appeals court has brought this protracted conflict to conclusion.

Witt-Bahls v. Bahls

Citation: 2016 Fla. App. LEXIS 1451
Date of decision: Feb. 3, 2016
Country: US
State/Jurisdiction: Florida
Court: Court of Appeals
Type of action: Marital Dissolution
Judge: Forst
SIC: 1629 Heavy Construction, NEC (except industrial nonbuilding structures, irrigation systems, sewage and water treatment plants, petrochemical plants and refineries, power generation plants [except hydroelectric dams] transmission and distribution stations
NAICS code: 237990 Heavy and Civil Engineering Construction

Court Rejects Bright-Line Rule for Valuing Appreciation of Nonmarital Assets

Active and passive appreciation of separate property is one of the most contentious issues in divorce cases, particularly in this age of entrepreneurship. Valuators know that much of the fight is over methodology—how to show conclusively that the increase in the value of the nonmarital asset is due to the efforts of the owner spouse or is due to market-related circumstances or the efforts of others in charge of the company. A recent case in Florida tackles the issue from the perspective of scope—how far should the nonowner spouse's right to share in the increased value of nonmarital assets extend?

Husband owns stock but not the company. This appreciation case differs from the familiar scenario featuring a spouse who built his or her business prior to the marriage. Here, the husband began working for a big, privately held, international company prior to the marriage and at that time bought a large number of company stock with a bank loan. During his tenure at the company, he had some supervisory responsibility. But, even at the peak of his career, several layers of management were above him. Also, during his marriage, while working for the company, he was twice demoted. He was ultimately terminated, and his stock was liquidated. The shares sold for substantially more than the outstanding balance on the loan the husband had used to buy them.

Testimony from the husband's CPA showed there were no payments on the loan other than interest payments.

The trial court determined the stock was separate property and its increase in value was passive and, therefore, not subject to marital distribution.

The wife appealed the ruling. The appeals court opinion states the wife asked for a rule "that all appreciation of the stock of a company for which a spouse works is a marital asset." The court's language suggests the wife either asked for a rule that would shift the burden of showing the appreciation was passive in nature and, therefore, not part of the marital estate to the stock-owning spouse or that the appreciation in value during the marriage was marital property as a matter of law.

Existing analysis stays in place. Either way, the Florida Court of Appeal rejected the wife's proposition and used the opportunity "to address the passivity of appreciation of stock in a marriage."

The court said with emphasis that, under the existing analytical framework, the increased value of stock from a company for which the owner spouse works *can* qualify as a marital asset and, thus, be subject to distribution. But it can also be a nonmarital asset. The crux of the matter is "whether the husband exerted the sort of 'effort' required to move the appreciation value from the nonmarital category to the marital one," the court stated.

The Court of Appeal went on to say that cases that have found the appreciation was a marital asset typically involve a family-owned or family-run business in which the stock-owning spouse holds a significant position. In the instant case, neither of these "key features" was present, the appeals court found. The company for which the husband worked was not owned or operated by his family. Moreover, he played no significant role in the management of the company. At most, he was a "middle manager," the court said. He did not contribute to the appreciation in the value of the company's stock, and the increase never converted into marital property. The wife had no claim on it.

The court cautioned that the wife's proposed rule might force trial courts into examining "how much of the increase in value of a multi-national corporation each and every hourly employee was responsible for." Such an expansion of the concept of marital assets was the province of the legislature, the Court of Appeal noted, upholding the trial court's ruling.

www.ingramcontent.com/pod-product-compliance
Lightning Source LLC
LaVergne TN
LVHW060250011026
849161LV00011B/2683